TOP
10
OF EVERYTHING
2012

TOP 10

2012

Caroline Ash and Alexander Ash

STERLING
New York

An Imprint of Sterling Publishing
387 Park Avenue South
New York, NY 10016

Russell Ash (1946–2010), was the originator and author of the *Top 10 of Everything* annual and series. For over 22 years his passion for facts, eye for detail, and pursuit of the curious fascinated and entertained millions of readers, and this edition is dedicated to his memory.

STERLING
New York

An Imprint of Sterling Publishing
387 Park Avenue South
New York, NY 10016

STERLING and the distinctive Sterling logo are registered trademarks of Sterling Publishing Co., Inc.

Publishing director: Colin Webb
Art director: Bernard Higton
Managing editor: Sonya Newland
Project editor: Emily Bailey
Picture researcher: Felicity Page

Top 10 of Everything was devised and created by Russell Ash

Copyright © Octopus Publishing Group Ltd 2011
Text copyright © Russell Ash Ltd 2011

ISBN 978-1-4027-9105-5

For information about custom editions, special sales, and premium and corporate purchases, please contact Sterling Special Sales at 800-805-5489 or specialsales@sterlingpublishing.com.

Manufactured in China

10 9 8 7 6 5 4 3 2 1

www.sterlingpublishing.com

CONTENTS

INTRODUCTION

23rd EDITION

23 is the smallest prime number with consecutive digits; a human cell has 23 pairs of chromosomes; Julius Caesar was stabbed 23 times when he was assassinated; William Shakespeare was born and died on April 23; John Forbes Nash, the Nobel Prize-winning mathematician and the subject of the film *A Beautiful Mind*, was obsessed with the number 23; Michael Jordan wore the number 23 throughout his career and David Beckham first started wearing the number 23 when he played for Real Madrid; Psalm 23, the "Shepherd Psalm," is the best known of all the psalms; there are 23 letters in the Latin alphabet (there is no J, U, or W); and this is the 23rd annual edition of *Top 10 of Everything*.

LISTMANIA

We are constantly bombarded with lists. The press and TV programs present rankings based on market research and polls, lists of the best places to live, the top universities, the greatest movies, the bestselling books, the worst crime rates, and so on. Ranked lists have become a way of managing what might otherwise be a daunting mass of facts and figures, putting our world into a perspective that we can readily grasp. *Top 10 of Everything* provides a unique collection of lists in a diverse array of categories that are—we hope—informative, educational, and entertaining.

THIS EVER-CHANGING WORLD

The majority of lists change from year to year—even "fixed" lists, such as those of the tallest mountains or deepest caves, are revised as more sophisticated measuring techniques are used or as deeper branches are discovered. The minimum entry requirements for Top 10 lists are in a constant state of flux as, for example, rich people get increasingly richer and build ever-bigger yachts, and movies with bigger and bigger budgets are released and achieve higher-earning opening weekends.

IT'S A FACT

Top 10 lists provide a shorthand glimpse of what is happing with the world economy, global warming, deforestation, the countries that will have the most people and the densest populations in the future, and other issues that concern us all. At the same time, the lists convey a fascinating and entertaining overview of the amazing diversity of our planet and its people, with lists on such subjects as the world's oldest people, the highest waterfalls, the heaviest mammals, the most venomous reptiles, the longest-serving presidents,

the tallest buildings, the longest bridges, the most-visited museums, the highest-grossing films, countries producing the most diamonds, the longest Shakespearean roles, companies with the most employees, the youngest American billionaires, leading chocolate consumers, latest air speed record holders, most widely spoken languages, countries with the most primary schools, bestselling albums and singles of all time, and the fastest men over 100 meters.

MORE THAN JUST THE NO. 1

All these lists follow a rule that has been true since the first edition of *Top 10 of Everything*, which is that every list has to be quantifiable—measurable in some way or other: the biggest, smallest, first, last, tallest, deepest, sunniest, dullest, worst, or chronologically the first or last. All the lists thus offer more than just the No. 1, and provide a perspective in which to compare the subjects of the list. There are no "bests," other than bestsellers, and "worsts" are of disasters, military losses, and murders, where they are measured by numbers of victims. Unless otherwise stated, movie lists are based on cumulative global earnings, irrespective of production or marketing budgets and—as is standard in the film industry—inflation is not taken into account, which means that recent releases

tend to feature disproportionately prominently. Countries are independent countries, not dependencies or overseas territories. All the lists are all-time and global unless a specific year or territory is noted.

CREDITS AND ACKNOWLEDGMENTS

Sources encompass international organizations, commercial companies and research bodies, specialized publications, and a network of experts around the world who have generously shared their knowledge. As always, their important contribution is acknowledged (see page 256 for a full list of credits), along with that of everyone who has been involved with the book at all stages of its development on this and the previous 22 annual editions.

OVER TO YOU

We hope you enjoy the book. Your comments, corrections, and suggestions for new lists are always welcome. Please contact us via the publishers or visit the *Top 10 of Everything* website www.top10ofeverything.com.

The Top 10 Team

1

THE UNIVERSE & THE EARTH

KUAFU SPACE MISSION

Launched by the Chinese in 2012, KuaFu will be the first space mission dedicated to the study of space weather—observing, monitoring, and recording activity, particularly solar storms, from their inception at the Sun to their arrival at the Earth's atmosphere. KuaFu comprises three spacecraft, one of which will be permanently situated 0.9 million miles (1.5 million km) away, while the other two will orbit Earth to provide the first continuous imaging of space weather. The erratic behavior of the Sun leads to solar storms, whose effects can wreak havoc on satellites and interfere to a dangerous degree with technology. Being able to accurately predict and monitor these storms will help to reduce their impact.

◄ **Sylvia**
The asteroid Sylvia is about 175 miles (280 km) in diameter and is orbited by two small moons.

▼ **Jupiter**
Composed primarily of hydrogen, Jupiter is the largest planet.

TOP 10 **LARGEST BODIES IN THE SOLAR SYSTEM**

	BODY	MAX. DIAMETER MILES	MAX. DIAMETER KM	SIZE COMPARED WITH EARTH
1	Sun	865,036	1,392,140	109.136
2	Jupiter	88,846	142,984	11.209
3	Saturn	74,898	120,536	9.449
4	Uranus	31,763	51,118	4.007
5	Neptune	30,775	49,528	3.883
6	Earth	7,926	12,756	1.000
7	Venus	7,521	12,104	0.949
8	Mars	4,228	6,805	0.533
9	Ganymede	3,270	5,262	0.413
10	Titan	3,200	5,150	0.404

TOP 10 **LARGEST ASTEROIDS**

NAME	NO.	DISCOVERED	MEAN DIAMETER* MILES	MEAN DIAMETER* KM
1 Ceres	1	Jan 1, 1801	592	952
2 Pallas	2	Mar 28, 1802	338	544
3 Vesta	4	Mar 29, 1807	329	529
4 Hygeia	10	Apr 12, 1849	268	431
5 Interamnia	704	Oct 2, 1910	203	326
6 Europa	52	Feb 4, 1858	187	301
7 Davida	511	May 30, 1903	180	289
8 Sylvia	87	May 16, 1866	178	286
9 Cybele	65	Mar 8, 1861	170	273
10 Eunomia	15	Jul 29, 1851	167	268

* Most asteroids are irregular in shape

Asteroids, also known as minor planets, but correctly (along with comets) now called "small Solar System bodies," are fragments of rock orbiting between Mars and Jupiter. In 2006, Ceres was redesignated as a dwarf planet (bodies over 466 miles/ 750 km in diameter), along with Pluto and Eris. Up to August 6, 2009, some 217,627 asteroids had been identified, but only 15,361 of them named.

► **Earth**
The third planet from the Sun, Earth was formed roughly 4.5 billion years ago.

▲ **Mars**
Iron oxide or its surface gives Mars its reddish appearance.

Asteroid Impact!

Large asteroids with a diameter of 0.62 miles (1 km) are likely to collide with Earth once every 500,000 years, and have the potential to cause extensive damage. Smaller asteroids with a diameter of 16–33 ft (5–10 m) enter the Earth's atmosphere roughly once a year, but frequently explode in the upper atmosphere and so fortunately do not cause much harm.

TOP 10 **BODIES* FARTHEST FROM THE SUN**

BODY	AVERAGE DISTANCE FROM THE SUN MILES	KM
1 Pluto	3,675,000,000	5,914,000,000
2 Neptune	2,794,000,000	4,497,000,000
3 Uranus	1,784,000,000	2,871,000,000
4 Chiron	1,740,000,000	2,800,000,000
5 Saturn	887,000,000	1,427,000,000
6 Jupiter	483,600,000	778,300,000
7 Mars	141,600,000	227,900,000
8 Earth	92,955,793	149,597,870
9 Venus	67,200,000	108,200,000
10 Mercury	36,000,000	57,900,000

* In the Solar System, excluding satellites and asteroids

◄ *Pluto*
Formerly the ninth planet in the Solar System, but now reclassified as a dwarf planet, Pluto is composed of rock and ice.

▲ *Neptune*
Farthest from the Sun, Neptune is the fourth-heaviest planet in the Solar System.

◄ *Saturn*
Saturn is surrounded by nine rings composed mainly of ice particles.

▶ *Halley's Comet*
Visible from Earth with the naked eye, Halley's Comet can be seen once every 75 years.

THE 10 **BODIES IN THE SOLAR SYSTEM WITH THE GREATEST ESCAPE VELOCITY**

BODY	ESCAPE VELOCITY (MILES/S)
1 Sun	383.70
2 Jupiter	37.42
3 Saturn	20.05
4 Neptune	14.85
5 Uranus	13.98
6 Earth	6.95
7 Venus	6.44
8 Mars	3.13
9 Mercury	2.64
10 Pluto	0.73

* Excluding satellites

Escape velocity is the speed a rocket has to attain upon launching to overcome the gravitational pull of the body it is leaving. The escape velocity of the Moon is 1.48 miles/s.

TOP 10 **COMETS COMING CLOSEST TO EARTH**

COMET	DATE*	AU#	DISTANCE MILES	KM
1 Comet of 1491	Feb 20, 1491	0.0094	873,784	1,406,220
2 Lexell	Jul 1, 1770	0.0151	1,403,633	2,258,928
3 Tempel-Tuttle	Oct 26, 1366	0.0229	2,128,688	3,425,791
4 IRAS-Araki-Alcock	May 11, 1983	0.0313	2,909,516	4,682,413
5 Halley	Apr 10, 837	0.0334	3,104,724	4,996,569
6 Biela	Dec 9, 1805	0.0366	3,402,182	5,475,282
7 Grischow	Feb 8, 1743	0.0390	3,625,276	5,834,317
8 Pons-Winnecke	Jun 26, 1927	0.0394	3,662,458	5,894,156
9 Comet of 1014	Feb 24, 1014	0.0407	3,783,301	6,088,633
10 La Hire	Apr 20, 1702	0.0437	4,062,168	6,537,427

* Of closest approach to Earth
# Astronomical Units: 1AU = mean distance from the Earth to the Sun (92,955,793 miles/ 149,597,870 km)

▲ *Andromeda galaxy*
The collision of two smaller galaxies formed Andromeda between five and nine billion years ago.

TOP 10 **GALAXIES NEAREST TO EARTH**

	GALAXY	DISCOVERED	APPROX. DIAMETER (1,000 LIGHT YEARS)	DISTANCE FROM EARTH
1	Sagittarius Dwarf	1994	10	82
2	Large Magellanic Cloud	Prehist.	30	160
3	Small Magellanic Cloud	Prehist.	16	190
4 =	Draco Dwarf	1954	3	205
=	Ursa Minor Dwarf	1954	2	205
6	Sculptor Dwarf	1937	3	254
7	Sextans Dwarf	1990	4	258
8	Carina Dwarf	1977	2	330
9	Fornax Dwarf	1938	6	450
10	Leo II	1950	3	660

Source: Peter Bond, Royal Astronomical Society

> As the Solar System and Earth are at the outer edge of the Milky Way galaxy, this is excluded.

TOP 10 **BRIGHTEST GALAXIES**

	GALAXY / NO.	DISTANCE FROM EARTH (MILLIONS OF LIGHT YEARS)	APPARENT MAGNITUDE
1	Large Magellanic Cloud	0.17	0.91
2	Small Magellanic Cloud	0.21	2.70
3	Andromeda Galaxy/NGC 224 M31	2.6	4.36
4	Triangulum Galaxy/NGC 598 M33	2.8	6.27
5	Centaurus Galaxy/NGC 5128	12.0	7.84
6	Bode's Galaxy/NGC 3031 M81	12.0	7.89
7	Silver Coin Galaxy/NGC 253	8.5	8.04
8	Southern Pinwheel Galaxy/ NGC 5236 M83	15.0	8.20
9	Pinwheel Galaxy/NGC 5457 M101	24.0	8.31
10	Cigar Galaxy/NGC 55	4.9	8.42

> Messier (M) numbers are named after French astronomer Charles Messier (1730–1817), who in 1781 compiled the first catalog of galaxies, nebulae, and star clusters. From 1888 onward, these were replaced by New General Catalogue (NGC) numbers.

TOP 10 **BRIGHTEST STARS***

STAR / CONSTELLATION / DISTANCE# / APPARENT MAGNITUDE

1
Sirius
Canis Major
8.61 / -1.44

2
Canopus
Carina
312.73 / -0.62

3
Arcturus
Boötes
36.39 / -0.05†

4
Alpha Centauri A
Centaurus
4.40 / -0.01

5
Vega
Lyra
25.31 / +0.03

6
Capella
Auriga
42.21 / +0.08

7
Rigel
Orion
772.91 / +0.18

8
Procyon
Canis Minor
11.42 / +0.40

9
Achernar
Eridanus
143.81 / +0.45

10
Beta Centauri
Centaurus
525.22 / +0.61

* Excluding the Sun
# From Earth in light years
† Variable

> This Top 10 is based on apparent visual magnitude as viewed from Earth—the lower the number, the brighter the star, since by convention 1 was considered a star of first magnitude and 6 the faintest visible to the naked eye. On this scale, the Sun would be -26.73 and the full Moon -12.6.

THE 10 **TYPES OF STAR**

	TYPE	SPECTRUM	MAX. SURFACE TEMPERATURE °F	°C
1	W	Bright lines	144,000	80,000
2	O	Bright and dark lines	72,000	40,000
3	B	Bluish-white	43,000	25,000
4	A	White	18,000	10,000
5	F	White/slightly yellow	13,500	7,500
6	G	Yellowish	11,000	6,000
7	K	Orange	9,000	5,000
8	M	Orange-red	6,000	3,400
9 =	C (formerly R & N)	Reddish	4,700	2,600
=	S	Red	4,700	2,600

Stars are classified by type according to their spectra—the colors by which they appear when viewed with a spectroscope. These vary according to the star's surface temperature. Within these types there are sub-types, with dwarfs generally hotter than giants.

TOP 10 **STARS NEAREST TO EARTH**

	STAR*	LIGHT YEARS	DISTANCE FROM EARTH MILES (MILLIONS)	KM (MILLIONS)
1	Proxima Centauri	4.22	24,792,500	39,923,310
2	Alpha Centauri	4.39	25,791,250	41,531,595
3	Barnard's Star	5.94	34,897,500	56,195,370
4	Wolf 359	7.78	45,707,500	73,602,690
5	Lalande 21185	8.31	48,821,250	78,616,755
6	Sirius	8.60	50,525,000	81,360,300
7	Luyten 726-8	8.72	51,230,000	82,495,560
8	Ross 154	9.69	56,928,750	91,672,245
9	Ross 248	10.32	60,630,000	97,632,360
10	Epsilon Eridani	10.49	61,628,750	99,240,645

* Excluding the Sun

Source: Peter Bond, Royal Astronomical Society

A spaceship traveling at 25,000 mph (40,237 km/h)—faster than any human has yet reached in space—would take more than 113,200 years to reach Earth's closest star, Proxima Centauri.

The World's Largest Telescope

The European Extremely Large Telescope (E-ELT) is currently being designed, and should be operational by 2018. The telescope's "eye" will be 138 ft (42 m) in diameter, made up of 906 hexagonal segments, and will gather 15 times more light than any of today's largest optical telescopes. It has an innovative design that includes advanced adaptive optics to correct for the Earth's turbulent atmosphere, giving exceptional image quality. It is likely to revolutionize our perception of the Universe.

Space Exploration

THE 10 **FIRST ANIMALS IN SPACE**

NAME / ANIMAL / STATUS	COUNTRY	DATE
1 Laika (female Samoyed husky) Died in space	USSR	Nov 3, 1957
2 =Laska and **Benjy** (mice) Re-entered Earth's atmosphere, but not recovered	USA	Dec 13, 1958
4 =Able (female rhesus monkey) and **Baker** (female squirrel monkey) Successfully returned to Earth	USA	May 28, 1959
6 =Otvazhnaya (female Samoyed husky) and an **unnamed rabbit** Successfully returned to Earth	USSR	Jul 2, 1959
8 Sam (male rhesus monkey) Successfully returned to Earth	USA	Dec 4, 1959
9 Miss Sam (female rhesus monkey) Successfully returned to Earth	USA	Jan 21, 1960
10 =Belka and **Strelka** (female Samoyed huskies) plus 40 mice and two rats First to orbit and return safely	USSR	Aug 19, 1960

The first animal to be sent up in a rocket—but not into space— was Albert 1, a male rhesus monkey, in a US Air Force converted German V2 rocket in 1948. He and his successor, Albert 2, died during the tests, as did a monkey and mice in 1951 tests, but a monkey and 11 mice were recovered after a launch in a US Aerobee rocket on 20 September 1951. The earliest Soviet experiments with launching animals in rockets involved monkeys, dogs, rabbits, cats, and mice, most of which died as a result. Laika, the first dog in space, went up in *Sputnik 2*, with no hope of coming down alive. Able and Baker, launched in a *Jupiter* missile, were the first animals to be recovered (although Able died a few days later).

SHQIPERIA 3 NËNDOR 1957 LAIKA 1

▲ *Space pioneers*
Laika (top) is actually the name of the breed to which the dog named Kudryavka, a female Samoyed husky, belonged. Baker (above) lived until 1984 after her safe return to Earth.

MOONWALKERS

Six of the 11 US *Apollo* manned missions resulted in successful Moon landings (*Apollo 13* was aborted after an oxygen tank exploded). During the last of these (*Apollo 17*, December 7–19 1972), Eugene A. Cernan (b. March 14, 1934) and Harrison H. Schmitt (b. July 3, 1935) became the final astronauts to date to have walked on the surface of the Moon, both spending a total of 22:04 in EVA.

◀ *Farewell to the Moon*
Eugene Cernan was the last of only 12 men to have left their footprints on the lunar surface.

INTERNATIONAL SPACE STATION

Completion of the International Space Station (ISS) is scheduled for 2012. This low Earth orbit research facility is the result of a collaboration between five space agencies—those of the USA, Russia, Japan, and China, as well as the European Space Agency. Construction began in 1998, when the first two modules were launched and joined in space. Two years later, the first crews arrived and the ISS has been manned constantly since then, with astronauts and cosmonauts conducting experiments that will help with future space exploration.

TOP 10 BODIES MOST VISITED BY SPACECRAFT

BODY / SPACECRAFT

1 Moon 66
2 Mars 32
3 Venus 26
4 Sun 14
5 Jupiter 7
6 Halley's Comet 5
7 Saturn 4
8 = Mercury 1
   = Neptune 1
   = Uranus 1

Arguably, Earth is the most visited body in the Solar System, with satellites constantly orbiting. With the exception of some visits to the Moon, all the visiting spacecraft were unmanned space probes known as flybys, landers, and orbiters. The US space probe *Voyager 2*, for instance, flew by Jupiter, Saturn, Uranus, and Neptune over a period of 12 years.

Venus
Around 80% of the surface of Venus is made up of volcanic lava plains.

MISSION TO MARS

The Mars Science Laboratory is expected to arrive on the red planet in autumn 2012. This, the latest of NASA's Mars missions, is intended to build on the success of the Mars rovers *Spirit* and *Opportunity*, which have been sending back information from the surface of the planet since 2004. Equipped with the latest technology, the Science Laboratory will be able to convey information about the Martian atmosphere, and its rocks and soil, in more detail than ever before.

ELEMENTARY

THE 10 **MOST COMMON ELEMENTS IN THE UNIVERSE**

ELEMENT (SYMBOL) / PARTS PER MILLION*

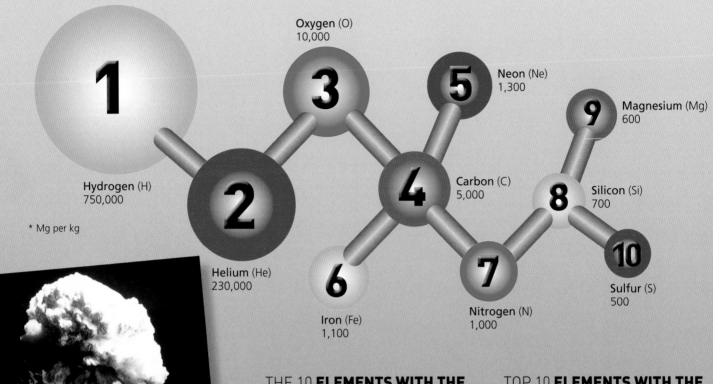

* Mg per kg

Hydrogen (H)
750,000

Helium (He)
230,000

Oxygen (O)
10,000

Carbon (C)
5,000

Neon (Ne)
1,300

Magnesium (Mg)
600

Silicon (Si)
700

Sulfur (S)
500

Iron (Fe)
1,100

Nitrogen (N)
1,000

H

Hydrogen
By far the commonest element in the Universe, hydrogen comprises some 930,000 out of every million atoms.

THE 10 **ELEMENTS WITH THE LOWEST BOILING POINTS**

	ELEMENT	SYMBOL	°F	°C
1	Helium	He	-452.07	-268.93
2	Hydrogen	H	-423.17	-252.87
3	Neon	Ne	-410.94	-246.08
4	Nitrogen	N	-320.42	-195.79
5	Fluorine	F	-306.62	-188.12
6	Argon	Ar	-302.40	-185.80
7	Oxygen	O	-297.20	-182.90
8	Krypton	Kr	-243.80	-153.22
9	Xenon	Xe	-162.00	-108.00
10	Radon	Rn	-79.10	-61.70

BOILING POINT

TOP 10 **ELEMENTS WITH THE HIGHEST BOILING POINTS**

	ELEMENT	SYMBOL	°F	°C
1	Rhenium	Re	10,105	5,596
2	Tungsten	W	10,031	5,555
3	Tantalum	Ta	9,856	5,458
4	Osmium	Os	9,054	5,012
5	Thorium	Th	8,708	4,820
6	Niobium	Nb	8,571	4,744
7	Molybdenum	Mo	8,382	4,639
8	Hafnium	Hf	8,317	4,603
9	Iridium	Ir	8,002	4,428
10	Zirconium	Zr	7,968	4,409

BOILING POINT

TOP 10 **METALLIC ELEMENTS WITH THE GREATEST RESERVES**

	ELEMENT (SYMBOL)	MIN. ESTIMATED GLOBAL RESERVES (TONS)				
1	Iron (Fe)	100,000,000,000	**6**	= Chromium (Cr)	1,000,000,000
2	Magnesium (Mg)	20,000,000,000		= Zirconium (Zr)	1,000,000,000
3	Potassium (K)	10,000,000,000	**8**	Titanium (Ti)	600,000,000
4	Aluminum (Al)	6,000,000,000	**9**	Barium (Ba)	400,000,000
5	Manganese (Mn)	3,000,000,000	**10**	Copper (Cu)	300,000,000

This list includes accessible reserves of commercially mined metallic elements (although magnesium is also extracted from seawater, where the reserves are vast), but excludes two, calcium and sodium, that exist in such huge quantities that their reserves are considered "unlimited" and unquantifiable.

Ne
Neon
Neon is used for signs because it glows red when an electrical discharge is passed through it.

TOP 10 **DEGREES OF HARDNESS**

MOHS SCALE NO. / SUBSTANCE

1	Talc	6	Orthoclase
2	Gypsum	7	Quartz
3	Calcite	8	Topaz
4	Fluorite	9	Corundum
5	Apatite	10	Diamond

He
Helium
Light, colorless, and odorless, helium also has the lowest melting point of any element in the periodic table.

The Mohs Scale, named after German mineralogist Friedrich Mohs (1773–1839), is used for comparing the relative hardness of minerals. Each mineral on the scale is softer, and hence capable of being scratched by all those below it.

THE 10 **FIRST ELEMENTS TO BE NAMED AFTER REAL PEOPLE**

	ELEMENT	SYMBOL	NAMED AFTER	YEAR
1	Samarium*	Sm	Vasili Samarsky-Bykhovets (Russia, 1803–70)	1879
2	Gadolinium#	Gd	Johan Gadolin (Finland, 1760–1852)	1880
3	Curium	Cm	Pierre† and Marie Curie† (France 1859–1906; Poland 1867–1934)	1944
4	Einsteinium	Es	Albert Einstein† (Germany, 1879–1955)	1952
5	Fermium	Fm	Enrico Fermi† (Italy, 1901–54)	1953
6	Nobelium	No	Alfred Nobel (Sweden, 1833–96)	1958
7	Lawrencium	Lr	Ernest Lawrence† (USA, 1901–58)	1961
8	Rutherfordium	Rf	Ernest Rutherford† (UK, 1871–1937)	1969
9	Seaborgium	Sg	Glenn T. Seaborg† (USA, 1912–99)	1974
10	Bohrium	Bh	Niels Bohr† (Denmark, 1885–62)	1981

* Named after mineral samarskite, which was named after Samarsky-Bykhovets
\# Named after mineral gadolinite, which was named after Gadolin
† Awarded Nobel Prize

▶ *Marie Curie*
With her husband, Marie Curie discovered the elements curium, radium, and polonium.

OCEANS & SEAS

Persian Gulf
Encompassing the world's largest offshore oilfield, the Persian Gulf adjoins eight countries.

TOP 10 LARGEST OCEANS AND SEAS

NAME / APPROX. AREA* (SQ MILES / SQ KM)

1 Pacific Ocean
60,060,900
155,557,000

2 Atlantic Ocean
29,637,977
76,762,000

3 Indian Ocean
26,469,622
68,556,000

4 Southern Ocean#
7,848,299
20,327,000

5 Arctic Ocean
5,427,053
14,056,000

6 Caribbean Sea
1,049,503
2,718,200

7 Mediterranean Sea
969,117
2,510,000

8 South China Sea
895,371
2,319,000

9 Bering Sea
884,908
2,291,900

10 Gulf of Mexico
614,984
1,592,800

* Excluding tributary seas
# As defined by the International Hydrographic Organization

THE 10 SMALLEST SEAS

SEA*/OCEAN	APPROX. AREA SQ MILES	SQ KM
1 Gulf of California, Pacific Ocean	59,100	153,070
2 Persian Gulf, Indian Ocean	88,800	230,000
3 Yellow Sea, Pacific Ocean	113,500	293,960
4 Baltic Sea, Atlantic Ocean	147,500	382,000
5 North Sea, Atlantic Ocean	164,900	427,090
6 Red Sea, Indian Ocean	174,900	452,990
7 Black Sea, Atlantic Ocean	196,100	507,900
8 Andaman Sea, Indian Ocean	218,100	564,880
9 East China Sea, Pacific Ocean	256,600	664,590
10 Hudson Bay, Atlantic Ocean	281,900	730,120

* Excludes landlocked seas

TOP 10 COUNTRIES WITH THE LARGEST AREAS OF CORAL REEF

COUNTRY / REEF AREA (SQ MILES) / % OF WORLD TOTAL

1 Indonesia
19,699 / 17.95

2 Australia
18,904 / 17.22

3 The Philippines
9,679 / 8.8

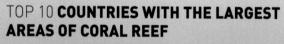

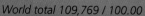

World total 109,769 / 100.00

* Clipperton, French Polynesia, Guadeloupe, Martinique, Mayotte, New Caledonia, Réunion, Wallis, and Futuna islands

Source: UNEP World Conservation Monitoring Centre, *World Atlas of Coral Reefs*

THE 10 **DEEPEST DEEP-SEA TRENCHES**

TRENCH*	DEEPEST POINT FT	M
1 Marianas	35,798	10,911
2 Tonga	35,702	10,882
3 Kuril-Kamchatka	34,587	10,542
4 Philippine	34,580	10,540
5 Kermadec	32,963	10,047
6 Bonin	32,789	9,994
7 New Britain	32,612	9,940
8 Izu	32,087	9,780
9 Puerto Rico	28,232	8,605
10 Yap	27,976	8,527

* With the exception of the Puerto Rico (Atlantic), all the trenches are in the Pacific

▲ *Canadian coast*
More than 50,000 offshore islands lie along Canada's extensive coastline.

Each of the eight deepest ocean trenches would be deep enough to submerge Mount Everest, which is 29,035 ft (8,850 m) above sea level.

▼ *Creature of the deep*
Fangtooth fish live at depths of up to 3 miles (5 km), where no light penetrates.

TOP 10 **COUNTRIES WITH THE LONGEST COASTLINES**

COUNTRY	COASTLINE LENGTH MILES	KM
1 Canada	125,567	202,080
2 Indonesia	33,999	54,716
3 Greenland	27,394	44,087
4 Russia	23,396	37,653
5 Philippines	22,549	36,289
6 Japan	18,486	29,751
7 Australia	16,007	25,760
8 Norway	15,626	25,148
9 USA	12,380	19,924
10 New Zealand	9,404	15,134
World	*300,780*	*484,058*

5 Papua New Guinea
5,344 / 4.87

4 France—overseas territories*
5,514 / 5.02

7 Maldives
3,444 / 3.14

9 Marshall Islands
2,359 / 2.15

6 Fiji
3,869 / 3.52

8 Saudi Arabia
2,571 / 2.34

10 India
2,236 / 2.04

WATER ON THE MOVE

TOP 10 **GREATEST* RIVER SYSTEMS**

RIVER SYSTEM# / CONTINENT	AVERAGE DISCHARGE AT MOUTH (CU FT/SEC)	(CU M/SEC)
1 Amazon South America	7,733,912	219,000
2 Congo (Zaïre) Africa	1,476,153	41,800
3 Orinoco South America	1,165,384	33,000
4 Yangtze (Chang Jiang) Asia	1,126,538	31,900
5 Paraná South America	907,587	25,700
6 Yenisei-Angara Asia	692,168	19,600
7 Brahmaputra (Tsangpo) Asia	678,042	19,200
8 Lena Asia	603,881	17,100
9 Madeira-Mamoré South America	600,349	17,000
10 Mississippi-Missouri North America	572,098	16,200

* Based on rate of discharge at mouth   # Excludes tributaries

Source: University of New Hampshire Global Composite Runoff Data Archive

▲ *Amazing Amazon*
Despite having a drainage area twice the size of India, the Amazon is not crossed by any bridges.

TOP 10 **LONGEST GLACIERS**

GLACIER / LOCATION / LENGTH (MILES/KM)

1 **Lambert** Antarctica
249 / 400

2 **Bering** Alaska, USA
118 / 190

3 **Beardmore** Antarctica
99 / 160

4 **Byrd** Antarctica
85 / 136

5 **Nimrod** Antarctica
84 / 135

6 **Amundsen** Antarctica
80 / 128

7 **Hubbard** Alaska, USA
76 / 122

8 **Slessor** Antarctica
75 / 120

9 **Denman** Antarctica
70 / 112

10 **Recovery** Antarctica
62 / 100

TOP 10 **LONGEST RIVERS**

RIVER / LOCATION	LENGTH MILES	KM
1 Amazon Bolivia, Brazil, Colombia, Ecuador, Peru, Venezuela	4,345	6,992
2 Nile Burundi, Dem. Rep. of Congo, Egypt, Eritrea, Ethiopia, Kenya, Rwanda, Sudan, Tanzania, Uganda	4,258	6,852
3 Yangtze (Chang Jiang) China	3,915	6,300
4 Mississippi-Missouri USA	3,899	6,275
5 Yenisei-Angara-Selenga Mongolia, Russia	3,442	5,539
6 Huang He (Yellow) China	3,395	5,464
7 Ob-Irtysh China, Kazakhstan, Russia	3,362	5,410
8 Congo-Chambeshi Angola, Burundi, Cameroon, Dem. Rep. of Congo, Rep. of Congo, Central African Republic, Rwanda, Tanzania, Zambia	2,920	4,700
9 Amur-Argun China, Mongolia, Russia	2,761	4,444
10 Lena Russia	2,734	4,400

TOP 10 **HIGHEST WATERFALLS**

WATERFALL* / RIVER / LOCATION / TOTAL DROP (FT / M)

1 Angel
Carrao, Venezuela
3,212 / 979#

2 Tugela
Tugela, South Africa
3,110 / 948

3 Ramnefjellsfossen
Jostedal Glacier, Nesdale, Norway
2,685 / 818

4 Mongefossen
Monge, Mongebekk, Norway
2,535 / 773

5 Gocta Cataracta
Cocahuayco, Peru
2,531 / 771

6 Mutarazi
Mutarazi River, Zimbabwe
2,499 / 762

7 Yosemite
Yosemite Creek,
California, USA
2,425 / 739

8 Østre Mardøla Foss
Mardals, Eikisdal, Norway
2,154 / 657

9 Tyssestrengane
Tysso, Hardanger, Norway
2,120 / 646

10 Cuquenán
Arabopo, Venezuela
2,000 / 610

* Waterfalls with year-round (non-seasonal) flow
and accurately recorded height
Longest single drop 2,648 ft (807 m)

▶ *Angel Falls*
The Falls are named after American pilot James Angel, who crash-landed his plane there in 1933 and trekked for 11 days back to civilization.

Bobby Leach, a Cornish circus stuntman, became the first man—and second person—ever to go over Niagara Falls in a barrel, on July 25, 1911. He broke both kneecaps and fractured his jaw.

TOP 10 **GREATEST* WATERFALLS**

WATERFALL / COUNTRY	AVERAGE FLOW CU FT/SEC	CU M/SEC
1 Inga Dem. Rep. of Congo	1,500,000	42,476
2 Livingstone Dem. Rep. of Congo	1,240,000	35,113
3 Boyoma (Stanley) Dem. Rep. of Congo	600,000	16,990
4 Khône Laos	410,000	10,783
5 Celilo USA	191,215	5,415
6 Salto Pará Venezuela	125,000	3,540
7 Paulo Afonso Brazil	100,000	2,832
8 Niagara (Horseshoe) Canada/USA	85,000	2,407
9 Iguaçu Argentina/Brazil	61,660	1,746
10 Victoria Zambia/Zimbabwe	38,430	1,088

* Based on volume of water

ISLANDS & LAKES

▲ *High island*
Lying between the Himalayas and the Andes, Puncak Jaya embodies one of very few ice-covered areas on the Equator.

TOP 10 **HIGHEST ISLANDS**

ISLAND / LOCATION / HIGHEST POINT	HIGHEST ELEVATION FT	M
1 New Guinea, Indonesia/Papua New Guinea; Puncak Jaya (Mount Carstensz)	16,024	4,884
2 Hawaii, USA; Mauna Kea	13,796	4,205
3 Borneo, Indonesia/Malaysia; Mount Kinabalu	13,455	4,101
4 Taiwan; Jade Mountain (Yu Shan)	12,966	3,952
5 Sumatra, Indonesia; Mount Kerinci	12,484	3,805
6 Ross, Antarctica; Mount Erebus	12,448	3,794
7 Honshu, Japan; Mount Fuji	12,387	3,776
8 South Island, New Zealand; Aorakim (Mount Cook)	12,320	3,755
9 Lombok, Indonesia; Mount Rinjani	12,224	3,726
10 Tenerife, Spain; Pico de Teide	12,198	3,718

THE 10 **SMALLEST ISLAND COUNTRIES**

COUNTRY / LOCATION / AREA (SQ MILES / SQ KM)

1 **Nauru**
Pacific Ocean 8.1 / 21.0

2 **Tuvalu**
Pacific Ocean 10.0 / 25.9

3 **Marshall Islands**
Pacific Ocean 69.9 / 181.0

4 **St. Kitts and Nevis**
Caribbean Sea 100.8 / 261.1

5 **Maldives**
Indian Ocean 115.1 / 298.1

6 **Malta**
Mediterranean Sea
122.0 / 316.0

7 **Grenada**
Caribbean Sea 132.8 / 344.0

8 **St. Vincent and the Grenadines**
Caribbean Sea 150.2 / 389.0

9 **Barbados**
Caribbean Sea 166.4 / 431.0

10 **Antigua and Barbuda**
Caribbean Sea 170.9 / 442.6

▼ *Island influx*
A commuter influx swells Manhattan's population to nearly three million during business hours.

TOP 10 **MOST DENSELY POPULATED ISLANDS***

ISLAND / LOCATION	AREA SQ MILES	SQ KM	TOTAL	POPULATION# PER SQ MILE	PER SQ KM
1 Salsette, India	168	435	13,180,000	78,452	30,291
2 Manhattan, New York, USA	23	60	1,629,000	70,826	27,346
3 Hong Kong, China	30	78	1,181,000	39,367	15,200
4 Singapore	269	679	4,620,000	17,175	6,631
5 Montreal Island, Canada	193	500	1,800,000	9,326	3,601
6 Long Island, New York, USA	1,401	3,629	7,536,000	5,379	2,077
7 Dakhin Shahbazbur, Bangladesh	556	1,440	1,675,000	3,013	1,163
8 Okinawa, Japan	446	1,115	1,250,000	2,803	1,082
9 Java, Indonesia	53,589	138,795	124,000,000	2,314	893
10 Cebu, Philippines	1,786	4,626	2,5360,000	1,942	750

* Includes only islands with populations of more than 1 million
# Latest available year

TOP 10 **LARGEST LAKES**

LAKE / LOCATION	APPROX. AREA SQ MILES	SQ KM
1 Caspian Sea, Azerbaijan/Iran/Kazakhstan/Russia/Turkmenistan	144,402	374,000
2 Michigan/Huron*, Canada/USA	45,342	117,436
3 Superior, Canada/USA	31,802	82,367
4 Victoria, Kenya/Tanzania/Uganda	26,828	69,485
5 Tanganyika, Burundi/Tanzania/Dem. Rep. of Congo/Zambia	12,700	32,893
6 Baikal, Russia	12,160	31,494
7 Great Bear, Canada	12,028	31,153
8 Malawi (Nyasa), Tanzania/Malawi/Mozambique	11,600	30,044
9 Great Slave, Canada	11,030	28,568
10 Erie, Canada/USA	9,930	25,719

* Now considered two lobes of the same lake

Source: ILEC, World Lake Database

▶ *Exploring Lake Baikal* Scientists use the same submarines that once explored the Titanic.

THE 10 **DEEPEST FRESHWATER LAKES**

LAKE / LOCATION	GREATEST DEPTH FT	M
1 Baikal, Russia	5,712	1,741
2 Tanganyika, Burundi/Tanzania/Dem. Rep. of Congo/Zambia	4,826	1,471
3 Vostok, Antarctica	3,281	1,000
4 Malawi (Nyasa) Tanzania/Malawi/Mozambique	2,316	706
5 Great Slave, Canada	2,014	614
6 Crater, Oregon, USA	1,949	594
7 Matana, Celebes, Indonesia	1,936	590
8 Toba, Sumatra, Indonesia	1,736	529
9 Hornindalsvatnet, Norway	1,686	514
10 Sarezskoye (Sarez), Tajikistan	1,657	505

Source: ILEC, World Lake Database

On Location
Containing roughly one-fifth of the world's surface freshwater, Lake Baikal is also the planet's oldest lake, having formed more than 25 million years ago.

ON TOP OF THE WORLD

TOP 10 **HIGHEST MOUNTAINS**

MOUNTAIN / LOCATION	FIRST ASCENT	TEAM NATIONALITY	HEIGHT* FT	M
1 Everest, Nepal/China	May 29, 1953	British/New Zealand	29,035	8,850
2 K2 (Chogori), Pakistan/China	Jul 31, 1954	Italian	28,251	8,611
3 Kangchenjunga, Nepal/India	May 25, 1955	British	28,169	8,586
4 Lhotse, Nepal/China	May 18, 1956	Swiss	27,940	8,516
5 Makalu I, Nepal/China	May 15, 1955	French	27,838	8,485
6 Cho Oyu, Nepal/China	Oct 19, 1954	Austrian	26,864	8,188
7 Dhaulagiri I, Nepal	May 13, 1960	Swiss/Austrian	26,795	8,167
8 Manaslu I (Kutang I), Nepal	May 9, 1956	Japanese	26,781	8,163
9 Nanga Parbat (Diamir), Pakistan	Jul 3, 1953	German/Austrian	26,657	8,125
10 Anapurna I, Nepal	Jun 3, 1950	French	26,545	8,091

* Height of principal peak; lower peaks of the same mountain are excluded

In 1852, the Great Trigonometrical Survey of India revealed that Everest (then called "Peak XV") was the world's tallest peak at 29,002 ft (8,840 m). Errors in measurement were corrected in 1955 to 29,029 ft (8,848 m) and in 1993 to 29,028 ft (8,847.7 m). In 1999, data beamed from sensors on Everest's summit to GPS satellites established a new height of 29,035 ft (8,850 m), which geographers accept as the current "official" figure.

TOP 10 **LONGEST MOUNTAIN RANGES**

RANGE / LOCATION	LENGTH MILES	KM
1 Andes, South America	4,500	7,242
2 Rocky Mountains, North America	3,750	6,035
3 Himalayas/Karakoram/Hindu Kush, Asia	2,400	3,862
4 Great Dividing Range, Australia	2,250	3,621
5 Trans-Antarctic Mountains, Antarctica	2,200	3,541
6 Brazilian East Coast Range, Brazil	1,900	3,058
7 Sumatran/Javan Range, Sumatra, Java	1,800	2,897
8 Tien Shan, China	1,400	2,253
9 Eastern Ghats, India	1,300	2,092
10 = Altai, Asia	1,250	2,012
= Central New Guinean Range, Papua New Guinea	1,250	2,012
= Urals, Russia	1,250	2,012

This Top 10 includes only ranges that are continuous (the Sumatran/Javan Range is divided only by a short interruption between the two islands). The Aleutian Range extends for 1,650 miles (2,655 km), but is fragmented across numerous islands of the northwest Pacific. As well as these ranges that lie above the surface of Earth, there are also several submarine ranges that are even longer.

▶ *Machu Picchu*
The Andes were originally inhabited by the Incas, and span seven countries and three capitals.

Ojos del Salado
The second highest peak in the Andes—and in the Southern Hemisphere—also contains the world's most elevated lake.

▶ **Piton de la Fournaise**
Meaning "Peak of the Furnace," this volcano has erupted 19 times in the last decade.

TOP 10 **HIGHEST VOLCANOES**

	VOLCANO	LOCATION	HEIGHT FT	M
1	Ojos del Salado	Chile	22,595	6,887
2	Llullaillaco	Chile	22,110	6,739
3	Tipas	Argentina	21,850	6,660
4	Nevado Incahuasi	Chile	21,722	6,621
5	Cerro el Cóndor	Argentina	21,430	6,532
6	Coropuna	Peru	20,922	6,377
7	Parinacota	Chile	20,827	6,348
8	Chimborazo	Ecuador	20,702	6,310
9	Pular	Chile	20,449	6,233
10	El Solo	Chile	20,308	6,190

Source: Smithsonian Institution

TOP 10 **COUNTRIES WITH THE HIGHEST ELEVATIONS***

	COUNTRY	PEAK	HEIGHT FT	M
1 =	China	Everest	29,035	8,850
=	Nepal	Everest	29,035	8,850
3	Pakistan	K2	28,238	8,607
4	India	Kangchenjunga	28,208	8,598
5	Bhutan	Khula Kangri	24,784	7,554
6	Tajikistan	Garmo (formerly Kommunizma)	24,590	7,495
7	Afghanistan	Noshaq	24,581	7,490
8	Kyrgyzstan	Pik Pobedy	24,406	7,439
9	Kazakhstan	Khan Tengri	22,949	6,995
10	Argentina	Cerro Aconcagua	22,834	6,960

* Based on the tallest peak in each country

TOP 10 **MOST ACTIVE VOLCANOES***

VOLCANO / LOCATION / CONTINUOUSLY ACTIVE SINCE

1 Mount Etna
Italy c. 1500 BC

2 Stromboli
Italy c. AD 4

3 Yasur
Vanuatu c. 1204

4 Piton de la Fournaise
Réunion 1920

5 Santa Maria
Guatemala 1922

6 Dukono
Indonesia 1933

7 Sangay
Ecuador 1934

8 Ambrym
Vanuatu 1935

9 Suwanose-jima
Japan 1949

10 Tinakula
Solomon Islands 1951

Sicily's 10,99-ft (3,350-m) Mount Etna may have been erupting for more than half a million years, with occasional dormant periods. Continuous activity has been recorded for the past 3,500 years, the eruption of 1843 killing 56, with a further nine in 1979 and two in 1987.

* Based on years of continuous eruption

LAND FEATURES

TOP 10 **LARGEST DESERTS**

DESERT / LOCATION	APPROX. AREA SQ MILES	SQ KM
1 Sahara, northern Africa	3,513,530	9,100,000
2 Arabian, southwest Asia	899,618	2,330,000
3 Gobi, central Asia	500,002	1,295,000
4 Patagonian, Argentina/Chile	259,847	673,000
5 Great Basin, USA	189,962	492,000
6 Great Victoria, Australia	163,707	424,000
7 Chihuahuan, Mexico/USA	140,000	362,600
8 Great Sandy, Australia	138,997	360,000
9 Karakum, Turkmenistan	135,136	350,000
10 Sonoran, Mexico/USA	120,078	311,000

◄ *Saharan sands*
Covering an area nearly the size of the USA, half of the Sahara receives less than 0.8 in (2 cm) of rain per year.

▼ *Coral collection*
With 1,190 coral islands, the Maldives' average height above sea level is only 4.9 ft (1.5 m).

THE 10 **COUNTRIES WITH THE LOWEST ELEVATIONS**

	COUNTRY*	HIGHEST POINT	ELEVATION FT	M
10	Singapore	Bukit Timah	544.6	166.0
9	Qatar	Qurayn Abu al Bawl	337.9	103.0
8	Kiribati	Unnamed on Banaba	265.7	81.0
7	Vatican City	Unnamed	246.1	75.0
6	Bahamas	Mount Alvernia on Cat Island	206.7	63.0
5	Nauru	Unnamed on plateau rim	200.1	61.0
4	Gambia	Unnamed	173.9	53.0
3	Marshall Islands	Unnamed on Likiep	32.8	10.0
2	Tuvalu	Unnamed	16.4	5.0
1	Maldives	Unnamed on Wilingili island in the Addu Atoll	7.8	2.4

* Excludes overseas possessions, territories, and dependencies

Source: CIA, *The World Factbook 2010*

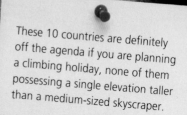

These 10 countries are definitely off the agenda if you are planning a climbing holiday, none of them possessing a single elevation taller than a medium-sized skyscraper.

▼ *Great depths*
The depth of the Krubera cave is equivalent to seven times the height of the Eiffel Tower

TOP 10 **LARGEST METEORITE CRATERS**

	CRATER / LOCATION	DIAMETER MILES	KM
1	Vredefort, South Africa	186	300
2	Sudbury, Ontario, Canada	155	250
3	Chicxulub, Yucatan, Mexico	107	170
4 =	Manicougan, Quebec, Canada	62	100
=	Popigai, Russia	62	100
6 =	Acraman, Australia	56	90
=	Chesapeake Bay, Virginia, USA	56	90
8	Puchezh-Katunki, Russia	50	80
9	Morokweng, South Africa	43	70
10	Kara, Russia	40	65

Source: Earth Impact Database, Planetary and Space Science Center, University of New Brunswick

▼ *Space debris*
Discovered by chance while a farmer was plowing, Hoba meteorite weighs more than six elephants.

THE 10 **DEEPEST CAVES**

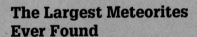

	CAVE SYSTEM / LOCATION	DEPTH FT	M
1	Krubera (Voronja), Georgia	7,188	2,191
2	Illyuzia-Mezhonnogo-Snezhnaya, Georgia	5,751	1,753
3	Lamprechtsofen Vogelschacht Weg Schacht, Austria	5,354	1,632
4	Gouffre Mirolda, France	5,335	1,626
5	Réseau Jean Bernard, France	5,256	1,602
6	Torca del Cerro del Cuevon/ Torca de las Saxifragas, Spain	5,213	1,589
7	Sarma, Georgia	5,062	1,543
8	Shakta Vjacheslav Pantjukhina, Georgia	4,948	1,508
9	Sima de la Conisa/Torca Magali, Spain	4,944	1,507
10	Cehi 2, Slovenia	4,928	1,502

In January 2001, a team of Ukrainian cave explorers in the Arabikskaja system in the western Caucasus mountains of the Georgian Republic found a branch of the Voronja, or "Crow's Cave," and established that its depth of 5,610 ft (1,710 m) far exceeded anything previously known.

The Largest Meteorites Ever Found

Meteorites have been known since early times: fragments of meteorite have been found mounted in a necklace in an Egyptian pyramid and in Native American burial sites. On November 16, 1492, there was a fall of a 118-kg (260-lb) meteorite, which was later preserved in the museum at Ensisheim in Switzerland. There have been nearly 40,000 documented meteorite finds, with the largest eight weighing over 20 tons. Estimates of the size of meteorites creating the largest craters dwarfs those that have actually been discovered. The meteorite producing Vredefort in South Africa is believed to have been between 3–6 miles (5–10 km) wide, weighing trillions of tonnes.

WORLD WEATHER

TOP 10 HOTTEST PLACES – AVERAGE

LOCATION* / AVERAGE TEMPERATURE# (°F / °C)

#	Location	°F	°C
1	Dalol, Ethiopia	94.3	34.6
2	Assab, Eritrea	86.8	30.4
3	Néma, Mauritania	86.5	30.3
4	Berbera, Somalia	86.2	30.1
5	Hombori, Mali	86.1	30.1
6	Perm Island, South Yemen	86.0	30.0
7	Djibouti, Djibouti	85.8	29.9
8	Atbara, Sudan	85.7	29.8
=	Bender Qaasim, Somalia	85.5	29.7
=	Kamarãn Island, North Yemen	85.5	29.7

* Maximum of two places per country listed

\# Highest long-term temperature averaged throughout year

TOP 10 PLACES WITH THE MOST CONTRASTING SEASONS*

#	LOCATION#	WINTER °F	WINTER °C	SUMMER °F	SUMMER °C	DIFFERENCE °F	DIFFERENCE °C
1	Verkhoyansk, Russia	-58.5	-50.3	56.5	13.6	115.0	63.9
2	Yakutsk, Russia	-49.0	-45.0	63.5	17.5	112.5	62.5
3	Manzhouli, China	-15.0	-26.1	69.0	20.6	84.0	46.7
4	Fort Yukon, Alaska, USA	-20.2	-29.0	61.4	16.3	81.6	45.3
5	Fort Good Hope, North West Territory, Canada	-21.8	-29.9	59.5	15.3	81.3	45.2
6	Brochet, Manitoba, Canada	-20.5	-29.2	59.7	15.4	80.2	44.6
7	Tunka, Mongolia	-16.0	-26.7	61.0	16.1	77.0	42.8
8	Fairbanks, Alaska, USA	-11.2	-24.0	60.1	15.6	71.3	39.6
9	Semipalatinsk, Kazakhstan	0.5	-17.7	69.0	20.6	68.5	38.3
10	Jorgen Bronlund Fjørd, Greenland	-23.6	-30.9	43.5	6.4	67.1	37.3

* Biggest differences between mean monthly temperatures in summer and winter
\# Maximum of two places per country listed

Source: Philip Eden

TOP 10 DRIEST PLACES – AVERAGE

#	LOCATION*	AVERAGE ANNUAL RAINFALL# IN	AVERAGE ANNUAL RAINFALL# MM
1	Arica, Chile	0.03	0.7
2	= Al'Kufrah, Peru	0.03	0.8
	= Aswân, Egypt	0.03	0.8
	= Luxor, Egypt	0.03	0.8
5	Ica, Peru	0.09	2.3
6	Wadi Halfa, Sudan	0.10	2.6
7	Iquique, Chile	0.20	5.0
8	Pelican Point, Namibia	0.32	8.0
9	= Aoulef, Algeria	0.48	12.0
	= Callao, Peru	0.48	12.0

* Maximum of two places per country listed
\# Annual total averaged over a long period

Source: Philip Eden

▼ Iquique
A commune in northern Chile, Iquique includes a popular port city and the Atacama Desert.

◀ The Republic of Djibouti
One of Africa's least populated countries, Djibouti's landscape is mostly semidesert.

TOP 10 **COLDEST PLACES**

LOCATION* / LOWEST RECORDED TEMPERATURE (°F / °C)

10 Prospect Creek Alaska, USA -79.8 -62.1

9 Mayo Yukon, Canada -80.0 -62.2

7 = Snag Yukon, Canada -81.4 -63.0
= Bulunkul Lake Tajikistan -81.4 -63.0

6 Eismitte# Greenland -85.0 -64.9

5 Northice# Greenland -87.0 -66.0

4 Verkhoyansk Russia -93.6 -69.8

3 Oymyakon Russia -96.2 -71.2

2 Sovietskaya# Antarctica -124.1 -86.7

1 Vostok# Antarctica -128.6 -89.2

* Maximum of two places per country listed
# Present or former scientific research base

Source: Philip Eden/Roland Bert

Vostok, a Russian research station, recorded the lowest temperature on Earth on July 21, 1983, and, though unofficial, an even colder one of -132°F (-91°C) in 1997. The station is situated at an altitude of 11,220 ft (3,420 m) and is susceptible to high speed katabatic (downhill) winds that can reach up to 200 mph (322 km/h).

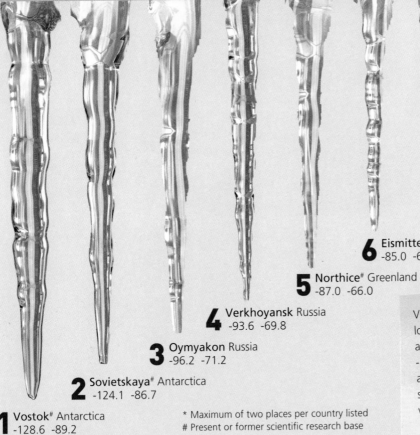

▼ *Oymyakon*
Known as the coldest populated place on Earth, Oymyakon has an average winter temperature of -49°F (-45°C).

TOP 10 **DULLEST PLACES** *

LOCATION#	% OF MAX. POSSIBLE HOURS SUNSHINE	AVERAGE ANNUAL HOURS SUNSHINE
1 Ben Nevis, Scotland	16	736
2 Hoyvik, Faeroes, Denmark	19	902
3 Maam, Ireland	19	929
4 Prince Rupert, British Columbia, Canada	20	955
5 Riksgransen, Sweden	20	965
6 Akureyri, Iceland	20	973
7 Raufarhöfn, Iceland	21	995
8 Nanortalik, Greenland	22	1,000
9 Dalwhinnie, Scotland	22	1,032
10 Karasjok, Norway	23	1,090

* Lowest yearly sunshine total, averaged over a long period of years
# Maximum of two places per country listed
Source: Philip Eden

NATURAL DISASTERS

THE 10 **DEADLIEST TYPES OF NATURAL DISASTER**

DISASTER /
ESTIMATED DEATHS 2000–10

Earthquake
680,361

> ► *Haiti earthquake*
> *The magnitude 7.0 earthquake caused $11 billion of damage and left 1.5 million homeless.*

Storm
173,699

Extreme temperature
148,249

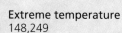

Epidemic
66,506

There are some discrepancies between the "official" death tolls in many of the world's worst earthquakes and the estimates of other authorities: a figure of 750,000 is sometimes quoted for the Tangshan earthquake of 1976, for example.

Flood
62,233

Mass movement (wet)
10,856

Drought
1,520

> ► *Indonesian eruption*
> *Around 1.8 billion cubic feet of volcanic material was released by the 2010 eruption of Mount Merapi in Indonesia.*

Wildfire
770

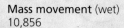

Volcanic eruption
560

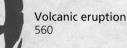

Mass movement (dry)
126

THE 10 **WORST EARTHQUAKES**

	LOCATION	DATE	ESTIMATED NO. KILLED
1	Near East/Mediterranean	May 20, 1202	1,100,000
2	Shenshi, China	Feb 2, 1556	820,000
3	Calcutta, India	Oct 11, 1737	300,000
4	Antioch, Syria	May 20, 526	250,000
5	Tangshan, China	Jul 28, 1976	242,419
6	Port-au-Prince, Haiti	Jan 12, 2010	230,000
7	Nanshan, China	May 22, 1927	200,000
8	Yeddo, Japan	Dec 30, 1703	190,000
9	Kansu, China	Dec 16, 1920	180,000
10	Messina, Italy	Dec 28, 1908	160,000

THE 10 **WORST EPIDEMICS**

	EPIDEMIC	LOCATION	DATE	ESTIMATED NO. KILLED
1	Black Death	Europe/Asia	1347–80s	75,000,000
2	Influenza	Worldwide	1918–20	20–40,000,000
3	AIDS	Worldwide	1981–	>25,000,000
4	Plague of Justinian	Europe/Asia	AD 541–90	<25,000,000
5	Bubonic plague	India	1896–1948	12,000,000
6 =	Antonine Plague (probably smallpox)	Roman Empire	AD 165–180	5,000,000
=	Plague	India	1896–1907	5,000,000
8	Typhus	Eastern Europe	1918–22	3,000,000
9 =	Smallpox	Mexico	1530–45	1,000,000
=	Cholera	Russia	1852–60	1,000,000

THE 10 **COUNTRIES WITH THE HIGHEST FLOOD-DAMAGE COST**

	COUNTRY	ESTIMATED COST ($) 2000–10
1	China	56,377,821,000
2	India	18,949,347,000
3	USA	15,565,330,000
4	UK	14,949,150,000
5	Germany	11,840,000,000
6	Pakistan	10,206,148,000
7	Italy	9,899,000,000
8	Australia	9,431,500,000
9	Japan	9,397,000,000
10	France	4,322,350,000
	World	212,197,295,000

Source: Emergency Events Database (EM-DAT)

Precise figures for deaths during the disruptions of epidemics are inevitably unreliable, but the Black Death, or bubonic plague, probably transmitted by fleas from infected rats, swept across Asia and Europe in the 14th century, destroying entire populations—including more than half the inhabitants of London, some 25 million in Europe and 50 million in Asia.

THE 10 **COUNTRIES WITH THE MOST DEATHS FROM NATURAL DISASTERS***

COUNTRY / ESTIMATED DEATHS FROM NATURAL DISASTERS / MOST DEADLY TYPE

1 China 12,710,201
Flood

2 India 9,114,324
Epidemic

3 USSR 3,868,439
Epidemic

4 Bangladesh 2,991,948
Drought

5 Ethiopia 416,056
Drought

6 Indonesia 239,462
Earthquake

7 Japan 221,700
Earthquake

8 Uganda 203,996
Epidemic

9 Niger 194,572
Epidemic

10 Pakistan 170,088
Earthquake

* Includes deaths from drought, earthquake, epidemic, extreme temperature, flood, insect infestation, landslides, storms, volcanoes, wave/surge, and wildfires.

▲ *Floodwaters in China*
China has suffered over 200 incidents of flooding in the last 100 years—the worst affecting a quarter of a billion people.

2

LIFE ON EARTH

EARTH SUMMIT 2012

The United Nations Conference on Sustainable Development takes place in June 2012—20 years after the influential first Earth Summit was held in Rio de Janeiro. The Rio+20 summit will provide a platform for world leaders to come together to address a number of globally important issues, including the financial, food, and energy crises, water scarcity, climate change, and the loss of biodiversity. The highly ambitious aim of the summit is to seek agreement from heads of state to work toward providing for a future in which each person has a decent standard of living while preserving ecosystems and natural resources.

EXTINCT!

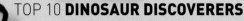

THE FIRST DINOSAUR TO BE NAMED

The first genus of dinosaur to be named was Megalosaurus, which means "great lizard" in Greek. It was described by William Buckland, a professor at Oxford University, UK, in a paper he wrote in 1824.

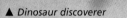

▲ *Dinosaur discoverer*
Dong Zhiming is the most prolific dinosaur hunter of modern times.

TOP 10 DINOSAUR DISCOVERERS

	DISCOVERER / COUNTRY	PERIOD	DINOSAURS NAMED*
1	Friedrich von Huene (Germany)	1902–61	46
2	Othniel Charles Marsh (USA)	1870–94	39
3	Dong Zhiming (China)	1973–2003	35
4 =	Edward Drinker Cope (USA)	1866–92	30
=	Harry Govier Seeley (UK)	1869–98	30
6	José Fernando Bonaparte (Argentina)	1969–2000	28
7	Richard Owen (UK)	1841–84	23
8 =	Barnum Brown (USA)	1873–1963	17
=	Henry Fairfield Osborn (USA)	1902–24	17
=	Yang Zhong-Jian ("C. C. Young") (China)	1937–82	17

* Including joint namings

TOP 10 HEAVIEST DINOSAURS EVER DISCOVERED

	NAME	ESTIMATED WEIGHT (TONS)
1	Bruhathkayosaurus	139
2	Amphicoelias	134
3	Puertasaurus	88–110
4	Argentinosaurus	66–97
5	Argyrosaurus	88
6	Antarctosaurus	76
7	Sauroposeidon	55–66
8	Paralititan	65
9	Turiasaurus	44–53
10	Supersaurus	39–44

Fossil remains of Bruhathkayosaurus were found in southern India. Some authorities have estimated it as having weighed as much as 240 tons—more than a blue whale—but such claims have been questioned.

▶ *Big bird*
At over 10 ft (3 m) tall, the elephant bird was once the world's largest.

TOP 10 TIMELINE: LAST SEEN ALIVE

These are the years when some notable creatures became extinct, especially as a result of human intervention. In the case of those that occurred in captivity, the precise date can be given.

1627
Aurochs
Extensively hunted, the last of these large oxen died in the Jaktorow Forest in Poland.

1649
Aepyornis
Also known as the "elephant bird," this wingless bird was a native of Madagascar.

1681
Dodo
Perhaps the most famous extinct creature ever, the last of these flightless birds was observed on Mauritius by Benjamin Harry.

1768
Steller's sea cow
This large marine mammal, named after its 1741 discoverer, was hunted to extinction.

1844
Great auk
The last surviving pair of great auks was killed on Eldey Island for Icelandic collector Carl Siemsen.

TOP 10 **LONGEST DINOSAURS EVER DISCOVERED**

	NAME	ESTIMATED LENGTH (FT)
1	Puertasaurus	115–131

Provisional estimates by palaeontologist Fernando Novas place this as the longest dinosaur yet discovered.

2	Sauroposeidon	112

It has been estimated that this creature was probably the tallest ever to walk on Earth, able to extend its neck to 60 ft (18 m).

3	Supersaurus	108–112

Claims of a length of up to 130 ft (40 m) have been made by some authorities.

4	Bruhathkayosaurus	92–112

As with claims of its record-breaking weight, those of a length of up to 145 ft (44 m) remain questionable.

5 =	Hudiesaurus	98

Although known only from incomplete remains found in China, this may have been one of the longest of all sauropods.

=	Turiasaurus	98

This long sauropod was named after Turia, the Latin name of Teruel, Spain, where it was found.

7	Giraffatitan	82–98

This lightly built but long dinosaur was found in Tanzania. A skeleton in the Humboldt Museum, Berlin, is the longest dinosaur on display.

8	Argentinosaurus	72–85

Estimates of the length of Argentinosaurus vary, some early claims putting it at up to 110 ft (35 m).

9 =	Argyrosaurus	66–98

This dinosaur from the late Cretaceous period is believed to have stood 26 ft (8 m) tall.

=	Diplodocus	66–98

As it was long and thin, Diplodocus was a relative lightweight in the dinosaur world. It was also probably one of the most stupid dinosaurs, having the smallest brain in relation to its body size. Diplodocus was given its name (which means "double beam") in 1878 by US palaeontologist Othniel C. Marsh.

▼ *Argentinosaurus*
This gigantic planteater lived in the forests of South America over 90 million years ago.

▶ **Back from the dead**
There have been nearly 4,000 unconfirmed sightings of the Tasmanian wolf since 1936.

1875 1883 1914 1932 1936

Tarpan
The last pure-bred tarpan, a European wild horse, died in a Moscow zoo.

Quagga
Found in South Africa, this zebra-like creature became extinct in the wild by 1883.

Passenger pigeon
Once seen in vast flocks, the last specimen died in Cincinnati Zoo on September 1, 1914.

Heath hen
The grouselike prairie chicken was extensively hunted in New England.

Tasmanian wolf
Also known as the thylacine, the last specimen died in captivity.

Endangered Animals

THE 10 COUNTRIES WITH THE MOST THREATENED ANIMAL SPECIES*

	COUNTRY	MAMMALS	BIRDS	REPTILES	AMPHIBIANS	FISHES	INVERTEBRATES	TOTAL
1	USA	37	74	32	56	177	531	907
2	Australia	55	52	43	47	100	489	786
3	Indonesia	183	119	31	32	138	246	749
4	Mexico	99	55	94	211	150	79	688
5	India	94	78	30	66	122	113	503
6	Malaysia	70	45	24	47	60	242	488
7	Philippines	39	72	38	48	65	213	475
8	Colombia	51	91	19	213	50	30	454
9	Ecuador	43	71	22	171	49	62	418
10	China	74	85	31	87	97	32	406
	UK	5	2	0	0	41	11	59

* Identified by the IUCN as Critically Endangered, Endangered, or Vulnerable

Source: IUCN, *2010 Red List of Threatened Species*

▲ **Symbol of hope**
After years of decline, giant panda numbers are thought to be increasing.

▲ **At risk**
The leatherback turtle, ranked as Critically Endangered, is close to extinction in the wild.

THE 10 MOST THREATENED CLASS OF ANIMAL

CLASS / CLASS THREATENED*

1 Amphibians 1,905
2 Fish 1,275
3 Birds 1,222
4 Mammals 1,141
5 Mollusks 978
6 Insects 626
7 Crustaceans 606
8 Reptiles 423
9 Corals 235
10 Arachnids 18

Total (including classes not in Top 10) 8,462

* Identified by the IUCN as Critically Endangered, Endangered, or Vulnerable

Source: IUCN, *2010 Red List of Threatened Species*

▶ **Galapagos hawk**
There are less than 150 mating pairs in existence, and these birds are now extinct on several Galapagos islands.

IN THE RED

The IUCN Red List system classifies the degree of threat posed to wildlife on a sliding scale from Vulnerable (at high risk of extinction), through Endangered (at very high risk of extinction), to Critically Endangered (facing an extremely high risk of extinction in the wild). Actual threats to species are many and varied, and include both human activity and natural events, ranging from habitat loss and degradation, invasions by alien species, hunting, and accidental destruction due to persecution, pollution, and natural disasters.

TOP 10 **CHIMPANZEE COUNTRIES**

COUNTRY / ESTIMATED CHIMPANZEE POPULATION*

1 Dem. Rep. of Congo 80,000–110,000
2 Gabon 27,000–64,000
3 Cameroon 34,000–44,000
4 Guinea 8,100–29,000
5 Côte d'Ivoire 8,000–12,000
6 Uganda 4,000–5,700
7 Mali 1,600–5,200
8 Liberia 1,000–5,000
9 Nigeria 2,000–3,000
10 Sierra Leone 1,500–2,500

World 172,700–299,700

* Ranked on estimated maximum

Source: IUCN

GLOBAL TIGER INITIATIVE

Faced with threats of poaching, habitat loss and fragmentation, if current trends persist the tiger faces extinction within this decade. The Global Tiger Recovery Program aims to double the population by 2022, through collaboration of 13 tiger-range countries, charities, and institutions. Tigers serve as an umbrella species—setting aside large areas protects many other species. Their habitat overlaps that of many other endangered animals, including Asian elephants, orangutans, and greater one-horned rhinoceroses.

▼ *Polar bears at drift*
With its habitat literally melting, global warming is considered the polar bear's most significant threat.

DEATHLY DECLINE

Biodiversity is being lost at 1,000 times the natural rate, with most serious decline in islands, dry forests, polar regions, and marine environments. Thirty percent of species are under threat because of climate change. Of the world's 5,490 mammals, 78 are extinct in the wild, 188 Critically Endangered, 450 Endangered, and 492 Vulnerable.

NATURE'S HEAVYWEIGHTS

TOP 10 **HEAVIEST LAND MAMMALS**

MAMMAL* / SCIENTIFIC NAME	LENGTH		WEIGHT	
	FT	M	LB	KG
1 African elephant (*Loxodonta africana*)	24.6	7.5	14,000	6,350
2 Hippopotamus (*Hippopotamus amphibius*)	14.0	4.2	8,000	3,629
3 White rhinoceros (*Ceratotherium simum*)	13.7	4.1	7,920	3,592
4 Giraffe (*Giraffa camelopardalis*)	19.0	6.0	2,800	1,270
5 American buffalo (*Bison bison*)	11.5	3.5	2,205	1,000
6 Moose (*Alces alces*)	10.1	3.1	1,820	825
7 Arabian camel (dromedary) (*Camelus dromedarius*)	11.5	3.5	1,600	726
8 Grizzly bear (*Ursus arctos*)	8.0	2.5	800	363
9 Siberian tiger (*Panthera tigris altaica*)	10.8	3.3	660	300
10 Gorilla (*Gorilla gorilla gorilla*)	6.5	2.0	485	220

* Heaviest species per genus; maximum weight, exclusively terrestrial, excluding seals, etc.

◄ **Land giant**
African elephants can be identified by their Africa-shaped ears, which they use to keep cool.

TOP 10 **HEAVIEST CARNIVORES**

CARNIVORE	LENGTH			WEIGHT	
	FT	IN	M	LB	KG
1 Southern elephant seal	20	0	6.0	8,800	4,000
2 Pacific walrus	12	6	3.8	3,086	1,400
3 Steller sea lion	9	3	2.8	2,425	1,100
4 Polar bear	8	0	2.5	1,600	726
5 Grizzly bear	8	0	2.5	800	363
6 Siberian tiger	10	7	3.3	660	300
7 American black bear	6	0	1.8	600	270
8 Lion	6	6	2.0	420	191
9 Spectacled bear	6	0	1.8	340	154
10 Giant panda	5	0	1.5	300	136

TOP 10 CARNIVORES WITH THE HEAVIEST NEWBORN

CARNIVORE / SCIENTIFIC NAME	BIRTH WEIGHT		
	LB	OZ	G
1 Lion (Panthera leo)	4	6	2,100
2 Spotted hyena (Crocuta crocuta)	3	5	1,500
3 Tiger (Panthera tigris)	2	11	1,255
4 Jaguar (Panthera onca)	1	13	816
5 Brown (grizzly) bear (Ursus arctos)	1	9	700
6 Polar bear (Ursus maritimus)	1	7	641
7 Leopard (Panthera pardus)	1	3	549
8 Snow leopard (Panthera uncia)	1	0	442
9 Grey wolf (Canis lupus)	0	15	425
10 Mountain lion (Puma concolor)	0	14	400

▶ **Queen of the jungle**
The gestation period for African lions is around 110 days, with lionesses giving birth to an average litter of two to three cubs.

TOP 10 HEAVIEST BIRDS

BIRD* / SCIENTIFIC NAME	HEIGHT		WEIGHT		
	IN	CM	LB	OZ	KG
1 Ostrich (Struthio camelus)	100.4	255	343	9	156.0
2 Northern cassowary (Casuarius unappendiculatus)	59.1	150	127	9	58.0
3 Emu (Dromaius novaehollandiae)	61.0	155	121	6	55.0
4 Emperor penguin (Aptenodytes forsteri)	45.3	115	101	4	46.0
5 Greater rhea (Rhea americana)	55.1	140	55	2	25.0
6 Mute swan# (Cygnus olor)	93.7	238	49	6	22.5
7 Kori bustard# (Ardeotis kori)	106.3	270	41	8	19.0
8 = Andean condor# (Vultur gryphus)	126.0	320	33	1	15.0
= Great white pelican# (Pelecanus onocrotalus)	141.7	360	33	1	15.0
10 European black vulture# (Old World) (Aegypius monachus)	116.1	295	27	5	12.5

* By species
# Flighted – all others are flightless

Source: Chris Mead

◀ **Southern elephant seal**
Adult male members of the southern elephant seal population are typically five to six times larger than the females.

▲ **Biggest bird**
The largest living species of bird, the ostrich also lays the biggest egg and has the top land speed of any living bird.

LONGEST & LARGEST

TOP 10 MAMMALS WITH THE LONGEST TAILS

MAMMAL / MAX. TAIL LENGTH (IN / CM)

Asian elephant   60 / 150

Leopard   55 / 140

African elephant   51 / 130

African buffalo   43 / 110
Giraffe   43 / 110
Red kangaroo   43 / 110

Langur   39 / 100
Lion   39 / 100
Snub-nosed monkey   39 / 100
Water buffalo   39 / 100
White-cheeked mangabey   39 / 100

▶ *Deadly grip*
The four largest snakes are all constrictors.

◀ *On the wing*
Weighing as much as 25 lb (11 kg), adult Andean condors can have a 10-ft (3-m) wingspan.

TOP 10 LARGEST BIRDS OF PREY*

	BIRD / SCIENTIFIC NAME	MAX. LENGTH IN	CM
1	Himalayan Griffon vulture (*Gyps himalayensis*)	59	150
2	Californian condor (*Gymnogyps californianus*)	53	134
3	Andean condor (*Vultur gryphus*)	51	130
4 =	Lammergeier (*Gypaetus barbatus*)	45	115
=	Lappet-faced vulture (*Torgos tracheliotus*)	45	115
6	Eurasian Griffon vulture (*Gyps fulvus*)	43	110
7	European black vulture (*Aegypus monachus*)	42	107
8	Harpy eagle (*Harpia harpyja*)	41	105
9	Wedge-tailed eagle (*Aquila audax*)	41	104
10	Ruppell's griffon (*Gyps rueppellii*)	40	101

* By length, diurnal only—hence excluding owls

TOP 10 BIGGEST BIG CATS

	SPECIES / SCIENTIFIC NAME	MAX. LENGTH FT	M
1	Tiger (*Panthera tigris*)	12.0	3.70
2	Lion (*Panthera leo*)	10.8	3.30
3	Leopard (*Panthera pardus*)	9.6	2.90
4	Clouded leopard (*Neofelis nebulosa*)	6.6	2.00
5	Jaguar (*Panthera onca*)	6.2	1.90
6	Snow leopard (*Uncia uncia*)	5.9	1.80
7	Cougar (*Puma concolor*)	4.9	1.50
8	Cheetah (*Acinonyx jubatus*)	4.9	1.50
9	Lynx (*Lynx lynx*, etc.)	4.2	1.30
10 =	Asian golden cat (*Pardofelis temminckii*)	3.2	1.00
=	Bobcat (*Lynx rufus*)	3.2	1.00
=	Ocelot (*Leopardus pardalis*)	3.2	1.00
=	Serval (*Leptailurus serval*)	3.2	1.00

TOP 10 OF EVERYTHING

TOP 10 **LARGEST WHALES**

	SPECIES / SCIENTIFIC NAME	ESTIMATED LENGTH FT	M
1	Blue whale (*Balaenoptera musculus*)	105.0	32.0
2	Fin whale (*Balaenoptera physalus*)	83.3	26.0
3	Humpback whale (*Megaptera novaeangliae*)	62.5	19.0
4	Sei whale (*Balaenoptera borealis*)	60.0	18.5
5	= Sperm whale (*Physeter macrocephalus*)	59.0	18.0
	= Bowhead whale (*Balaena mysticetus*)	59.0	18.0
7	Northern right whale (*Eubalaena glacialis/Eubalaena australis*)	55.0	17.0
8	Grey whale (*Eschrichtius robustus*)	50.0	15.3
9	Bryde's whale (*Balaenoptera brydei*)	47.5	14.5
10	Baird's whale (*Berardius bairdii*)	42.0	12.8

TOP 10 **LONGEST SNAKES**

	SNAKE / SCIENTIFIC NAME	MAX. LENGTH FT	M
1	Reticulated (royal) python (*Python reticulatus*)	32.8	10.0
2	Indian python (*Python molurus molurus*)	29.5	9.0
3	Anaconda (*Eunectes murinus*)	27.9	8.5
4	Diamond python (*Morelia spilota spilota*)	21.0	6.4
5	King cobra (*Opiophagus hannah*)	19.0	5.8
6	Boa constrictor (*Boa constrictor*)	18.0	5.5
7	Bushmaster (*Lachesis muta*)	12.1	3.7
8	Giant brown snake (*Oxyuranus scutellatus*)	11.2	3.4
9	Diamondback rattlesnake (*Crotalus atrox*)	8.9	2.7
10	Indigo or gopher snake (*Drymarchon corais*)	7.9	2.4

▼ *Spotted climber*
Skilled climbers, leopards can drag whole carcasses into trees.

▲ *Underwater acrobat*
Known for their singing and acrobatics, humpback whales weigh about 1 ton per foot.

TOP 10 **LONGEST FOUR-LEGGED ANIMALS**

	ANIMAL* / SCIENTIFIC NAME	MAX. LENGTH FT	M
1	African elephant (*Loxodonta africana*)	24.0	7.3
2	Southern elephant seal (*Mirounga leonina*)	22.5	6.0
3	Estuarine crocodile (*Crocodylus porosus*)	20.6	6.3
4	Giraffe (*Giraffa camelopardalis*)	19.0	5.8
5	White rhinoceros (*Ceratotherium simum*)	13.8	4.2
6	West Indian manatee (*Trichechus manatus*)	13.5	4.1
7	Hippopotamus (*Hippopotamus amphibius*)	13.1	4.0
8	American bison (*Bison bison*)	12.8	3.9
9	Arabian camel (*Camelus dromedarius*)	11.5	3.5
10	Siberian tiger (*Panthera tigris altaica*)	10.8	3.3

* Longest representative of each species

FASTEST & SLOWEST

TOP 10 FASTEST BIRDS

BIRD / SCIENTIFIC NAME / MAX. RECORDED SPEED (MPH / KM/H)

1 Grey-headed albatross
(*Thalassarche chrysostama*)
80 / 127

2 Common eider
(*Somateria mollissima*)
47 / 76

3 Bewick's swan
(*Cygnus columbianus*)
45 / 72

4 = Barnacle goose
(*Branta leucopsis*)
42 / 68

= Common crane
(*Grus grus*)
42 / 68

6 Mallard
(*Anas platyrhynchos*)
40 / 65

7 = Red-throated loon
(*Gavia stellata*)
38 / 61

= Wood pigeon
(*Columba palumbus*)
38 / 61

9 Oystercatcher
(*Haematopus ostralegus*)
36 / 58

10 = Ring-necked pheasant
(*Phasianus colchichus*)
33 / 54

= White-fronted goose
(*Anser albifrons*)
33 / 54

► *Quick off the mark*
Cheetahs can run at top speed only in very short bursts, but can accelerate from 0 to 100 km/h (62 mph) in about three seconds.

TOP 10 FASTEST FISH

FISH / SCIENTIFIC NAME / MAX. RECORDED SPEED (MPH / KM/H)

1 Sailfish (*Istiophorus platypterus*)
68 / 110*

2 Striped marlin (*Tetrapturus audax*)
50 / 81

3 Wahoo (peto, jack mackerel)
(*Acanthocybium solandri*)
49 / 80

4 Southern bluefin tuna
(*Thunnus maccoyii*)
47 / 76

5 = Bonefish (*Albula vulpes*)
40 / 64

= Swordfish (*Xiphias gladius*)
40 / 64

7 Atlantic needlefish
(*Strongylura marina*)
38 / 61*

8 Four-winged flying fish
(*Hirundichthys affinis*)
37 / 60*

9 Tarpon (ox-eye herring)
(*Megalops cyprinoides*)
35 / 56*

10 Blue shark (*Prionace glauca*)
25 / 39

* "Flying" or leaping through air

▲ *Fast fish*
Sailfish have the ability to alter their body color, and turn light blue when excited.

TOP 10 FASTEST MAMMALS

MAMMAL / SCIENTIFIC NAME / MAX. RECORDED SPEED* (MPH / KM/H)

1 Cheetah (*Acinonyx jubatus*)
62 / 110

2 Pronghorn antelope
(*Antilocapra americana*)
53 / 86

3 Grant's gazelle (*Gazella granti*)
51 / 82

4 = Blue wildebeest (brindled gnu)
(*Connochaetes taurinus*)
50 / 80

= Lion (*Panthera leo*)
50 / 80

= Springbok (*Antidorcas marsupialis*)
50 / 80

7 Red fox (*Vulpes vulpes*)
48 / 77

8 Thomson's gazelle
(*Gazella thomsonii*)
47 / 76

9 = Brown hare (*Lepus capensis*)
45 / 72

= Horse (*Equus caballus*)
45 / 72

* Of those species for which data available

TOP 10 **MAMMALS WITH THE LONGEST GESTATION PERIODS***

MAMMAL / SCIENTIFIC NAME	AVERAGE GESTATION (DAYS)
1 African elephant (*Loxodonta africana*)	660
2 Asian elephant (*Elephas maximus*)	645
3 = White rhinoceros (*Ceratotherium simum*)	480
= Walrus (*Odobenus rosmarus*)	480
5 = Black rhinoceros (*Diceros bicornis*)	450
= Arabian camel (dromedary) (*Camelus dromedarius*)	450
7 Giraffe (*Giraffa camelopardalis*)	435
8 Bactrian camel (*Camelus bactrianus*)	410
9 Tapir (*Tapirus*)	400
10 = Ass (*Equus africanus asinus*)	365
= Grant's zebra (*Equus quagga*)	365

* Excluding whales

▼ **Big baby**
An elephant calf is enormous—weighing about 200 lb (91 kg) and about 3 ft (1 m) tall.

▲ **Slow mover**
Three-toed sloths are extremely sedentary, and sleep for 15 to 20 hours a day.

THE 10 **SLOWEST MAMMALS**

MAMMAL / SCIENTIFIC NAME	AVERAGE SPEED* MPH	KM/H
1 Three-toed sloth (*Bradypus variegatus*)	0.06–0.19	0.1–0.3
2 Short-tailed (giant mole) shrew (*Blarina brevicauda*)	1.4	2.2
3 = Pine vole (*Microtus pinetorum*)	2.6	4.2
= Red-backed vole (*Clethrionomys gapperi*)	2.6	4.2
5 Opossum (order *Didelphimorphia*)	2.7	4.4
6 Deer mouse (order *Peromyscus*)	2.8	4.5
7 Woodland jumping mouse (*Napaeozapus insignis*)	3.3	5.3
8 Meadow jumping mouse (*Zapus hudsonius*)	3.4	5.5
9 Meadow mouse or meadow vole (*Microtus pennsylvanicus*)	4.1	6.6
10 White-footed mouse (*Peromyscus leucopus*)	4.2	6.8

* Of those species for which data available

Mammals with the Shortest Gestation Periods

The short-nosed bandicoot and the opossum have the shortest gestation period of any mammal (12 days and 12–14 days respectively). Both are marsupial mammals, whose newborn offspring are extremely small, and transfer to a pouch to complete their development. A baby opossum is no bigger than a bee.

NATURE BY NUMBERS

▼ *Old man of the forest*
Indonesia's orang-utans are threatened by logging, poaching, and forest fires.

TOP 10 **LONGEST-LIVED MARINE ANIMALS***

ANIMAL / SCIENTIFIC NAME / LIFESPAN (YEARS)

1 Quahog (marine clam) (*Arctica islandica*) 221

2 Bowhead whale (*Balaena mysticetus*) 211

3 Alligator snapping turtle (*Macrochelys temminckii*) 150

4 Whale shark (*Rhincodon typus*) 80

5 Sea anemone (*Actinia mesembryanthemum*, etc.) 70

6 European eel (*Anguilla anguilla*) 85

7 Lake sturgeon (*Acipenser fulvescens*) 82

8 Freshwater mussel (*Palaeoheterodonta* – various) 80

9 Dugong (*Dugong dugon*) 73

10 Spiny dogfish (*Squalus acanthias*) 70

* Longest-lived of each genus listed

TOP 10 **COUNTRIES WITH THE MOST MAMMAL SPECIES**

COUNTRY / MAMMAL SPECIES

1 Indonesia 667

2 Brazil 578

3 Mexico 544

4 China 502

5 USA 468

6 Colombia 467

7 Peru 441

8 Dem. Rep. of Congo 430

9 India 422

10 Kenya 407

TOP 10 **COUNTRIES WITH THE MOST ELEPHANTS**

COUNTRY / ELEPHANTS

1 Botswana 133,829

2 Tanzania 108,816

3 Zimbabwe 84,461

4 India 28,250

5 Kenya 23,353

6 South Africa 17,847

7 Zambia 16,562

8 Mozambique 14,079

9 Namibia 12,531

10 Uganda 2,337

▼ *Old man of the sea*
Snapping turtles are among the largest freshwater turtles in the world.

Source: EarthTrends/World Conservation Monitoring Centre of the United Nations Environment Programme (UNEP-WCMC)

▲ *Royal albatross*
Albatrosses spend
almost all their lives at
sea, returning to land
primarily to breed.

TOP 10 **LONGEST BIRD MIGRATIONS**

SPECIES / SCIENTIFIC NAME / APPROX. DISTANCE (MILES / KM)

1 Pectoral sandpiper
(*Calidris melanotos*)
11,806* / 19,000

2 Wheatear
(*Oenanthe oenanthe*)
11,184 / 18,000

3 Slender-billed shearwater
(*Puffinus tenuirostris*)
10,874* / 17,500

4 Ruff
(*Philomachus pugnax*)
10,314 / 16,600

5 Willow warbler
(*Phylloscopus trochilus*)
10,128 / 16,300

6 Arctic tern
(*Sterna paradisaea*)
10,066 / 16,200

7 Parasitic jaeger
(*Stercorarius parasiticus*)
9,693 / 15,600

8 Swainson's hawk
(*Buteo swainsoni*)
9,445 / 15,200

9 Knot
(*Calidris canutus*)
9,320 / 15,000

10 Barn swallow
(*Hirundo rustica*)
9,258 / 14,900

* Thought to be only half of the path taken
during a whole year

Source: Chris Mead

TOP 10 **LONGEST-LIVED RINGED WILD BIRDS**

BIRD / SCIENTIFIC NAME / AGE* (YRS / MTHS)

1 Northern royal albatross
(*Diomedea sanfordi*)
51 / 10

2 Fulmar
(*Fulmarus glacialis*)
40 / 11

3 Manx shearwater
(*Puffinus puffinus*)
37 / 0

4 Gannet
(*Morus bassanus*)
36 / 4

5 Oystercatcher
(*Haematopus ostralegus*)
36 / 0

6 White (fairy) tern
(*Gygis alba*)
35 / 11

7 Common eider
(*Somateria mollissima*)
35 / 0

8 Lesser Black-backed gull
(*Larus fuscus*)
34 / 10

9 Pink-footed goose
(*Anser brachyrhynchus*)
34 / 2

10 Great frigate bird
(*Fregata minor*)
33 / 9

* Elapsed time between marking and report

Source: RSPB

Wild Mammals with the Largest Litters

With up to 32 young per litter, the common
tenrec takes the top prize, and females
possess up to 29 teats—more than any
other mammal. The southern opossum
has an average litter size of 10, and can
have up to three litters in a single year.
The meadow vole probably holds the
world record for most offspring produced
in a season, as it can have up to 17 litters in
rapid succession, bringing up to 150 young
into the world.

DEADLIEST ANIMALS

THE 10 **TYPES OF SHARK THAT HAVE ATTACKED AND KILLED THE MOST HUMANS**

	SHARK / SCIENTIFIC NAME	UNPROVOKED ATTACKS* TOTAL	FATALITIES[#]
1	Great white (Carcharodon carcharias)	244	65
2	Tiger (Galeocerdo cuvier)	88	27
3	Bull (Carcharhinus leucas)	82	25
4	Requiem (Carcharhinus sp.)	39	7
5	Blue (Prionace glauca)	13	4
6	Sand tiger (Carcharias taurus)	32	3
7	= Blacktip (Carcharhinus limbatus)	28	1
	= Shortfin mako (Isurus oxyrinchus)	8	1
	= Oceanic whitetip (Carcharhinus longimanus)	5	1
	= Dusky (Carcharhinus obscurus)	3	1
	= Galapagos (Carcharhinus galapagensis)	1	1

* 1580–2009
\# Where fatalities are equal, entries are ranked by total attacks

Source: *International Shark Attack File*, Florida Museum of Natural History

Requiem is actually a family of sharks. However, many Requiem sharks are difficult to identify so the International Shark Attack File groups together attacks by unidentified Requiems, hence its inclusion at No. 4.

▲ Great white
These enormous fish are frequently up to 6 m (20 ft) long.

THE 10 **PLACES WHERE MOST PEOPLE ARE ATTACKED BY SHARKS**

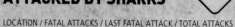

LOCATION / FATAL ATTACKS / LAST FATAL ATTACK / TOTAL ATTACKS

1 USA (excluding Hawaii) 33 / 2008 — **885**
2 Australia 117 / 2008 — **330**
3 South Africa 44 / 2009 — **212**
4 Hawaii 8 / 2004 — **96**
5 Brazil 21 / 2006 — **87**
6 Papua New Guinea 24 / 2000 — **47**
7 New Zealand 8 / 1968 — **44**
8 Mexico 19 / 2008 — **35**
9 The Bahamas 1 / 1968 — **26**
10 Iran 8 / 1985 — **23**

* Confirmed unprovoked attacks, including nonfatal, 1580–2009

Source: *International Shark Attack File*, Florida Museum of Natural History

THE 10 **BODY PARTS MOST OFTEN INJURED IN SHARK ATTACKS ON DIVERS**

BODY PART INJURED / % OF ATTACKS*

1 Calf/knee 35.2
2 Arm 30.2
3 Thigh 23.9
4 Foot 22.0
5 Hand 13.2
6 = Abdomen/stomach 8.8
 = Buttocks 8.8
 = Chest 8.8
9 = Back 6.9
 = Shoulder 6.9

* As of July 2009

Source: *International Shark Attack File*, Florida Museum of Natural History

THE 10 **MOST VENOMOUS SPIDERS**

SPIDER / SCIENTIFIC NAME / RANGE

1 Banana spider
(*Phonenutria nigriventer*)
Central and South America

2 Sydney funnel web
(*Atrax robustus*)
Australia

▶ **Lethal hunter**
*Wolf spiders are
hunters, chasing their
prey, which includes
crickets and lizards.*

3 Wolf spider
(*Lycosa raptoria/erythrognatha*)
Central and South America

4 Black widow
(*Latrodectus* sp.)
Widespread

5 Violin spider/Recluse spider
(*Loxesceles reclusa*)
Widespread

6 Sac spider
(*Cheiracanthium
punctorium*)
Central Europe

7 Tarantula
(*Eurypelma
rubropilosum*)
Neotropics

8 Tarantula
(*Acanthoscurria atrox*)
Neotropics

9 Tarantula
(*Lasiodora klugi*)
Neotropics

10 Tarantula
(*Pamphobeteus* sp.)
Neotropics

◀ **Killer cobra**
*The Indian cobra is the most venomous
of all reptiles.*

THE 10 **MOST VENOMOUS REPTILES AND AMPHIBIANS**

	CREATURE*	TOXIN	FATAL AMOUNT (MG)[#]
1	Indian cobra	Peak V	0.009
2	Mamba	Toxin 1	0.02
3	Brown snake	Texilotoxin	0.05
4 =	Inland taipan	Paradotoxin	0.10
=	Mamba	Dendrotoxin	0.10
6	Taipan	Taipoxin	0.11
7 =	Indian cobra	Peak X	0.12
=	Poison arrow frog	Batrachotoxin	0.12
9	Indian cobra	Peak 1X	0.17
10	Krait	Bungarotoxin	0.50

* Excluding bacteria
# Quantity required to kill an average-sized human adult

This list ranks spiders according to their "lethal potential"—their venom yield divided by their venom potency. The banana spider, for example, yields 6 mg of venom, with 1 mg the estimated lethal dose in humans. However, few spiders are capable of killing people—there were just 14 recorded deaths caused by black widows in the USA in the whole of the 19th century—since their venom yield is relatively low compared with that of the most dangerous snakes.

The venom of these creatures is almost unbelievably powerful: 1 mg (the approximate weight of a banknote) of Mamba Toxin 1 would be sufficient to kill 50 people. Other than reptiles, such creatures as scorpions (0.5 mg) and black widow spiders (1.0 mg) fall just outside the Top 10. Were bacteria included, 12 kg of the deadly Botulinus Toxin A (fatal dose just 0.000002 mg) would easily kill the entire population of the world.

CATS & DOGS

◀ *Clever Collie* In 2011 a border collie was reported to have learned the names of 1,022 objects.

TOP 10 **PEDIGREE CAT BREEDS IN THE USA**

BREED

1 Persian
2 Exotic
3 Maine coon
4 Siamese
5 Ragdoll
6 Abyssinian
7 Sphynx
8 American shorthair
9 Birman
10 Oriental

Source: The Cat Fanciers' Association

▶ *Popular pedigree* Siamese cats are among the best-loved pedigree pets.

THE 10 **MOST INTELLIGENT DOG BREEDS**

BREED

1 Border collie
2 Poodle
3 German shepherd (Alsatian)
4 Golden retriever
5 Doberman pinscher
6 Shetland sheepdog
7 Labrador retriever
8 Papillon
9 Rottweiler
10 Australian cattle dog

Source: Stanley Coren, *The Intelligence of Dogs* (Scribner, 1994)

▶ *Bottom of the class* Seemingly based on physical rather than intellectual strength, 39 US universities use a bulldog as their mascot.

THE 10 **LEAST INTELLIGENT DOG BREEDS**

BREED

1 Afghan hound
2 Basenji
3 Bulldog
4 Chow Chow
5 Borzoi
6 Bloodhound
7 Pekinese
8 = Beagle
= Mastiff
10 Bassett Hound

Dog owners who have criticized the results of American psychology professor Stanley Coren's intelligence tests (mostly those whose own pets scored badly) maintain that dogs are bred for specialized abilities, such as speed or ferocity, and obedience to their human masters is only one feature of their "intelligence."

TOP 10 **CAT NAMES IN THE USA**

1 Max
2 Chloe
3 Bella
4 Oliver
5 Tiger
6 Smokey
7 Tigger
8 Lucy
9 Shadow
10 Angel

Source: Veterinary Pet Insurance Co., 2009

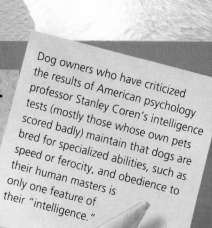

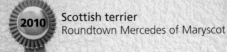
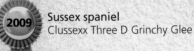

◀ **Labrador**
The labrador is often considered the most popular breed in the world.

TOP 10 **PEDIGREE DOG BREEDS IN THE USA, 2009**

BREED

1 Labrador retriever
2 German shepherd
3 Yorkshire terrier
4 Golden retriever
5 Beagle
6 Boxer
7 Bulldog
8 Dachsund
9 Poodle
10 Shih Tzu

Source: The American Kennel Club

THE 10 **LATEST WINNERS OF THE WESTMINSTER SHOW**

YEAR / BREED / NAME

2010 Scottish terrier
Roundtown Mercedes of Maryscot

2009 Sussex spaniel
Clussexx Three D Grinchy Glee

2008 Beagle
K-Run's Park Me In First

2007 English springer spaniel
Felicity's Diamond Jim

2006 Bull Terrier
Rocky Top's Sundance Kid

2005 Pointer
Kan-Point's VJK Autumn Roses

2004 Newfoundland
Darbydale's All Rise Pouch Cove

2003 Kerry Blue Terrier
Torums Scarf Michael

2002 Miniature poodle
Surrey Spice Girl

2001 Bichons Frises
Special Times Just Right

TOP 10 **DOG MOVIES**

	MOVIE	YEAR
1	Scooby-Doo	2004
2	One Hundred and One Dalmatians*	1961
3	Marley & Me	2008
4	101 Dalmatians	1996
5	Bolt	2008
6	Beverly Hills Chihuahua	2008
7	Lady and the Tramp	1955
8	Cats & Dogs	2001
9	Scooby-Doo 2: Monsters Unleashed	2004
10	Eight Below	2006

* Animated version

▲ **Pampered pooch**
Drew Barrymore provided the voice for Chloe the Chihuahua in the 2008 film.

TOP 10 **TEA-PRODUCING COUNTRIES**

COUNTRY / TEA HARVEST (TONS)*

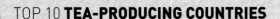

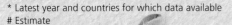

1 China 1,405,870

2 India 887,559

3 Kenya 381,179

4 Sri Lanka 351,307

5 Turkey 218,308

6 Vietnam 192,794

7 Indonesia 166,285

8 Japan 106,373

9 Argentina# 83,775

10 Thailand 67,855

Source (all lists): Food and Agriculture Organization of the United Nations

* Latest year and countries for which data available
# Estimate

TOP 10 **COFFEE-PRODUCING COUNTRIES**

COUNTRY / COFFEE PRODUCED*: BEANS (TONS) / CUPS# (1000)

1 Brazil 3,083,084 / 391,569,780
2 Vietnam 1,176,607 / 149,436,000
3 Colombia 759,140 / 96,415,200
4 Indonesia 752,810 / 95,611,320
5 Peru 301,791 / 38,329,200
6 Ethiopia 301,372 / 38,276,000
7 Mexico 293,013 / 37,214,380
8 India 288,806 / 36,680,000
9 Guatemala 274,050 / 34,805,960
10 Uganda 190,808 / 24,233,720

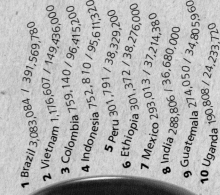

* Latest year and countries for which data available
# Based on 7g of coffee per cup

TOP 10 **STRAWBERRY-PRODUCING COUNTRIES**

COUNTRY / PRODUCTION (TONS)*

1 USA 1,400,700

2 Turkey 321,870

3 Spain 290,679

4 Egypt 220,462

5 Poland 219,257

6 Japan 203,928

7 Russia 174,165

8 Germany 165,457

9 Morocco 143,300

10 Ukraine 63,823

World total 3,426,003

* Latest year and countries for which data available

TOP 10 **PIG COUNTRIES**

	COUNTRY	PIGS*
1	China	451,177,581
2	USA	67,148,000
3	Brazil	37,000,000
4	Vietnam	27,627,700
5	Germany	26,886,500
6	Spain	26,289,600
7	Russia	16,161,860
8	Mexico	16,100,000
9	France	14,810,000
10	Poland	14,278,647
	World total	941,212,507

* Latest year and countries for which data available

▲ **China pigs**
Pigs were domesticated around 10,000 years ago, and provide over a billion Chinese people with their main source of meat.

▶ **Ruler of the roost**
The world chicken population produces one trillion eggs a year, over 150 per person.

TOP 10 **CROPS**

	COMMODITY	PRODUCTION (TONS)*
1	Sugar cane	1,854,724,505
2	Maize	900,710,156
3	Wheat	751,683,541
4	Rice	748,125,778
5	Potatoes	363,274,311
6	Cassava	265,645,431
7	Sugar beet	252,969,749
8	Soybeans	245,009,527
9	Oil palm fruit	228,539,567
10	Barley	165,646,055

* Latest year and countries for which data available; includes semi-official and estimated data

TOP 10 **TYPES OF LIVESTOCK**

	ANIMAL	WORLD STOCKS*
1	Chickens	18,457,445,000
2	Cattle	1,382,241,378
3	Ducks	1,173,438,000
4	Sheep	1,071,274,348
5	Pigs	941,212,507
6	Goats	867,968,573
7	Turkeys	548,880,000
8	Geese and guinea fowl	357,438,000
9	Buffaloes	188,306,103
10	Horses	59,019,729

* Latest year and countries for which data available; includes semi-official and estimated data

TREES & FORESTS

TOP 10 COUNTRIES WITH THE LARGEST AREAS OF FOREST

COUNTRY	SQ MILES	% OF TOTAL	SQ KM
1 Russia	3,123,910	49	8,090,900
2 Brazil	2,005,890	62	5,195,220
3 Canada	1,197,430	34	3,101,340
4 USA	1,173,840	33	3,040,220
5 China	798,690	22	2,068,610
6 Dem. Rep. of Congo	595,120	68	1,541,350
7 Australia	576,450	19	1,493,000
8 Indonesia	364,600	52	944,320
9 Sudan	270,070	29	699,490
10 India	264,423	23	684,340
World total	*15,571,73*	*31*	*40,330,600*

Source: Food and Agriculture Organization of the United Nations

▲ *Brazilian rainforest*
The Amazon rainforest covers over a billion acres, with the largest area contained in Brazil.

TOP 10 COUNTRIES WITH THE LARGEST AREAS OF BAMBOO FOREST

COUNTRY / AREA (SQ MILES / SQ KM)

World total 141,997 / 367,770

Source: Food and Agriculture Organization of the United Nations

1 India
43,865
113,610

2 Brazil
35,908
93,000

3 China
21,019
54,440

4 Indonesia
8,035
20,810

5 Lao People's Dem. Rep.
6,224
16,120

6 Nigeria
6,139
15,900

TOP 10 **MOST COMMON TREES IN THE USA**

TREE	% OF TOTAL FOREST AREA
1 Douglas fir (*Pseudotsuga menziesii*)	12.8
2 Loblolly pine (*Pinus taeda*)	6.6
3 Ponderosa pine (*Pinus ponderosa*)	4.1
4 Red maple (*Acer rubrum*)	3.9
5 Western hemlock (*Tsuga heterophylla*)	3.6
6 =Lodgepole pine (*Pinus contorta*)	3.2
=White oak (*Quercus alba*)	3.2
8 Sugar maple (*Acer saccharum*)	2.7
9 Yellow poplar (*Liriodendron tulipifera*)	2.6
10 Northern red oak (*Quercus rubra*)	2.4

Source: US Forest Service

TOP 10 **TALLEST TREES IN THE USA***

	TREE	LOCATION	HEIGHT FT	HEIGHT M
1	Coast redwood (*Sequoia sempervirens*)	Jedediah Smith Redwoods State Park, CA	321	97.8
2	Coast Douglas fir (*Pseudotsuga menziesii var. menziesii*)	Jedediah Smith Redwoods State Park, CA	301	91.7
3	Giant sequoia (*Sequoiadendron giganteum*)	Sequoia National Park, CA	274	83.5
4	Grand fir (*Abies grandis*)	Redwood National Park, CA	257	78.3
5	Port Orford cedar (*Chamaecyparis lawsoniana*)	Siskiyou National Forest, OR	242	73.8
6	Ponderosa pine (*Pinus ponderosa var. ponderosa*)	Trinity, CA	240	73.2
7	Western hemlock (*Tsuga heterophylla*)	Olympic National Park, WA	237	72.2
8	Noble fir (*Abies procera*)	Mount St. Helens National Monument, WA	227	69.2
9	Pacific silver fir (*Abies amabilis*)	Olympic National Park, WA	218	66.4
10	California white fir (*Abies concolor var. lowiana*)	Yosemite National Park, CA	217	66.1

* Tallest example of each species

Source: Big Tree Register

▼ **Asian devastation**
In the past 20 years, Indonesia has lost 20% of its forest cover.

TOP 10 **DEFORESTING COUNTRIES***

	COUNTRY	ANNUAL FOREST LOSS 2005–10 SQ MILES	ANNUAL FOREST LOSS 2005–10 SQ KM
1	Brazil	11,931	30,900
2	Nigeria	1,583	4,100
3	Tanzania	1,556	4,030
4	Zimbabwe	1,263	3,270
5	Dem. Rep. of Congo	1,201	3,110
6	Indonesia	1,197	3,100
7	Myanmar	1,193	3,090
8	Venezuela	1,112	2,880
9	Bolivia	1,046	2,710
10	Argentina	973	2,520
	World total	*18,691*	*48,410*

* Countries for which data available

Source: Food and Agriculture Organization of the United Nations, *Global Forest Resources Assessment 2010*

7 Chile	8 Myanmar	9 Ethiopia	10 Vietnam
3,475	3,317	3,278	3,139
9,000	8,590	8,490	8,130

3

THE HUMAN WORLD

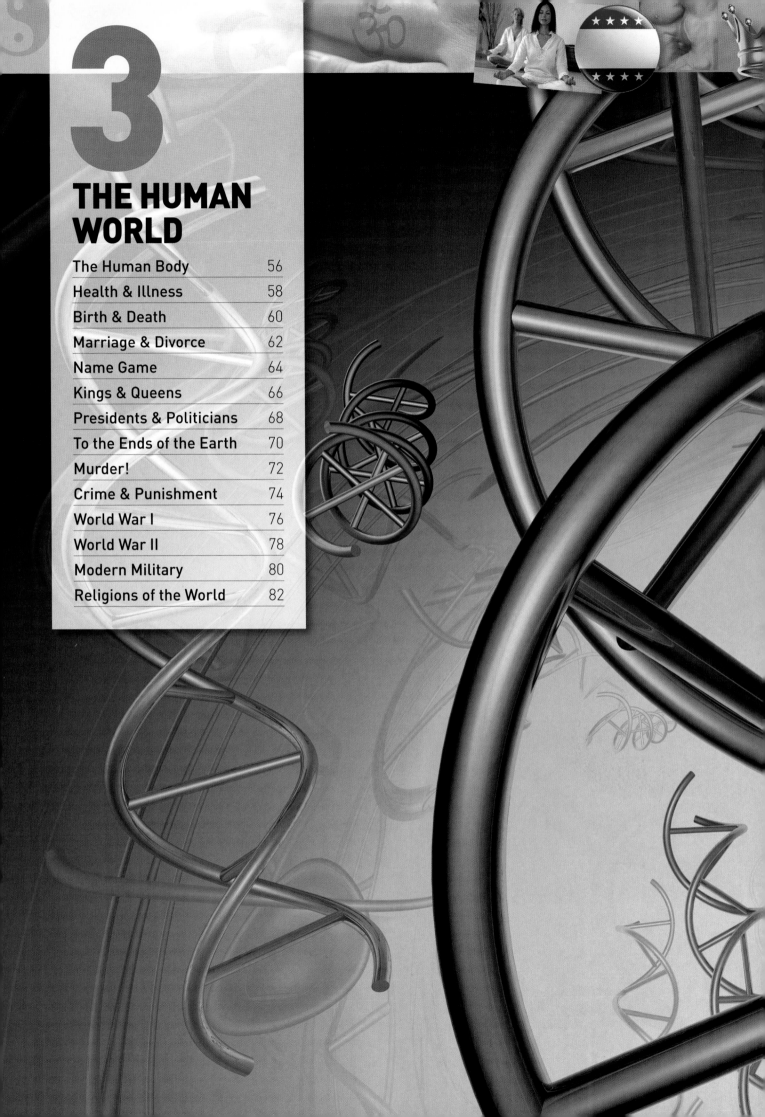

DISCOVERING THE DOUBLE HELIX

Fifty years ago—in 1962—James Watson and Francis Crick were awarded the Nobel Prize for Medicine for their discovery of the molecular structure of DNA (deoxyribonucleic acid). This is the complex molecule that carries genetic information in the body, and is formed of strands of the bases A (adenine), T (thymine), C (cytosine), and G (guanine). Each molecule comprises two twisted strands, which form a spiral configuration (like a spiral staircase or a spring) and run in opposite directions to form a double helix. Watson and Crick's work was a huge scientific breakthrough, and enhanced understanding of how DNA is replicated from cell to cell, and how it passes from generation to generation.

THE HUMAN BODY

◀ Facing the facts
More than 10 million cosmetic procedures are performed every year in the USA.

TOP 10 COSMETIC SURGERY PROCEDURES IN THE USA

PROCEDURE / NO.

1 Breast augmentation (women) 311,957

2 Liposuction 283,735

3 Cosmetic eyelid surgery 149,943

4 Nose reshaping 138,258

5 Tummy tuck 127,923

6 Breast reduction (women) 113,511

7 Breast lift 98,279

8 Facelift 94,247

9 Forehead lift 30,789

10 Cosmetic ear surgery 21,817

Source: American Society for Aesthetic Plastic Surgery

While women account for over 90% of cosmetic surgery in the USA, the number of men seeking treatment continues to increase, with liposuction being the most common procedure, followed by nose reshaping, eyelid surgery, breast reduction, and hair transplantation.

TOP 10 MOST COMMON ELEMENTS IN THE HUMAN BODY

ELEMENT / SYMBOL / AVERAGE ADULT* TOTAL (OZ / G)

1 Oxygen# O 1,721 / 48,800

2 Carbon C 649 / 18,400

3 Hydrogen# H 282 / 8,000

4 Nitrogen N 73 / 2,080

5 Calcium Ca 39.5 / 1,120

6 Phosphorus P 31.0 / 880

7 = Potassium K 5.6 / 160

= Sulfur S 5.6 / 160

9 Sodium Na 4.0 / 112

10 Chlorine Cl 3.4 / 96

* 176 lb male
# Mostly combined as water

THE 10 LATEST PEOPLE TO HOLD THE RECORD AS "WORLD'S OLDEST"

NAME / COUNTRY	YRS	DAYS	BORN	DIED
1 Besse Cooper, USA	114	218	Aug 26, 1896	*
2 Eunice Sanborn, USA	115	195	Jul 20, 1896	Jan 31, 2011
2 Anna Eugénie Blanchard, France	114	261	Feb 16, 1896	Nov 4, 2010
3 Kama Chinen, Japan	114	357	May 10, 1895	May 2, 2010
4 Gertrude Baines, USA	115	158	Apr 6, 1894	Sep 11, 2009
5 Maria (de Jesus) dos Santos, Portugal	115	114	Sep 10, 1893	Jan 2, 2009
6 Edna Ruth (Scott) Parker, USA	115	220	Apr 20, 1893	Nov 26, 2008
7 Yone Minagawa, Japan	114	221	Jan 4, 1893	Aug 13, 2007
8 Emma Fanchon (Faust) Tillman, USA	114	67	Nov 22, 1892	Jan 28, 2007
9 Emiliano Mercano Del Toro, Puerto Rico	115	156	Aug 21, 1891	Jan 24, 2007

* Alive as of April 1, 2011

This list is based on the longevity of the successive holders of the record as "world's oldest" among people for whom there is undisputed evidence of their birth date. None of those in the past 10 years has come within five years of the 122-year 5-month 15-day lifespan of Jeanne Calment (France), who lived from February 21, 1875 to August 4, 1997.

TOP 10 TALLEST PEOPLE

	NAME / DATES	COUNTRY	FT	IN (HEIGHT)	CM
1	Robert Pershing Wadlow (1918–40)	USA	8	11.1	272
2	John William Rogan (1868–1905)	USA	8	9.8	268
3	John Aasen (1887–1938)	USA	8	9.7	267
4	John F. Carroll (1932–69)	USA	8	7.6	264
5	Al Tomaini (1918–62)	USA	8	4.4	255
6	Trijntje Keever* (1616–33)	Netherlands	8	3.3	254
7	Edouard Beaupré (1881–1904)	Canada	8	2.5	250
8	=Bernard Coyne (1897–1921)	USA	8	1.2	249
	=Don Koehler (1925–81)	USA	8	1.2	249
10	=Jeng Jinlian* (1964–82)	China	8	1.1	248
	=Väinö Myllyrinne (1909–63)	Finland	8	1.1	248

* Female; all others male

TOP 10 HEAVIEST PEOPLE

	NAME / DATES*	LB (MAX. WEIGHT)	KG
1	Carol Yager (1960–94)	1,600	726
2	Jon Brower Minnoch (1941–83)	1,400	635
3	Manuel Uribe Garza (b. 1965), Mexico	1,234	560
4	Rosalie Bradford (1943–2006)	1,200	544
5	Walter Hudson (1944–91)	1,197	543
6	Francis John Lang aka Michael Walker (b. 1934)	1,187	538
7	Johnny Alee (1853–87)	1,132	513
8	Michael Hebranko (b. 1953)	1,100	499
9	Patrick Deuel (b. 1962)	1,072	486
10	Robert Earl Hughes (1926–58)	1,069	485

* All USA unless otherwise stated

◄ **Robert Wadlow**
At the time of his death at age 22, Robert Wadlow was still growing.

What weighs 1600 lb?

Carol Yager, the world's heaviest person, weighed 1,600 lb (726 kg) at her peak weight. This is roughly the same as:

▪ An adult domestic water buffalo—sometimes referred to as "living tractors of the East."

▪ A Smart Fortwo (1,609 lb/ 730 kg), one of the lightest cars on the European market.

▪ The Rosetta Stone. Though only part of its original size, the stone weighs approximately 1,700 lb (760 kg).

HEALTH & ILLNESS

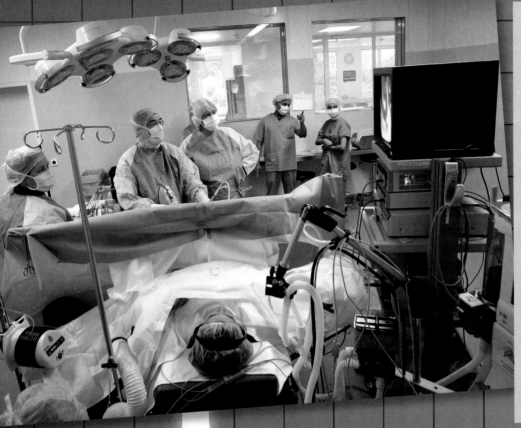

TOP 10 **COUNTRIES SPENDING THE MOST ON HEALTH CARE**

COUNTRY	HEALTH SPENDING PER CAPITA ($)
1 Luxembourg	6,763
2 Norway	6,184
3 Monaco	5,492
4 Iceland	4,927
5 Denmark	4,690
6 Ireland	3,676
7 Sweden	3,673
8 France	3,655
9 Switzerland	3,620
10 Netherlands	3,481
USA	3,317

Source: World Health Organization, *World Health Statistics 2010*

◀ *Swiss surgery*
Healthcare in Switzerland is universal, and all Swiss residents are required to purchase basic health insurance.

TOP 10 **DISEASE BURDENS**

	DISEASE	% OF DALYS*
1	Lower respiratory infections	6.2
2	Diarrheal diseases	4.8
3	Depression	4.3
4	Coronary heart disease	4.1
5	HIV/AIDS	3.8
6	Cerebrovsacular disease	3.1
7	Premature and low weight birth	2.9
8 =	Birth asphyxia and trauma	2.7
=	Road traffic injuries	2.7
=	Neonatal infections	2.7

* All ages; latest available year

Source: World Health Organization

▶ *Medical ratio*
With one doctor for every 170 residents, Cuba has the highest doctor-to-patient ratio in the world.

TOP 10 **COUNTRIES WITH THE MOST DOCTORS***

	COUNTRY	DOCTORS PER 1,000
1	Cuba	
2	Greece	6.4
3	Belarus	5.4
4	Russia	4.9
5	Belgium	4.3
6 =	Lithuania	4.2
=	Switzerland	4.0
8 =	Kazakhstan	4.0
=	Netherlands	3.9
=	Norway	3.9

* Where known 3.9

Source: World Health Organization, *The World Health Report*

DALYs—Disability-adjusted Life Years—are potential healthy years of life that are lost as a result of contracting diseases or as a result of an injury or other disability. This is used as a measure of the "burden of disease" that affects not only the individual sufferer, but also has an effect on the cost of the provision of health services and consequent loss to a country's economy. These are world averages, but there are variations from country to country.

THE 10 **LEAST HEALTHY COUNTRIES**

	COUNTRY	HEALTHY LIFE EXPECTANCY AT BIRTH*
1	Sierra Leone	35
2	Afghanistan	36
3	Zimbabwe	39
4	= Chad	40
	= Lesotho	40
	= Zambia	40
7	= Guinea-Bissau	42
	= Mozambique	42
	= Central African Republic	42
	= Swaziland	42
	= Uganda	42

* Average number of years expected to be spent in good health

Source: World Health Organization, *World Health Statistics 2010*

HALE (Health Adjusted Life Expectancy) is a method used by the WHO to compare the state of health of nations, and illustrates the contrast between developed and developing countries.

◄ *Sierra Leone*
Almost one out of three children born in Sierra Leone dies before reaching the age of five.

TOP 10 **HEALTHIEST COUNTRIES**

	COUNTRY	HEALTHY LIFE EXPECTANCY AT BIRTH*
1	Japan	76
2	San Marino	75
3	= Spain	74
	= Sweden	74
	= Australia	74
	= Iceland	74
	= Italy	74
8	= Canada	73
	= France	73
	= Germany	73
	= Ireland	73
	= Israel	73
	= Luxembourg	73
	= Monaco	73
	= Netherlands	73
	= Norway	73
	USA	*72*

* Average number of years expected to be spent in good health

Source: World Health Organization, *World Health Statistics 2010*

▼ *Japan*
Japan has one of the lowest infant mortality rates in the world.

THE 10 **COUNTRIES SPENDING THE LEAST ON HEALTH CARE**

	COUNTRY	HEALTH SPENDING PER CAPITA ($)
1	Myanmar >$1	
2	Dem. Rep. of Congo $2	
3	Guinea $3	
4	= Guinea Bissau $4	
	= Eritrea $4	
	= Sierra Leone $4	
7	= Bangladesh $5	
	= Ethiopia $5	
9	= Central African Republic $6	
	= Liberia $6	
	= Tajikistan $6	

Source: World Health Organization, *World Health Statistics 2010*

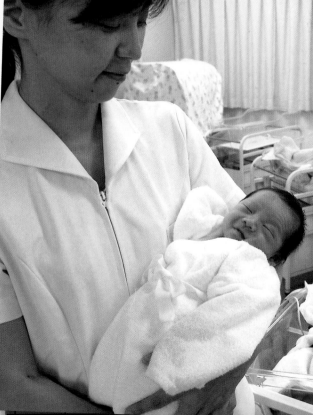

BIRTH & DEATH

THE 10 MOST COMMON CAUSES OF DEATH IN THE USA

	DISEASE	NO. OF DEATHS
1	Diseases of the heart	616,067
2	Cancer	562,875
3	Cerebrovascular diseases (e.g. stroke)	135,952
4	Chronic lower respiratory diseases	127,924
5	Accidents (unintentional injuries)	123,706
6	Alzheimer's disease	74,632
7	Diabetes	71,382
8	Pneumonia and influenza	52,717
9	Nephritis, nephrotic syndrome and nephrosis	46,448
10	Septicemia	34,828
	Total (all causes)	2,423,712

Source: US Department of Health and Human Services, *National Vital Statistics Reports*, 2010

The latest year for which data is available on death causes in the USA is 2007, when a total of 2,423,712 deaths were registered—or 760.2 deaths per 100,000 of the population. Outside this Top 10, other death causes include suicide (at No. 11) and murder (at No. 15), with 34,598 and 18,361 deaths respectively. The rise in the numbers of suicides and of those dying from chronic liver disease (No. 12) were the most dramatic from the previous year, while victims of the top three diseases in this list decreased. Life expectancy in the same year rose to an average of 77.9 years across both sexes, with women expecting to live a full five years longer than men.

TOP 10 COUNTRIES WITH THE HIGHEST BIRTH RATE

	COUNTRY	ESTIMATED BIRTH RATE (PER 1,000 LIVE BIRTHS), 2012
1	Niger	50.1
2	Uganda	47.4
3	Mali	45.2
4	Zambia	43.5
5	Burkina Faso	43.2
6	Ethiopia	42.6
7	Angola	42.5
8	Somalia	42.3
9	Burundi	40.6
10	Dem. Rep. of Congo	40.1
	USA	13.8
	World average	19.0

Source: US Census Bureau, *International Data Base*

The countries with the highest birth rates are amongst the poorest in the world. In these countries, people often deliberately have large families so that the children can help with earning income for the family when they are older. The list of the 10 countries with the highest birth rate therefore corresponds very closely with that of countries with the highest fertility rate—the average number of children born to each woman in the country.

THE 10 COUNTRIES WITH THE MOST DEATHS

	COUNTRY	ESTIMATED DEATHS, 2012
1	China	9,631,030
2	India	8,953,697
3	USA	2,650,305
4	Nigeria	2,503,085
5	Russia	2,213,457
6	Indonesia	1,558,798
7	Brazil	1,312,474
8	Japan	1,305,160
9	Pakistan	1,293,980
10	Ethiopia	1,012,275
	World	57,081,617

Source: US Census Bureau, *International Data Base*

▲ **Happy families**
The total fertility rate (TFR) per woman in Uganda is estimated at 6.69 children in 2011. This represents a slight drop from recent years, but remains one of the highest in the world.

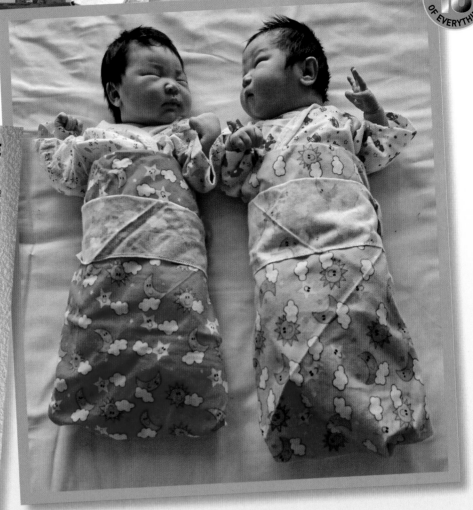

▶ *Asian baby boom*
China's total fertility rate (TFR) is 1.54 children born for every woman.

THE 10 COUNTRIES WITH THE MOST BIRTHS

COUNTRY	ESTIMATED BIRTHS, 2012
1 India	24,824,516
2 China	16,535,283
3 Nigeria	5,529,888
4 Pakistan	4,624,074
5 Indonesia	4,408,320
6 USA	4,370,790
7 Ethiopia	3,995,623
8 Bangladesh	3,629,218
9 Brazil	3,595,931
10 Dem. Rep. of Congo	3,300,799
World	133,145,854

Source: US Census Bureau, *International Data Base*

As India's birth rate is maintained and China's subject to curbs, the population of India is set to overtake that of China by 2025.

THE 10 COUNTRIES WITH THE HIGHEST INFANT MORTALITY

COUNTRY	ESTIMATED DEATH RATE (PER 1,000 LIVE BIRTHS), 2012
1 Angola	173.7
2 Afghanistan	146.9
3 Niger	110.0
4 Mali	109.1
5 Somalia	103.7
6 Mozambique	99.9
7 Central African Republic	97.2
8 Guinea-Bissau	94.4
9 Chad	93.6
10 Nigeria	90.1
World average	40.9

Source: US Census Bureau, *International Data Base*

Deaths as a ratio of live births is a commonly employed measure of a country's medical and social conditions. In sharp contrast to many western countries, these figures represent the most disadvantaged.

THE 10 COUNTRIES WITH THE LOWEST INFANT MORTALITY

COUNTRY / ESTIMATED DEATH RATE (PER 1,000 LIVE BIRTHS), 2012

| **1** Monaco 1.8 | **2** Singapore 2.3 | **3** Sweden 2.7 | **4** Japan 2.8 | **5** Iceland 3.2 | **6** France 3.3 |

| **7** Spain 3.4 | **8** Norway 3.6 | **9** Malta 3.7 | **10** = Czech Republic = Andorra 3.8 |

Source: US Census Bureau, *International Data Base*

MARRIAGE & DIVORCE

THE 10 US STATES WITH THE MOST DIVORCES

STATE*	COUPLES DIVORCED#
1 Florida	84,373
2 Texas	77,810
3 New York	55,068
4 Ohio	38,884
5 North Carolina	36,205
6 Pennsylvania	35,508
7 Michigan	34,502
8 Illinois	33,239
9 Virginia	29,516
10 New Jersey	25,687

* Figures not available for California, Georgia, Indiana, and Louisiana
\# Latest year for which data available

California is most likely to have the highest divorce rate—the number of men divorcing in 2007 was 119,315 and women 145,281. However, no figures are available for the number of partners divorcing so the state cannot be ranked here.

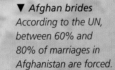

TOP 10 COUNTRIES WITH THE HIGHEST PROPORTION OF TEEN BRIDES

COUNTRY	% OF 15–19-YEAR-OLD GIRLS WHO HAVE EVER BEEN MARRIED*
1 Dem. Rep. of Congo	74.2
2 Niger	61.9
3 Congo	55.5
4 Afghanistan	53.7
5 Bangladesh	51.3
6 Uganda	49.8
7 Mali	49.7
8 Guinea	49.0
9 Chad	48.6
10 Mozambique	47.1
USA	3.9

* In those countries/latest year for which data available

Source: United Nations

▼ *Afghan brides*
According to the UN, between 60% and 80% of marriages in Afghanistan are forced.

TOP 10 **COUNTRIES WITH THE MOST MARRIAGES**

COUNTRY	MARRIAGES PER ANNUM*
1 China	9,914,000
2 USA	2,205,000
3 Russia	1,262,500
4 Brazil	916,006
5 Iran	841,107
6 Japan	719,822
7 Turkey	638,311
8 Egypt	614,848
9 Mexico	595,209
10 Italy	250,041

* In those countries/latest year for which data available

Source: United Nations

▲ **Hearts and flowers**
The average age of first marriage in China is 33.8 for men and 29.1 for women.

THE 10 **COUNTRIES WITH THE LOWEST MARRIAGE RATES**

	COUNTRY	MARRIAGES PER 1,000 PER ANNUM*
1	Qatar	2.6
2	Andorra	3.1
3	Slovenia	3.2
4	=Panama	3.4
	=Venezuela	3.4
6	=Argentina	3.5
	=Bolivia	3.5
	=Ireland	3.5
9	=China	3.9
	=Bulgaria	3.9

* In those countries/latest year for which data available

Source: United Nations

THE 10 **COUNTRIES WITH THE HIGHEST DIVORCE RATES**

	COUNTRY	DIVORCE RATE PER 1,000*
1	Russia	4.5
2	Ukraine	3.8
3	Moldova	3.5
4	=Belarus	3.3
	=Lithuania	3.3
6	=Cuba	3.2
	=Latvia	3.2
8	Czech Republic	3.1
9	=Belgium	2.8
	=Estonia	2.8

* In those countries/latest year for which data available

Source: United Nations

THE 10 **COUNTRIES WITH THE LOWEST DIVORCE RATES**

	COUNTRY	DIVORCE RATE PER 1,000*
1	Guatemala	0.1
2	Chile	0.2
3	=Tajikistan	0.4
	=Bosnia and Herzegovina	0.4
5	Georgia	0.5
6	Mongolia	0.6
7	=Jamaica	0.7
	=Mexico	0.7
	=Macedonia	0.7
10	Ireland	0.8

* In those countries/latest year for which data available

Source: United Nations

The countries that figure among those with the lowest divorce rates represent a range of cultures and religions, which either condone or condemn divorce to varying extents, thus affecting its prevalence or otherwise. In some countries, legal and other obstacles make divorce difficult or costly.

NAME GAME

TOP 10 **FIRST NAMES IN ENGLAND AND WALES, 2009**

BOYS		BIRTHS
1	Oliver	7,364
2	Jack	7,090
3	Harry	6,143
4	Alfie	5,536
5	Joshua	5,526
6	Thomas	5,520
7	Charlie	5,409
8	William	5,247
9	James	4,544
10	Daniel	4,444
	Top 10 total	56,823

Source: Office for National Statistics, 2010

GIRLS		BIRTHS
1	Olivia	5,201
2	Ruby	4,555
3	Chloe	4,479
4	Emily	4,462
5	Sophie	4,452
6	Jessica	4,291
7	Grace	4,208
8	Lily	3,967
9	Amelia	3,625
10	Evie	3,389
	Top 10 total	42,629

Since 2008, Jack has been replaced by Oliver as the most popular boys' name, after 14 years in the top position. However, regionally, Jack remains in top place in Wales and the north-east and north-west of England. Olivia is the top girls' name for the second year running. Regionally, Isabella appears at No. 6 in London, while Ava and Lucy are popular in the north-east of England, listed at Nos. 8 and 10 respectively.

TOP 10 **FIRST NAMES IN THE USA**

	BOYS / BIRTHS	GIRLS / BIRTHS
1	Jacob 20,858	Isabella 22,067
2	Ethan 19,664	Emma 17,716
3	Michael 18,677	Olivia 17,246
4	Alexander 18,025	Sophia 16,743
5	William 17,696	Ava 15,730
6	Joshua 17,418	Emily 15,204
7	Daniel 17,336	Madison 15,097
8	Jayden 17,082	Abigail 14,232
9	Noah 17,061	Chloe 11,785
10	Anthony 16,139	Mia 11,319
	Top 10 total 179,902	Top 10 total 157,139

Source: Social Security Administration, 2009

TOP 10 **FIRST NAMES IN THE USA 100 YEARS AGO**

	GIRLS	BOYS
1	Mary	John
2	Helen	William
3	Dorothy	James
4	Margaret	Robert
5	Ruth	Joseph
6	Mildred	George
7	Anna	Charles
8	Elizabeth	Edward
9	Frances	Frank
10	Marie	Thomas

TOP 10 **FIRST NAMES IN AUSTRALIA**

GIRLS		BOYS
Isabella	1	William
Ruby	2	Jack
Chloe	3	Oliver
Olivia	4	Joshua
Charlotte	5	Thomas
Mia	6	Lachlan
Lily	7	Cooper
Emily	8	Noah
Ella	9	Ethan
Sienna	10	Lucas

* Based on registrations in New South Wales, 2010

TOP 10 **FIRST NAMES IN CANADA** *

GIRLS		BOYS
Olivia	1	Ethan
Ava	2	Liam
Isabella	3	Jacob
Emily	4	Logan
Sophia	5	Noah
Alexis	6	Alexander
Ella	7	Benjamin
Sarah	8	Owen
Chloe	9	William
Hailey	10	Lucas

* Based on registrations in Alberta, 2009

KINGS & QUEENS

TOP 10 LONGEST-REIGNING LIVING MONARCHS

MONARCH / COUNTRY*	ACCESSION	YRS	REIGN# MTHS	DAYS	MONARCH / COUNTRY*	ACCESSION	YRS	REIGN# MTHS	DAYS
1 Bhumibol Adulyadej Thailand	Jun 9, 1946	64	6	21	6 Carl XVI Gustaf Sweden	Sep 15, 1973	37	3	16
2 Elizabeth II UK	Feb 6, 1952	58	10	25	7 Juan Carlos Spain	Nov 22, 1975	35	1	9
3 Haji Hassanal Bolkiah Brunei	Oct 5, 1967	43	2	26	8 Beatrix Netherlands	Apr 30, 1980	30	8	1
4 Sayyid Qaboos ibn Said al-Said Oman	Jul 23, 1970	40	5	7	9 Mswati Swaziland	Mar 25, 1986	24	9	6
5 Margrethe II Denmark	Jan 14, 1972	38	11	17	10 Emperor Akihito Japan	Jan 7, 1989	21	11	2

* Sovereign states only
\# As of March 31, 2011

THE 10 LATEST COUNTRIES TO ABOLISH MONARCHIES

	COUNTRY	LAST MONARCH	MONARCHY ABOLISHED
1	Nepal	Gyanendra I	2008
2	Samoa	Malietoa Tanumafili II	2007
3	Central Africa	Bokassa I	1979
4	Iran	Mohammad Reza Pahlavi	1979
5	Laos	Savang Vatthana	1975
6	Ethiopia*	Haile Selassie I	1974
7	Afghanistan	Mohammed Zahir Shah	1973
8	Greece#	Konstantinos II	1973
9	Cambodia†	Norodom Sihanouk	1970
10	Libya	Idris I	1969

* Emperor deposed 1974
\# King exiled 1967
† Restored 1993

This list excludes countries that detached from British rule and became republics or no longer exist as a state.

◀ Bokassa I
A dictator who ruled with an iron fist, Bokassa I was overthrown in 1979.

► **Ruler of Brunei**
One of the richest men in the world, the sultan has an estimated fortune of $20 billion.

► **Heads of state**
The portrait used for the Queen's Head stamp is the most reproduced work of art in the world.

TOP 10 **LONGEST-REIGNING QUEENS**

	QUEEN*	COUNTRY	REIGN	REIGN YEARS
1	Victoria	UK	1837–1901	63
2	Elizabeth II	UK	1952–	59#
3	Wilhelmina	Netherlands	1890–1948	58
4	Wu Chao	China	AD 655–705	50
5	Salote Tubou	Tonga	1918–65	47
6	Elizabeth I	England	1558–1603	44
7	Maria Theresa	Hungary	1740–80	40
8	Maria I	Portugal	1777–1816	39
9	Joanna I	Italy	1343–81	38
10	Suiko Tenno	Japan	AD 592–628	36

* Queens and empresses who ruled in their own right, not as consorts of kings or emperors
\# As of March 31, 2011

TOP 10 **LONGEST-SERVING BRITISH ROYAL CONSORTS**

	CONSORT / MONARCH	BECAME CONSORT	CEASED TO BE CONSORT	YRS	MTHS	DAYS
1	Duke of Edinburgh Queen Elizabeth II	Feb 6, 1952	–	59	1	24*
2	Charlotte of Mecklenburg-Strelitz George III	Sep 8, 1761	Nov 17, 1818	57	2	9
3	Philippa of Hainault Edward III	Jan 24, 1328	Aug 15, 1369	41	6	22
4	Eleanor of Provence Henry III	Jan 14, 1236	Nov 16, 1272	36	10	2
5	Eleanor of Aquitaine Henry II	Oct 25, 1154	Jul 6, 1189	34	8	11
6	Anne of Denmark James I	Nov 23, 1589	Mar 4, 1619	29	3	9
7	Margaret of Anjou Henry VI	Apr 23, 1445	May 21, 1471	26	0	28
8	Mary of Teck George V	May 6, 1910	Jan 20, 1936	25	8	14
9	Catherine of Aragon Henry VIII	Jun 11, 1509	May 23, 1533	23	11	12
10	Henrietta Maria of France Charles I	Jun 13, 1625	Jan 30, 1649	23	7	17

* As of March 31, 2011

▲ **Queen and consort**
The royal couple celebrate their 64th wedding anniversary on November 20, 2011.

PRESIDENTS & POLITICIANS

▲ **Kennedy's last moments**
Kennedy's assassination spawned a wealth of conspiracy theories that continue to this day.

THE 10 LAST US PRESIDENTS AND VICE-PRESIDENTS TO DIE IN OFFICE

	NAME / PRESIDENT/ VICE-PRESIDENT	DEATH DATE
1	John F. Kennedy* (P)	Nov 22, 1963
2	Franklin D. Roosevelt (P)	Apr 12, 1945
3	Warren G. Harding (P)	Aug 2, 1923
4	James S. Sherman (V-P)	Oct 30, 1912
5	William McKinley* (P)	Sep 14, 1901
6	Garret A. Hobart (V-P)	Nov 21, 1899
7	Thomas A. Hendricks (V-P)	Nov 25, 1885
8	James A. Garfield* (P)	Sep 19, 1881
9	Henry Wilson (V-P)	Nov 10, 1875
10	Abraham Lincoln* (P)	Apr 15, 1865

* Assassinated

John F. Kennedy was the 15th and last US president or vice-president to die in office, and the fourth to die by an assassin's bullet. Prior to Lincoln, two presidents (Zachary Taylor and William Harrison) and three vice-presidents (William Rufus de Vane King, Elbridge Gerry, and George Clinton) had all died in office.

TOP 10 LONGEST-SERVING PRESIDENTS TODAY*

	PRESIDENT / COUNTRY	TOOK OFFICE
1	Colonel Mu'ammar Gaddafi# Libya	Sep 1, 1969
2	Ali Abdullah Saleh Yemen	Jul 18, 1978†
3	Teodoro Obiang Nguema Mbasogo Equatorial Guinea	Aug 3, 1979
4	José Eduardo dos Santos Angola	Sep 21, 1979
5	Paul Biya Cameroon	Nov 7, 1982
6	Yoweri Museveni Uganda	Jan 29, 1986
7	Blaise Compaoré Burkina Faso	Oct 15, 1987
8	Robert Mugabe Zimbabwe	Dec 1, 1987
9	Omar al-Bashir Sudan	Jun 30, 1989
10	Idriss Déby Chad	Dec 2, 1990

* As of March 31, 2011
# Since a reorganization in 1979, Colonel Gaddafi has held no formal position, but continues to rule under the ceremonial title of "Leader and Guide of the Revolution"
† Became president of North Yemen; of combined country since May 22, 1990

Youngest US Presidents

When Barack Obama assumed the office of president on January 20, 2009, he was 47 years old. He became the fifth youngest US president, and was almost exactly a year older than Bill Clinton, who was 46 when he took office. John F. Kennedy maintains the title of the youngest president—he was 43 years old when he was elected. The US Constitution requires that a president must be at least 35 years old on taking office.

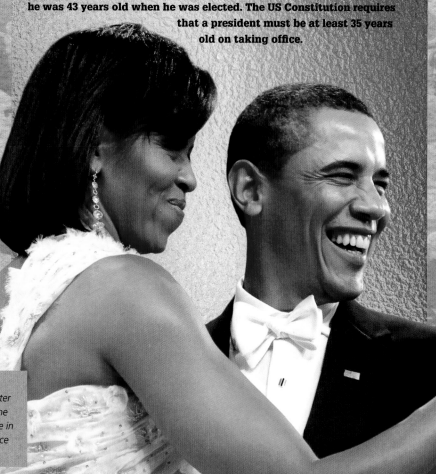

▶ **Young couple**
The Obamas' daughter Sasha (b. 2001), is the youngest child to live in the White House since John F. Kennedy, Jr.

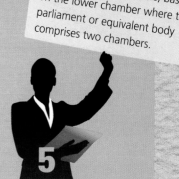

This list is based on the most recent general election results for 145 democratic countries, based on the lower chamber where the parliament or equivalent body comprises two chambers.

TOP 10 **PARLIAMENTS WITH THE HIGHEST PERCENTAGE OF WOMEN MEMBERS***

PARLIAMENT / LATEST ELECTION / WOMEN MEMBERS / TOTAL MEMBERS / % WOMEN

1 Rwanda (2008)
45 / 80 / 56.3%

2 Sweden (2010)
157 / 349 / 45.0%

3 South Africa (2009)
178 / 400 / 44.5%

4 Cuba (2008)
265 / 614 / 43.2%

5 Iceland (2009)
27 / 63 / 42.9%

6 Netherlands (2010)
61 / 150 / 40.7%

7 Norway (2009)
67 / 169 / 39.6%

8 Belgium (2010)
59 / 150 / 39.3%

9 Mozambique (2009)
98 / 250 / 39.2%

10 Angola (2008)
85 / 220 / 38.6%

USA 73 / 435 / 17.0%

* As of September 30, 2010   Source: Inter-Parliamentary Union

THE 10 **YOUNGEST BRITISH PRIME MINISTERS**

PRIME MINISTER / DATES	TOOK OFFICE	AGE* YRS	AGE* DAYS
1 William Pitt (1759–1806)	1783	24	205
2 Duke of Grafton (1735–1811)	1768	33	16
3 Marquess of Rockingham (1730–82)	1765	35	61
4 Duke of Devonshire (1720–64)	1756	c. 36	–
5 Lord North (1732–92)	1770	37	290
6 Earl of Liverpool (1770–1828)	1812	42	1
7 Henry Addington (1757–1844)	1801	43	291
8 David Cameron (b. 9 Oct 1966)	2010	43	214
9 Tony Blair (b. 6 May 1953)	1997	43	360
10 Sir Robert Walpole (1676–1745)	1721	44	107

* Where a prime minister served in more than one ministry, only the first is listed

▶ *Young blood*
In 2010, David Cameron became the youngest British prime minister for nearly 200 years.

To the Ends of the Earth

THE 10 FIRST PEOPLE TO REACH THE SOUTH POLE

NAME / AGE / NATIONALITY / DATE

#	Name	Age	Nationality	Date
1	Roald Amundsen	47	Norwegian	Dec 14, 1911
2	Olav Bjaaland	50	Norwegian	Dec 14, 1911
3	Helmer Hanssen	41	Norwegian	Dec 14, 1911
4	Sverre Hassel	35	Norwegian	Dec 14, 1911
5	Oscar Wisting	40	Norwegian	Dec 14, 1911
6	Robert Falcon Scott	43	English	Jan 17, 1912
7	Henry Bowers	29	Scottish	Jan 17, 1912
8	Edgar Evans	36	Welsh	Jan 17, 1912
9	Lawrence Oates	31	English	Jan 17, 1912
10	Edward Wilson	39	English	Jan 17, 1912

In 1910, Robert Falcon Scott set out to reach the South Pole, and "secure for the British Empire the honor of this achievement." After hauling a sled for more than 800 miles (1,290 km), on January 17, 1912 he was greeted by the Norwegian flag. He had been beaten by Roald Amundsen.

▶ **Pole position**
Making use of sled dogs and skis, Amundsen's 99-day journey was relatively uneventful.

▶ **Scott's team**
8,000 people applied to be part of Scott's Terra Nova expedition, many volunteering to help and contributing to its funds.

THE FIRST EXPEDITIONS TO REACH THE NORTH POLE OVERLAND

American Robert Peary claimed to have reached the pole on April 7, 1909. However, due to the speeds and route claimed, this is widely disputed, and later studies suggest he was several dozen miles short. The first undisputed surface conquest, verified by the United States Air Force, was made by Ralph Plaisted, Walt Pederson, Gerry Pitzl, and Jean Luc Bombardier, on April 19, 1968. Traveling by snowmobile, the expedition lasted 43 days and covered 825 miles (1,328 km).

SCOTT'S LAST JOURNEY

Upon reaching the pole, Scott proclaimed "Great God! This is an awful place." After planting the flag, they returned homeward the next day. Faced with abnormally cold weather, all five members perished, succumbing to frostbite, gangrene, and starvation. Scott's last diary entry reads:

> Since the 21st we have had a continuous gale from W.S.W. and S.W. We had fuel to make two cups of tea apiece and bare food for two days on the 20th. Every day we have been ready to start for our depot 11 miles away, but outside the door of the tent it remains a scene of whirling drift. I do not think we can hope for any better things now. We shall stick it out to the end, but we are getting weaker, of course, and the end cannot be far. It seems a pity, but I do not think I can write more.
> R. Scott

▲ **Captain Scott's depot**
Scott's hut at Cape Evans, which survives to this day, is insulated by quilted seaweed.

THE HEROIC AGE OF ANTARCTIC EXPLORATION

In 1895, the Sixth International Geographic Congress meeting in London proclaimed that "This congress record its opinion that the exploration of the Antarctic Regions is the greatest piece of geographical exploration still to be undertaken."

SHACKLETON AND THE ENDURANCE

> "Men wanted for hazardous journey. Low wages, bitter cold, long hours of complete darkness. Safe return doubtful. Honor and recognition in event of success."
> Advertisement for Shackleton's expedition

Two years after Scott's expedition, Ernest Shackleton attempted to cross the Antarctic continent via the pole. However, his ship got trapped and crushed in the ice, leaving the crew of 28 marooned, far from land, and with only three lifeboats for survival. After months in makeshift camps on the ice, the party reached the uninhabited Elephant Island. From there, Shackleton and five others sailed to reach help at a whaling station on South Georgia, some 800 miles (1,300 km) away. They returned four months later with a borrowed Chilean boat to pick up the remaining crew.

▲ **Endurance**
Hailed as the strongest wooden ship ever built, Endurance lasted eight months trapped in ice.

MURDER!

THE 10 **MOST PROLIFIC POISONERS**

POISONER* / CIRCUMSTANCES / VICTIMS

1 Dr. Harold Shipman
In January 2000, British doctor Shipman was found guilty of the murder of 15 women patients; the official enquiry into his crimes put the figure at 215, with 45 possible further cases, but some authorities believe that the total could be as high as 400.

2 Susannah Olah
Hungarian nurse Susi Olah "predicted" the demise of up to 100 people, who subsequently met their deaths as a result of arsenic poisoning. When the law finally caught up with her in 1929, she committed suicide.

3 Gesina Margaretha Gottfried
Having poisoned her first husband and two children with arsenic in 1815, German murderess Gesina Mittenberg then killed her next husband, Michael Gottfried. After a trial, at which she admitted to more than 30 murders, she was executed.

4 Nora Kelley (aka Jane Toppan)
Boston-born Nora Kelley trained as a nurse. After numerous patients in her care had died bodies were exhumed, revealing traces of morphine and atropine poisoning. She may have claimed as many as 30 victims.

5 Hélène Jegado
Jegado was a French housemaid who was believed to have committed some 23 murders by arsenic. She was tried at Rennes in 1851, found guilty and guillotined in 1852.

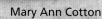
▲ **Harold Shipman**
Shipman is the only British doctor to be found guilty of murdering his patients.

6 Mary Ann Cotton
Over a 20-year period, it seems probable that former nurse Cotton (b. 1832) disposed of 14–20 victims, including her husband, children, and stepchildren by arsenic poisoning.

7 =Dr. William Palmer
Dubbed the "Rugeley Poisoner," Palmer (b.1824) may have killed at least 13, including his wife, brother, and children, in order to claim insurance. He was hanged at Stafford, UK, on June 14, 1856.

=Sadamichi Hirasawa
On January 26, 1948, Hirasawa entered the Shiinamachi branch of the Imperial Bank of Tokyo. Posing as a doctor, he administered what he claimed was a medicine but was in fact cyanide to 16 members of staff, 14 of whom died.

9 Johann Otto Hoch
German-born Hoch (1862–1906) preyed on widows, many of whom he married before murdering them, usually with poison. He certainly killed 12 and, according to some authorities, as many as 50 before being hanged in 1906.

10 Marie Becker
In the autumn of 1932 Becker poisoned her husband Charles with digitalis, followed by her lover Lambert Bayer. In order to finance her own extravagant lifestyle, she then embarked on a series of murders of elderly women whom she nursed, using the same drug.

◄ **Arsenic**
The fact that it is odorless and flavorless has made arsenic a favorite method for poisoners.

* Excluding poisoners where evidence is so confused with legend (such as that surrounding the Borgia family) as to be unreliable

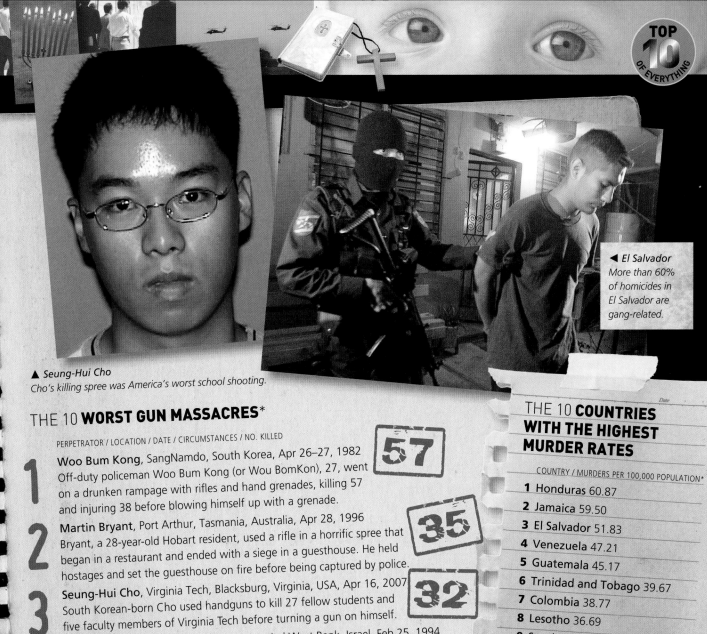

▲ *Seung-Hui Cho*
Cho's killing spree was America's worst school shooting.

◄ *El Salvador*
More than 60% of homicides in El Salvador are gang-related.

THE 10 **WORST GUN MASSACRES***

PERPETRATOR / LOCATION / DATE / CIRCUMSTANCES / NO. KILLED

1 **Woo Bum Kong**, SangNamdo, South Korea, Apr 26–27, 1982
Off-duty policeman Woo Bum Kong (or Wou BomKon), 27, went on a drunken rampage with rifles and hand grenades, killing 57 and injuring 38 before blowing himself up with a grenade. **57**

2 **Martin Bryant**, Port Arthur, Tasmania, Australia, Apr 28, 1996
Bryant, a 28-year-old Hobart resident, used a rifle in a horrific spree that began in a restaurant and ended with a siege in a guesthouse. He held hostages and set the guesthouse on fire before being captured by police. **35**

3 **Seung-Hui Cho**, Virginia Tech, Blacksburg, Virginia, USA, Apr 16, 2007
South Korean-born Cho used handguns to kill 27 fellow students and five faculty members of Virginia Tech before turning a gun on himself. **32**

4 = **Baruch Kappel Goldstein**, Hebron, occupied West Bank, Israel, Feb 25, 1994
Goldstein, a 42-year-old US immigrant doctor, carried out a gun massacre of Palestinians at prayer at the Tomb of the Patriarchs, before being beaten to death by the crowd. **29**

= **Matsuo Toi**, Tsuyama, Japan, May 21, 1938
21-year-old Toi used a rifle and swords to kill 29 of his neighbors before committing suicide.

6 **Campo Elias Delgado**, Bogota, Colombia, Dec 4, 1986
Delgado, a Vietnamese war veteran and electronics engineer, stabbed two and shot a further 26 people before being killed by police. **28**

7 = **George Jo Hennard**, Killeen, Texas, USA, Oct 16, 1991
Hennard drove his pickup truck through the window of Luby's Cafeteria and, in 11 minutes, killed 22 with semi-automatic pistols before shooting himself.

= **James Oliver Huberty**, San Ysidro, California, USA, Jul 18, 1984
Huberty, aged 41, opened fire in a McDonald's restaurant, killing 21 before being shot dead by a SWAT marksman. A further 19 were wounded, including a victim who died the following day. **22**

9 = **Thomas Hamilton**, Dunblane, Stirling, UK, Mar 13, 1996
Hamilton, 43, shot 16 children and a teacher in Dunblane Primary School before killing himself in the UK's worst ever shooting incident. **17**

= **Robert Steinhäuser**, Erfurt, Germany, Apr 26, 2002
Former student Steinhäuser returned to Johann Gutenberg Secondary School and killed 14 teachers, two students, and a police officer before shooting himself.

* By individuals, excluding terrorist and military actions; totals exclude perpetrator

THE 10 **COUNTRIES WITH THE HIGHEST MURDER RATES**

COUNTRY	MURDERS PER 100,000 POPULATION*
1 Honduras	60.87
2 Jamaica	59.50
3 El Salvador	51.83
4 Venezuela	47.21
5 Guatemala	45.17
6 Trinidad and Tobago	39.67
7 Colombia	38.77
8 Lesotho	36.69
9 South Africa	36.54
10 St. Kitts and Nevis	35.25

* In latest year for which data available

Source: United Nations

THE 10 COUNTRIES REPORTING THE MOST BURGLARIES

COUNTRY / BURGLARIES REPORTED

1. USA
2,222,200

2. UK
581,546

3. Germany
380,684

4. France
298,173

5. Australia
241,690

6. Canada
209,755

7. Spain
174,761

8. Japan
162,111

9. Poland
124,066

10. Turkey
114,234

Source: United Nations Office on Drugs and Crime

▲ American prisoners
With numbers increasing four-fold over the last 20 years, the USA houses a quarter of the world's prison population.

THE 10 COUNTRIES WITH THE MOST KIDNAPPINGS

COUNTRY* / KIDNAPPINGS

1. India
23,911

2. Turkey
10,509

3. Canada
4,671

4. France
2,074

5. UK
2,034

6. Belgium
1,165

7. United Arab Emirates
971

8. Australia
782

9. Mexico
713

10. Russia
698

* For which data available

Source: United Nations Office on Drugs and Crime

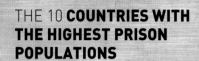

THE 10 **COUNTRIES WITH THE HIGHEST PRISON POPULATIONS**

	COUNTRY	PRISONERS PER 100,000 OF POPULATION	TOTAL PRISONERS*
1	USA	748	2,297,400
2	China	120	1,620,000
3	Russia	585	829,300
4	Brazil	253	494,237
5	India	32	384,753
6	Mexico	202	222,550
7	Thailand	313	212,058
8	Iran	223	166,979
9	South Africa	319	160,026
10	Ukraine	334	152,169

* As at date of most recent data

Source: International Centre for Prison Studies

▲ Crowded conditions
Despite an official capacity of 438, the national penitentiary in Port-au-Prince, Haiti, actually houses 3,100 inmates.

THE 10 **COUNTRIES WITH THE MOST OVERCROWDED PRISONS**

COUNTRY / PRISON OCCUPANCY RATE (%)*

	COUNTRY	OCCUPANCY RATE (%)
1	Haiti	335.7
2	Benin	307.1
3	Bangladesh	275.0
4	Burundi	268.1
5	Sudan	255.3
6	El Salvador	253.5
7	Pakistan	232.7
8	Kenya	223.3
9	Mali	223.0
10	Uganda	218.0

* Occupancy level based on official capacity

Source: International Centre for Prison Studies

THE 10 **LARGEST LOCAL POLICE FORCES IN THE USA**

POLICE FORCE

	POLICE FORCE	OFFICERS
1	New York	35,973
2	Chicago	13,469
3	Los Angeles	9,307
4	Philadelphia	6,853
5	Houston	5,350
6	Detroit	3,837
7	Washington	3,632
8	Baltimore	3,258
9	Miami	3,178
10	Dallas	2,943

Source: US Bureau of Justice

THE 10 **COUNTRIES WITH THE HIGHEST PROPORTION OF FOREIGN PRISONERS**

COUNTRY / % FOREIGN PRISONERS

1 United Arab Emirates 92.2
2 Monaco 91.2
3 Andorra 81.7
4 Saudi Arabia 72.0
5 Switzerland 70.2
6 Luxembourg 69.5
7 Gambia 66.7
8 Qatar 59.7
9 Cyprus 59.6
10 Austria 45.8

Source: International Centre for Prison Studies

WORLD WAR I

▲ **Facing the enemy**
An estimated 2,000,000
German soldiers lost their
lives in the war.

THE 10 **COUNTRIES WITH THE GREATEST MERCHANT SHIPPING LOSSES IN WORLD WAR I**

	COUNTRY	VESSELS SUNK NO.	TONNAGE
1	UK	2,038	6,797,802
2	Italy	228	720,064
3	France	213	651,583
4	USA	93	372,892
5	Germany	188	319,552
6	Greece	115	304,992
7	Denmark	126	205,002
8	Netherlands	74	194,483
9	Sweden	124	192,807
10	Spain	70	160,383

THE 10 **LARGEST ARMED FORCES OF WORLD WAR I**

	COUNTRY	PERSONNEL*
1	Russia	12,000,000
2	Germany	11,000,000
3	British Empire	8,904,467
4	France	8,410,000
5	Austria-Hungary	7,800,000
6	Italy	5,615,000
7	USA	4,355,000
8	Turkey	2,850,000
9	Bulgaria	1,200,000
10	Japan	800,000

* Total at peak strength

THE 10 **SMALLEST ARMED FORCES OF WORLD WAR I**

	COUNTRY	PERSONNEL*
1	Montenegro	50,000
2	Portugal	100,000
3	Greece	230,000
4	Belgium	267,000
5	Serbia	707,343
6	Romania	750,000
7	Japan	800,000
8	Bulgaria	1,200,000
9	Turkey	2,850,000
10	USA	4,355,000

* Total at peak strength

THE 10 **COUNTRIES SUFFERING THE GREATEST MILITARY LOSSES IN WORLD WAR I**

	COUNTRY	KILLED
1	Germany	1,773,700
2	Russia	1,700,000
3	France	1,357,800
4	Austria-Hungary	1,200,000
5	British Empire*	908,371
6	Italy	650,000
7	Romania	335,706
8	Turkey	325,000
9	USA	116,516
10	Bulgaria	87,500

* Including Australia, Canada, India, New Zealand, South Africa, etc.

THE 10 **COUNTRIES WITH THE MOST PRISONERS OF WAR, 1914–18**

	COUNTRY	POWS
1	Russia	2,500,000
2	Austria-Hungary	2,200,000
3	Germany	1,152,800
4	Italy	600,000
5	France	537,000
6	Turkey	250,000
7	British Empire	191,652
8	Serbia	152,958
9	Romania	80,000
10	Belgium	34,659

TOP 10 **GERMAN AIR ACES OF WORLD WAR I**

PILOT / KILLS CLAIMED

1	Rittmeister Manfred von Richthofen	*80*
2	Oberleutnant Ernst Udet	*62*
3	Oberleutnant Erich Loewenhardt	*53*
4	Leutenant Werner Voss	*48*
5	= Hauptmann Bruno Loerzer = Leutnant Fritz Rumey	*45*
7	Hauptmann Rudolph Berthold	*44*
8	Leutnant Paul Bäumer	*43*
9	Leutnant Josef Jacobs	*41*
10	= Hauptmann Oswald Boelcke = Leutnant Franz Büchner = Oberleutnant Lothar Freiherr von Richthofen	*40*

The claims of top World War I ace Rittmeister Manfred, Baron von Richthofen (right)—whose brother also merits a place in this list—of 80 kills has been disputed, since only 60 of them have been completely confirmed. Richthofen, known as the "Red Baron" and leader of the so-called "Flying Circus" (because the aircraft of his squadron were painted in distinctive bright colors), shot down 21 allied fighters in the single month of April 1917. His own end a year later, on April 21, 1918, has been the subject of controversy, and it remains uncertain whether he was shot down in aerial combat with British pilot Captain A. Roy Brown, or downed by shots from Australian machine gunners on the ground.

WORLD WAR II

TOP 10 BRITISH AND COMMONWEALTH AIR ACES OF WORLD WAR II

PILOT / NATIONALITY — KILLS CLAIMED

1 Sqd. Ldr. Marmaduke Thomas St. John Pattle — **>40**
South African

2 Gp. Capt. James Edgar "Johnny" Johnson — **33.91**
British

3 Wng. Cdr. Brendan "Paddy" Finucane — **32**
Irish

4 Flt. Lt. George Frederick Beurling — **31.93**
Canadian

5 Wng. Cdr. John Randall Daniel Braham — **29**
British

6 Gp. Capt. Adolf Gysbert "Sailor" Malan — **28.66**
South African

7 Wng. Cdr. Clive Robert Caldwell — **28.5**
Australian

8 Sqd. Ldr. James Harry "Ginger" Lacey — **28**
British

9 Sqd. Ldr. Neville Frederick Duke — **27.83**
British

10 Wng. Cdr. Colin F. Gray — **27.7**
New Zealander

▶ **Success in the skies**
The Battle of Britain was a turning point for Britain, as the RAF defeated the Luftwaffe.

Kills expressed as fractions refer to those that were shared with others, the number of fighters involved, and the extent of each pilot's participation determining the proportion allocated to him. Thus, while some overall totals may be approximations, as a result of this precise reckoning of the shared kills, British pilot James Harry "Ginger" Lacey, with 28, misses sharing 10th place with Gray by one-third of a kill.

TOP 10 TANKS OF WORLD WAR II

	TANK / INTRODUCED	COUNTRY	WEIGHT (TONS)	NO. PRODUCED
1	M4A3 Sherman (1942)	USA	34.7	41,530
2	T34 Model 42 (1940)	USSR	31.9	35,120
3	T34/85 (1944)	USSR	35.8	29,430
4	M3 General Stuart (1941)	USA	13.7	14,000
5	Valentine II (1941)	UK	19.6	8,280
6	M3A1 Lee/Grant (1941)	USA	30.0	7,400
7	Churchill VII (1942)	UK	44.8	5,640
8	=Panzer IVD (pre-war)	Germany	22.4	5,500
	=Panzer VG (1943)	Germany	50.2	5,500
10	Crusader I (1941)	UK	21.3	4,750

The Sherman's weaponry comprised two machine guns and, originally, a 3-inch cannon, but after 1944 about half the Shermans in operation had their cannons replaced by one capable of firing a powerful 17-lb shell or a 12-lb armor-piercing shell.

TOP 10 LARGEST ARMED FORCES OF WORLD WAR II

	COUNTRY	PERSONNEL*
1	USSR	12,500,000
2	USA	12,364,000
3	Germany	10,000,000
4	Japan	6,095,000
5	France	5,700,000
6	UK	4,683,000
7	Italy	4,500,000
8	China	3,800,000
9	India	2,150,000
10	Poland	1,000,000

* Total at peak strength

Allowing for deaths and casualties, the total forces mobilized during the course of the war is, of course, greater than the peak strength figures: that of the USSR, for example, has been put as high as 20 million, the USA 16,354,000, Germany 17.9 million, Japan 9.1 million, and the UK 5,896,000.

◀ *Ground control*
Swiftly designed and mass-produced by the USA, the iconic Sherman tank was technically uncomplicated but extremely reliable.

TOP 10 US NAVY SUBMARINE COMMANDERS OF WORLD WAR II

COMMANDER / SUBMARINES COMMANDED / SHIPS SUNK

1 **Richard H. O'Kane**
Tang
 31

2 **Eugene B. Fluckley**
Barb
 25

3 **Slade D. Cutter**
Seahorse
 21

4 **Samuel D. Dealey**
Harder
 20.5

5 **William S. Post, Jr.**
Gudgeon and Spot
 19

6 **Reuben T. Whitaker**
S-44 and Flasher
 18.5

7 **Walter T. Griffith**
Bowfin and Bullhead
 17*

8 **Dudley W. Morton**
R-5 and Wahoo
 17*

9 **John E. Lee**
S-12, Grayling and Croaker
 16

10 **William B. Sieglaff**
Tautog and Tench
15

* Gross tonnage used to determine ranking order

THE 10 COUNTRIES SUFFERING THE GREATEST MILITARY LOSSES IN WORLD WAR II

COUNTRY / LOSSES

10 Italy 279,800
9 USA 292,131
8 Yugoslavia 305,000
7 Poland 320,000
6 Romania 350,000
5 British Empire# (UK 264,000) 357,116
4 Japan 1,140,429
3 China 1,324,516
1 USSR 13,600,000*
2 Germany 3,300,000

Total 21,268,992

* Total, of which 7.8 million battlefield deaths
# Including Australia, Canada, India, New Zealand, etc.

MODERN MILITARY

TOP 10 COUNTRIES WITH THE MOST ATTACK HELICOPTERS

	COUNTRY	HELICOPTERS
1	USA	1,273
2	Spain	665
3	Russia	646
4	France	228
5	Germany	192
6	Ukraine	139
7	Egypt	120
8	Israel	103
9	Taiwan	101
10	Japan	80
	World	*5,015*

Source: CIA, *The World Factbook 2010*

◄ *Air combat*
America's Boeing Apache fleet has clocked over two million flight hours in numerous global peacekeeping operations.

TOP 10 COUNTRIES WITH THE LARGEST ARMIES

	COUNTRY	PERSONNEL
1	China	1,400,000
2	India	1,100,000
3	North Korea	1,002,000
4	South Korea	560,000
5	Pakistan	520,000
6	USA	512,000
7	Vietnam	412,000
8	Turkey	402,000
9	Iran	350,000
10	Myanmar	325,000

▼ *People's Army*
In addition to its million-plus active members, North Korea's People's Army has over eight million reserve personnel.

TOP 10 RANKS OF THE US NAVY, ARMY, AND AIR FORCE

	NAVY	ARMY	AIR FORCE
1	Fleet Admiral	General	General
2	Admiral	Lieutenant-General	Lieutenant-General
3	Vice-Admiral	Major-General	Major-General
4	Rear-Admiral (Upper Half)	Brigadier-General	Brigadier-General
5	Rear-Admiral (Lower Half)	Colonel	Colonel
6	Captain	Lieutenant-Colonel	Lieutenant-Colonel
7	Commander	Major	Major
8	Lieutenant Commander	Captain	Captain
9	Lieutenant	First Lieutenant	First Lieutenant
10	Lieutenant (Junior Grade)	Second Lieutenant	Second Lieutenant

TOP 10 CONTRIBUTORS TO UN PEACEKEEPING OPERATIONS

	COUNTRY	PERSONNEL
1	Bangladesh	10,862
2	Pakistan	10,733
3	India	8,783
4	Nigeria	5,837
5	Egypt	5,258
6	Nepal	5,186
7	Ghana	3,911
8	Jordan	3,769
9	Rwanda	3,663
10	Uruguay	2,516

Source: United Nations

Although no one has been appointed to the naval rank of Fleet Admiral since 1945, it is regarded as active, whereas General of the Army has not been conferred since Omar Bradley in 1950, and is unlikely to be used in the future. General of the Armies ranks above General of the Army, but has been awarded only to John J. Pershing in 1919 and retrospectively in 1976 to George Washington. As it has since been decreed that no one may ever outrank Washington, it is no longer valid.

▼ **American arms**
The USA's four largest arms companies—Lockheed Martin, Boeing, Northrop Grumman, and General Dynamics—employ over half a million people.

TOP 10 ARMS-IMPORTING COUNTRIES

	COUNTY	IMPORTS VALUE ($)
1	India	2,116,000,000
2	Singapore	1,729,000,000
3	Malaysia	1,494,000,000
4	Greece	1,269,000,000
5	South Korea	1,172,000,000
6	Pakistan	1,146,000,000
7	Algeria	942,000,000
8	USA	831,000,000
9	Australia	757,000,000
10	Turkey	675,000,000
	World	22,640,000,000

Source: Stockholm International Peace Research Institute

TOP 10 ARMS-EXPORTING COUNTRIES

	COUNTRY	EXPORTS VALUE ($)	MAIN TRADE PARTNER
1	USA	6,090,000,000	Singapore
2	Russia	4,469,000,000	India
3	Germany	2,473,000,000	South Korea
4	France	1,851,000,000	Singapore
5	UK	1,024,000,000	Saudi Arabia
6	Spain	925,000,000	Norway
7	China	870,000,000	Pakistan
8	Israel	760,000,000	Turkey
9	Netherlands	608,000,000	Portugal
10	Italy	588,000,000	Malaysia
	World	22,640,000,000	

Source: Stockholm International Peace Research Institute

RELIGIONS OF THE WORLD

TOP 10 **LARGEST HINDU POPULATIONS**

COUNTRY / HINDUS

Top 10 total / 936,719,230
World total / 942,871,282

Source: World Christian Database

1 India 887,059,081

2 Nepal 20,249,772

3 Bangladesh 15,587,198

4 Indonesia 3,429,712

5 Sri Lanka 2,662,954

6 Pakistan 2,436,797

7 Malaysia 1,749,669

8 USA 1,478,555

9 South Africa 1,204,106

10 Myanmar 861,386

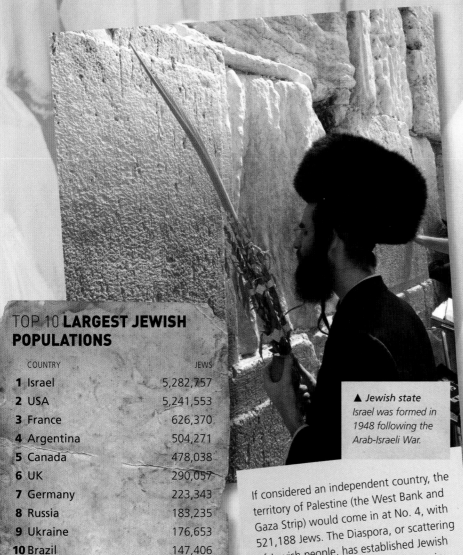

▲ *Jewish state*
Israel was formed in 1948 following the Arab-Israeli War.

TOP 10 **LARGEST JEWISH POPULATIONS**

COUNTRY	JEWS
1 Israel	5,282,757
2 USA	5,241,553
3 France	626,370
4 Argentina	504,271
5 Canada	478,038
6 UK	290,057
7 Germany	223,343
8 Russia	183,235
9 Ukraine	176,653
10 Brazil	147,406
Top 10 total	*13,674,871*
World total	*14,822,687*

Source: World Christian Database

If considered an independent country, the territory of Palestine (the West Bank and Gaza Strip) would come in at No. 4, with 521,188 Jews. The Diaspora, or scattering of Jewish people, has established Jewish communities in almost every country in the world. In 1939, the estimated total Jewish population was 17 million. Some 6 million fell victim to Nazi persecution, reducing the figure to about 11 million, since when it has grown to more than 14 million.

TOP 10 **BELIEFS IN THE USA**

RELIGION	FOLLOWERS
1 Christians	257,935,642
2 Agnostics	38,695,319
3 Jews	5,241,553
4 Muslims	4,805,776
5 Buddhists	4,047,598
6 New religionists	1,662,922
7 Hindus	1,478,555
8 Atheists	1,328,803
9 Ethnoreligionists	1,109,997
10 Baha'is	525,046

Source: World Christian Database

▶ *Christian symbol*
About one-third of the world's population is Christian.

▼ *Brazilian worship*
Nearly 75% of the Brazilian population claims to be Roman Catholic.

TOP 10 **LARGEST CHRISTIAN POPULATIONS**

	COUNTRY	CHRISTIANS
1	USA	257,935,642
2	Brazil	177,737,086
3	China	114,364,041
4	Russia	114,041,632
5	Mexico	106,058,166
6	Philippines	83,077,538
7	Nigeria	72,023,815
8	Dem. Rep. of Congo	64,685,125
9	Germany	58,016,298
10	India	57,550,490
	Top 10 total	*1,105,489,833*
	World total	*2,159,141,594*

Source: World Christian Database

TOP 10 **COUNTRIES WITH MOST ATHEISTS AND AGNOSTICS**

	COUNTRY	ATHEISTS	AGNOSTICS	TOTAL
1	China	96,860,601	428,644,836	525,505,437
2	USA	1,328,803	38,695,319	40,024,122
3	Germany	2,056,011	17,773,652	17,793,663
4	Vietnam	5,888,435	11,258,775	17,147,210
5	North Korea	3,737,875	13,360,858	17,098,733
6	Japan	3,643,341	12,919,880	16,563,221
7	India	1,937,586	14,076,698	16,014,284
8	France	2,589,310	10,281,764	12,871,074
9	Russia	1,484,731	8,495,922	9,980,653
10	Italy	2,162,156	7,749,533	9,911,689
	Top 10 total	*121,688,849*	*563,257,237*	*682,910,086*
	World total	*137,845,884*	*659,922,513*	*797,768,397*

Source: World Christian Database

TOP 10 **LARGEST MUSLIM POPULATIONS**

	COUNTRY	MUSLIMS
1	Indonesia	183,700,584
2	Pakistan	177,658,575
3	India	166,097,980
4	Bangladesh	146,090,117
5	Iran	74,021,861
6	Turkey	73,745,237
7	Egypt	73,609,345
8	Nigeria	71,845,953
9	Algeria	34,685,807
10	Morocco	32,012,962
	USA	*4,805,776*

Source: World Christian Database

▼ *Islamic domes*
The domes on the mosques of Islam symbolize the vaults of heaven and the sky.

4

TOWN & COUNTRY

POPULATION EXPLOSION

On September 1, 1962, the UN announced that the world population totaled more than 3 billion people. By the end of the 20th century this figure had reached 6 billion, meaning that the number of people in the world had doubled in a little under 40 years. If this astronomical population growth continued it would be unsustainable for our planet, but fortunately the growth rate has slowed substantially, although the actual population will continue to rise. There will be an estimated population of just over 7 billion people by June 2012, rising to 9.3 billion by 2050.

COUNTRIES OF THE WORLD

TOP 10 LARGEST COUNTRIES

	COUNTRY	SQ MILES	% OF AREA SQ KM	WORLD TOTAL (%)
1	Russia	6,601,669	17,098,242	11.5
2	Canada	3,855,103	9,984,670	6.7
3	USA	3,717,813	9,629,091	6.5
4	China	3,704,408	9,596,961	6.4
5	Brazil	3,287,613	8,514,877	5.7
6	Australia	2,969,907	7,692,024	5.2
7	India	1,269,219	3,287,263	2.3
8	Argentina	1,073,519	2,780,400	2.0
9	Kazakhstan	1,052,090	2,724,900	1.8
10	Sudan	967,500	2,505,813	1.7

Source: United Nations Statistics Division

THE 10 MOST RECENT INDEPENDENT COUNTRIES

	COUNTRY	INDEPENDENCE
1	Kosovo	Feb 17, 2008
2	Montenegro	Jun 3, 2006
3	Serbia	Jun 5, 2006
4	Timor-Leste	May 20, 2002
5	Palau	Oct 1, 1994
6	Eritrea	May 24, 1993
7	= Czech Republic	Jan 1, 1993
	= Slovakia	Jan 1, 1993
9	Bosnia and Herzegovina	Mar 1, 1992
10	Kazakhstan	Dec 16, 1991

Kazungula, on the Zambezi River, is a point at which the borders of Botswana, Namibia, Zambia, and Zimbabwe all meet, each thus theoretically having a border length of zero. There are also many island countries that have no borders with any other countries.

TOP 10 SHORTEST BORDERS

	COUNTRIES	LAND BORDERS MILES	KM
1	Vatican City/Italy	2.0	3.2
2	Monaco/France	2.7	4.4
3	Azerbaijan/Turkey	5.6	9.0
4	North Korea/Russia	11.8	19.0
5	Cuba/USA (Guantanamo Bay)	18.0	29.0
6	Liechtenstein/Austria	21.7	34.9
7	Armenia/Iran	21.7	35.0
8	San Marino/Italy	24.2	39.0
9	Liechtenstein/Switzerland	25.5	41.1
10	Andorra/France	35.2	56.6

Source: CIA, *The World Factbook 2010*

▶ *Small state*
Monaco is the second smallest country in the world (after Vatican City), covering an area of only 0.78 sq miles (2 sq km).

▲ *Brazil*
The entire Brazilian coastline—stretching nearly 4,660 miles (7,500 km) lies on the Atlantic Ocean.

THE 10 COUNTRIES WITH THE LOWEST COASTLINE/AREA RATIO

	COUNTRY	AREA (SQ KM)	COASTLINE (KM)	RATIO (M/SQ KM)
1	Dem. Rep. of Congo	2,267,600	37	0.016
2	Iraq	432,162	58	0.134
3	Jordan	91,971	26	0.283
4	Sudan	2,376,000	853	0.359
5	Bosnia and Herzegovina	51,197	20	0.391
6	Algeria	2,381,740	998	0.419
7	Republic of the Congo	341,500	169	0.495
8	Mauritania	1,030,400	754	0.732
9	Cameroon	469,440	402	0.856
10	Brazil	8,456,510	7,491	0.886

Source: CIA, *The World Factbook 2010*

There are some 44 landlocked countries in the world. Landlocked countries often suffer through having to rely on their neighbors for trade routes. In times of conflict this makes them especially vulnerable to blockades. Two countries in the world are actually doubly landlocked—completely surrounded by other landlocked countries—so anyone leaving the country would have to cross two borders before reaching a sea coast. They are Liechtenstein, which is surrounded by Austria and Switzerland, and Uzbekistan, surrounded by Afghanistan, Kazakhstan, Kyrgyzstan, Tajikistan, and Turkmenistan.

TOP 10 LARGEST LANDLOCKED COUNTRIES

	COUNTRY / NEIGHBORS	AREA SQ MILES	AREA SQ KM
1	Kazakhstan — China, Kyrgyzstan, Russia, Turkmenistan, Uzbekistan	1,049,156	2,717,300
2	Mongolia — China, Russia	603,908	1,564,116
3	Niger — Algeria, Benin, Burkina Faso, Chad, Libya, Mali, Nigeria	489,075	1,266,699
4	Chad — Cameroon, Central African Republic, Libya, Niger, Nigeria, Sudan	486,180	1,259,201
5	Mali — Algeria, Burkina Faso, Côte d'Ivoire, Guinea, Mauritania, Niger, Senegal	471,044	1,219,999
6	Ethiopia — Djibouti, Eritrea, Kenya, Somalia, Sudan	435,186	1,127,127
7	Bolivia — Argentina, Brazil, Chile, Paraguay, Peru	424,164	1,098,580
8	Zambia — Angola, Dem. Rep. of Congo, Malawi, Mozambique, Namibia, Tanzania, Zimbabwe	290,585	752,614
9	Afghanistan — China, Iran, Pakistan, Tajikistan, Turkmenistan, Uzbekistan	250,001	647,500
10	Central African Republic — Cameroon, Chad, Congo, Dem. Rep. of Congo, Sudan	240,535	622,984

POPULATION PROJECTIONS

TOP 10 **MOST DENSELY POPULATED COUNTRIES, 2050**

	COUNTRY	AREA (SQ MILES)	ESTIMATED POPULATION (2050)	POPULATION PER SQ MILE
1	Monaco	0.8	29,810	29,810
2	Singapore	265	4,635,110	17,491
3	Hong Kong	407	6,172,723	15,166
4	Bangladesh	50,258	250,155,274	4,977
5	Maldives	115	444,429	3,865
6	Bahrain	286	980,431	3,428
7	Rwanda	9,524	27,506,207	2,888
8	Burundi	9,915	27,148,888	2,738
9	Malta	122	295,639	2,423
10	Comoros	863	1,837,671	2,129
	USA	*3,537,455*	*439,010,253*	*124*

Source (all lists): US Census Bureau, *International Data Base*

TOP 10 **MOST POPULATED COUNTRIES, 2011**

	COUNTRY	ESTIMATED POPULATION (2011)
1	China	1,336,718,015
2	India	1,189,172,906
3	USA	313,232,044
4	Indonesia	245,613,043
5	Brazil	203,429,773
6	Pakistan	187,342,721
7	Bangladesh	158,570,535
8	Nigeria	152,217,341
9	Russia	139,390,205
10	Japan	126,804,433
	Top 10 total	*3,772,611,166*
	World total	*6,929,098,151*

TOP 10 **MOST POPULATED COUNTRIES, 2050**

	COUNTRY	ESTIMATED POPULATION (2050)
1	India	1,656,553,632
2	China	1,303,723,332
3	USA	439,010,253
4	Indonesia	313,020,847
5	Pakistan	290,847,790
6	Ethiopia	278,283,137
7	Nigeria	264,262,405
8	Brazil	260,692,493
9	Bangladesh	250,155,274
10	Congo (Kinshasa)	189,310,849
	Top 10	*5,245,860,012*
	World	*9,284,107,424*

Estimates of national populations in 2050 present a striking change as long-time world leader China is eclipsed by India, a reversal that is projected to take place around the year 2025.

▼ *People power*
India has a rapidly growing population as well as an increasingly important economy.

THE 10 **COUNTRIES WITH THE GREATEST POPULATION GROWTH, 2011–50**

COUNTRY / ESTIMATED POPULATION 2010 / ESTIMATED POPULATION 2050 / % GROWTH

1 Uganda
34,612,250 / 128,007,514 / 269.83%

2 Niger
16,468,886 / 55,304,449 / 235.81%

3 Burkina Faso
16,751,455 / 47,429,509 / 183.14%

4 Zambia
13,881,336 / 38,371,544 / 176.43%

5 Congo (Kinshasa)
73,179,859 / 189,310,849 / 158.69%

6 Somalia
10,399,807 / 26,024,500 / 150.24%

7 Rwanda
11,370,425 / 27,506,207 / 141.91%

8 Malawi
15,879,252 / 37,406,745 / 135.57%

9 Liberia
3,786,764 / 8,192,118 / 116.34%

10 Chad
10,758,945 / 20,473,601 / 90.29%

As all these countries are in sub-Saharan Africa, this list demonstrates that the population in this part of the world is set to increase dramatically in the next 40 years, with the population of Uganda predicted to increase to more than three times its current level during this period.

▶ *Greatest growth*
Despite substantial growth in the coming decades, Africa will remain considerably underpopulated compared to Asia.

THE 10 **LEAST DENSELY POPULATED COUNTRIES, 2050**

	COUNTRY	AREA (SQ MILES)	ESTIMATED POPULATION (2050)	POPULATION PER SQ MILE
1	Namibia	317,874	2,149,815	6.8
2	Mongolia	599,831	4,340,496	7.2
3	Iceland	38,707	350,922	9.0
4	Australia	2,966,153	29,012,740	9.8
5	Suriname	60,232	617,249	10.2
6	=Canada	3,511,023	41,135,648	11.7
	=Guyana	76,004	888,494	11.7
8	Botswana	218,816	2,871,345	13.1
9	Kazakhstan	1,030,777	15,099,700	14.6
10	Libya	679,362	10,871,760	16.0

▶ *Namibia*
It is estimated that the population of Namibia will increase by a mere 2,230 people by 2050.

PEOPLE ON THE MOVE

TOP 10 ORIGINAL NATIONALITIES OF REFUGEES AND ASYLUM SEEKERS

NATIONALITY / REFUGEES/ASYLUM SEEKERS*

1 Afghanistan
2,805,100

2 Iraq
1,876,000

3 Myanmar
754,100

4 Somalia
530,400

5 Sudan
424,100

6 Columbia
394,700

7 Congo (Kinshasa)
361,100

8 Vietnam
319,300

9 Burundi
256,000

10 Eritrea
224,700

* Latest available year

Source: US Committee for Refugees

TOP 10 ANCESTRIES OF THE US POPULATION

ANCESTRY GROUP / NO.

1 German 42,800,000
2 Irish 30,500,000
3 Afro-American 24,900,000
4 English 24,500,000
5 American 20,200,000
6 Mexican 18,400,000
7 Italian 15,600,000
8 Polish 9,000,000
9 French 8,300,000
10 American Indian 7,900,000

Source: US Census Bureau

TOP 10 MOST COMMON COUNTRIES OF BIRTH OF US RESIDENTS

COUNTRY / TOTAL*

1 Mexico 11,413,000
2 Philippines 1,685,000
3 India 1,623,000
4 China 1,361,000
5 Vietnam 1,138,000
6 El Salvador 1,095,000
7 Korea 1,031,000
8 Cuba 975,000
9 Canada 819,000
10 Dominican Republic 772,000

* Latest available year

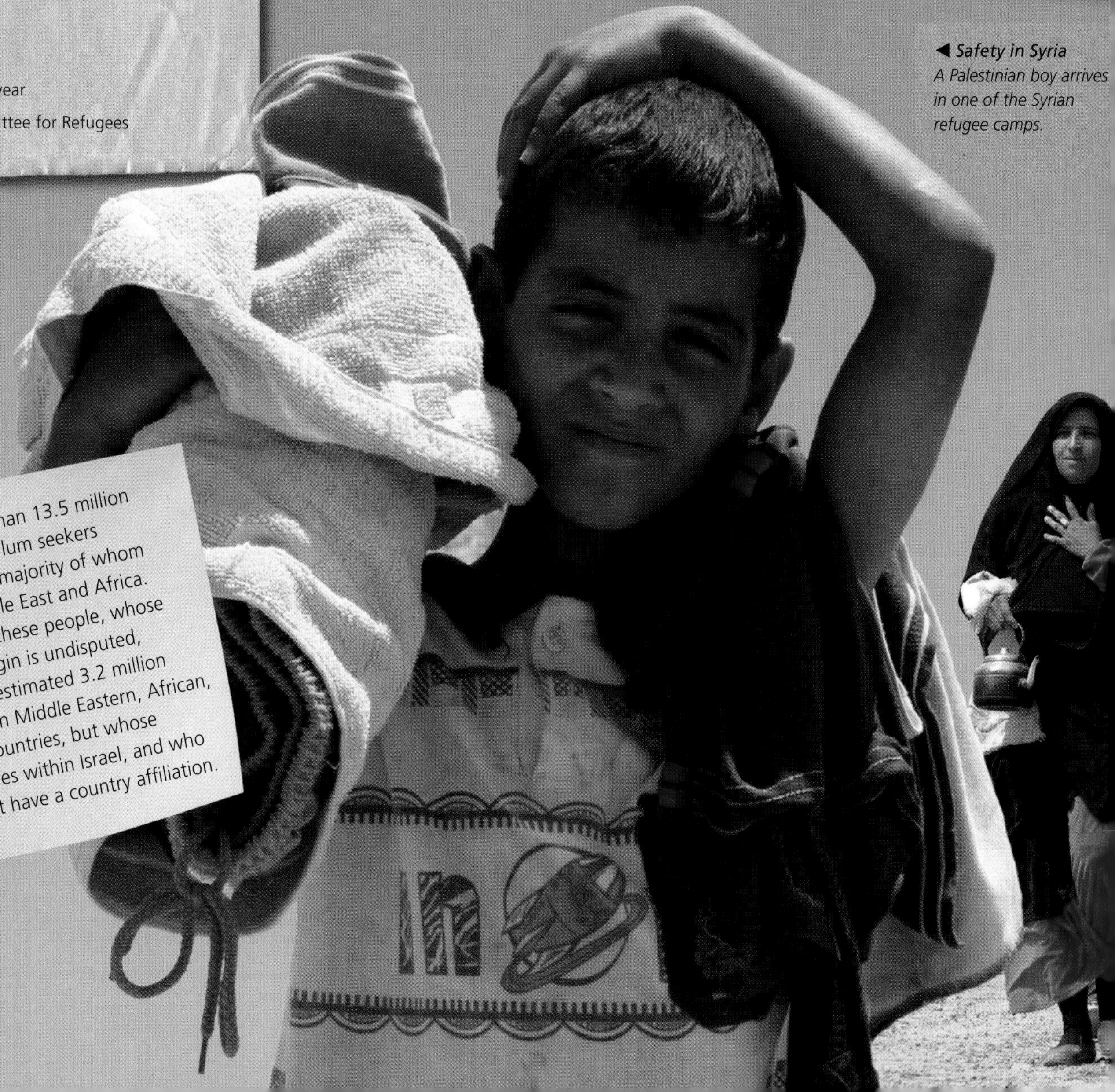

◀ *Safety in Syria*
A Palestinian boy arrives in one of the Syrian refugee camps.

There are more than 13.5 million refugees and asylum seekers worldwide, the majority of whom are in the Middle East and Africa. In addition to these people, whose country of origin is undisputed, there are an estimated 3.2 million Palestinians in Middle Eastern, African, and other countries, but whose homeland lies within Israel, and who thus do not have a country affiliation.

TOP 10 COUNTRIES/TERRITORIES RECEIVING THE MOST REFUGEES AND ASYLUM SEEKERS

COUNTRY/TERRITORY / REFUGEE/ASYLUM SEEKER POPULATION*

#	Country/Territory	Population
1	Pakistan	1,776,000
2	Syria	1,764,000
3	Gaza Strip	1,066,000
4	Iran	994,000
5	West Bank	762,000
6	Jordan	622,000
7	India	411,000
8	Kenya	377,000
9	Thailand	369,000
10	Lebanon	334,000

* Latest available year

Source: US Committee for Refugees

TOP 10 COUNTRIES RECEIVING REMITTANCES FROM MIGRANTS*

COUNTRY / RECEIPTS 2008 ($)

#	Country	Receipts 2008 ($)
1	India	52,000,000,000
2	China	40,600,000,000
3	Mexico	26,300,000,000
4	Philippines	18,600,000,000
5	Poland	10,700,000,000
6	Nigeria	10,000,000,000
7	Egypt	9,500,000,000
8	Romania	9,400,000,000
9	Bangladesh	9,000,000,000
10	Vietnam	7,200,000,000

* Nationals working overseas

Source: World Bank

▼ *Iraq's dispossesed*
At least 15% of the Iraqi population have become long-term refugees since 2003.

CITIES

TOP 10 **MOST POPULOUS CITIES**

CITY / COUNTRY	POPULATION
1 Tokyo, Japan	34,000,000
2 =Guangzhou, China	24,200,000
=Seoul, South Korea	24,200,000
4 Mexico City, Mexico	23,400,000
5 Delhi, India	23,200,000
6 Mumbai, India	22,800,000
7 New York, USA	22,200,000
8 São Paulo, Brazil	20,900,000
9 Manila, Philippines	19,600,000
10 Shanghai, China	18,400,000
Top 10 total	232,900,000

Source: Th. Brinkhoff: The Principal Agglomerations of the World, www.citypopulation.de © Thomas Brinkhoff 2010-01-23

◄ *Tokyo*
27% of the total population of Japan live in this enormous conurbation.

TOP 10 **COUNTRIES WITH THE MOST MILLION-PLUS CITIES**

COUNTRY	CITIES WITH POPULATIONS OF OVER 1 MILLION*
1 China	76#
2 USA	53
3 India	48
4 Brazil	21
5 Russia	15
6 =Japan	13
=Mexico	13
8 Germany	10
9 =Pakistan	8
=UK	8

* As of January 1, 2011
# 81 including Taiwan

THE 10 **FIRST CITIES WITH POPULATIONS OF MORE THAN ONE MILLION**

CITY / COUNTRY

Rome's population was reckoned to have exceeded one million some time in the second century BC, and Alexandria soon after. Angkor and Hangchow had both reached this figure by about AD 900 and 1200 respectively, but all subsequently declined. No other city attained one million until London in the early years of the 19th century.

► *Ankor*
Prior to industrialization, Angkor was the largest city in the world, and was the center of the Khmer Empire from the 9th to the 13th centuries.

1 Rome — Italy
2 Alexandria — Egypt
3 Angkor — Cambodia
4 Hangchow (Hangzhou) — China
5 London — UK

TOP 10 **MOST URBANIZED COUNTRIES**

	COUNTRY	% OF POPULATION LIVING IN URBAN AREAS (2010)
1	= Singapore	100.0
	= Hong Kong	100.0
	= Monaco	100.0
	= Nauru	100.0
5	Kuwait	98.4
6	Belgium	97.4
7	Qatar	95.8
8	Malta	94.7
9	= Venezuela	93.4
	= Iceland	93.4
	USA	*82.3*

Source: United Nations, *Human Development Report 2010*

▲ *Singapore*
This hi-tech city-state has a population density of nearly 9,500 people per sq mile.

THE 10 **LEAST URBANIZED COUNTRIES**

	COUNTRY	% OF POPULATION LIVING IN URBAN AREAS (2010)
1	Burundi	11.0
2	Papua New Guinea	12.5
3	Uganda	13.3
4	Trinidad and Tobago	13.9
5	= Liechtenstein	14.3
	= Sri Lanka	14.3
7	Ethiopia	16.7
8	Niger	17.1
9	= Nepal	18.6
	= Solomon Islands	18.6

Source: United Nations, *Human Development Report 2010*

◄ *Burundi*
Despite having the lowest urban population, Burundi claims the highest rate of urbanzation.

6 Paris
France

7 Peking (Beijing)
China

8 Canton Guangzhou)
China

9 Berlin
Prussia

10 New York
USA

Skyscrapers

TOP 10 **TALLEST HABITABLE BUILDINGS IN 2012**

	BUILDING / LOCATION	YEAR COMPLETED	FLOORS	HEIGHT FT	HEIGHT M
1	Burj Khalifa, Dubai, UAE	2010	163	2,717	828
2	Makkah Royal Clock Tower Hotel, Makkah, Saudi Arabia	2011	95	1,972	601
3	Taipei 101, Taipei, Taiwan, China	2004	101	1,667	508
4	Shanghai World Financial Centre, Shanghai, China	2008	101	1,614	492
5	International Commerce Centre, Hong Kong, China	2010	108	1,588	484
6 =	Petronas Tower 1, Kuala Lumpur, Malaysia	1998	88	1,483	452
=	Petronas Tower 2, Kuala Lumpur, Malaysia	1998	88	1,483	452
8	Nanjing Greenland Financial Center, Nanjing, China	2010	66	1,476	450
9	Willis (formerly Sears) Tower, Chicago, USA	1974	108	1,451	442
10	Guangzhou International Finance Center, Guangzhou, China	2010	103	1,435	438

Source: Council on Tall Buildings and Urban Habitat

TOP 10 **TALLEST BUILDINGS IN 1912**

	BUILDING / LOCATION	YEAR COMPLETED	HEIGHT FT	HEIGHT M
1	Eiffel Tower, Paris, France	1889	984	300
2	Metropolitan Life Tower, New York, USA	1909	700	213
3	City Hall, Philadelphia, USA	1901	548	167
4	14 Wall Street, New York, USA	1912	540	165
5	Ulm Minster, Ulm, Germany	1890	530	162
6	Cologne Cathedral, Cologne, Germany	1880	516	157
7	Park Row Building, New York, USA	1898	391	119
8	Domtoren, Utrech, Netherlands	1382	369	112
9	Nieuwe Kerk, Delft, Netherlands	1496	358	109
10	Our Lady Tower, Amersfoort, Netherlands	1444	323	98

Source: Council on Tall Buildings and Urban Habitat

▼ *Onwards and upwards*
For the past 100 years the height of the world's tallest building has grown, on average, by over 20 ft per year. In the last decade this figure has risen to nearly 130 ft per year.

The Top 10 tallest buildings in the world has undergone drastic change in the last few years. Half of the buildings in the Top 10 have been completed since 2009. Such is the pace of construction that Taipei 101, previously the world's highest, only held the title for six years, whereas previous record-holders, such as the Empire State Building, enjoyed the top spot for over 40 years.

▼ On top of the world
Over 3,000 workers spent seven million man-hours constructing the Empire State Building.

STANDING UP TO THE STORMS

The taller a building is, the more prone it is to lightning strikes. The 22-story television antenna at the top of the Empire State Building acts as a lightning rod, absorbing about 100 lightning strikes a year. Many tall buildings contain tuned mass dampers, which are huge weights near the top of the building that act like pendulums to exert an equal and opposite push to high winds, typhoons and earthquakes.

EMPIRE STATE BUILDING

Containing 10 million bricks, the Empire State Building is one of the American Society of Civil Engineers' Seven Wonders of the Modern World. It held the title of "World's Tallest Building" from 1931 to 1972, overtaking the Chrysler Building (seen in the background on the right), and was the first structure ever built that was more than 1,000 ft (305 m) high.

SKYSCRAPER FACTS AND FIGURES

Speedy ascent Taipei 101's elevators ascend at 56 ft (17 m) per second, or 0.62 mile (1 km) per minute—faster than a jumbo jet's climb during takeoff.

Great weight The concrete, reinforced steel, and aluminum alone in the Burj Khalifa weigh over 800,000 tons. Yet this is only one-eighth of the weight of the Great Pyramid of Giza.

High climb The Burj Khalifa has 2,909 stairs from the ground floor to the 160th floor, and is expected to hold 35,000 people at any one time.

Windows on the world The Petronas Towers (below) have so many windows that window cleaners take a month to clean each tower.

▲ Record heights
The Shanghai World Financial Centre has the world's highest restaurant and observation deck, on the 94th and 100th floors respectively.

SUPERSTRUCTURES

TOP 10 **TALLEST FERRIS WHEELS**

FERRIS WHEEL / LOCATION / YEAR / HEIGHT (FT / M)

1 **Singapore Flyer**
Singapore, 2008
541 / 165

▶ *View from the top*
The 28-mile view radius of the Singapore Flyer enables visitors to see as far as Malaysia.

2 **Star of Nanchang**
China, 2006
525 / 160

3 **Jeddah Eye**
Saudi Arabia,
2012*
492 / 150

* Under construction—
scheduled completion

4 **London Eye**
UK, 2000
443 / 135

▼ *Gateway to the globe*
56 miles (90 km) of conveyor belts transport baggage around the terminal at Dubai International Airport.

5 = **Suzhou Ferris Wheel**
China, 2009
394 / 120

= **Southern Star**
Australia, 2008
394 / 120

= **Tianjin Eye**
China, 2008
394 / 120

= **Changsha Ferris Wheel**
China, 2004
394 / 120

= **Zhengzhou Ferris Wheel**
China, 2003
394 / 120

= **Sky Dream**
Fukuoka, Japan, 2002
394 / 120

TOP 10 **LARGEST BUILDINGS**

BUILDING / LOCATION	FLOOR SPACE	
	SQ FT	SQ M
1 Dubai International Airport Terminal 3, Dubai, UAE	12,755,000	1,185,000
2 CentralWorld, Bangkok, Thailand	11,022,000	1,024,000
3 Aalsmeer Flower Auction, Aalsmeer, Netherlands	10,656,000	990,000
4 Beijing Capital International Airport Terminal 3, Beijing, China	10,613,000	986,000
5 The Venetian, Macau, China	10,549,000	980,000
6 The Palazzo, Las Vegas, USA	6,953,000	646,000
7 The Pentagon, Virginia, USA	6,566,000	610,000
8 K-25, Tennessee, USA	6,555,000	609,000
9 Air Force Plant 4, Texas, USA	6,501,000	604,000
10 Marina Bay Sands, Singapore	6,254,000	581,000

TOP 10 **TALLEST CHIMNEYS**

CHIMNEY / LOCATION / YEAR / HEIGHT (FT / M)

1 GRES-2 power station
Ekibastuz, Kazakhstan, 1987
1,378 / 420

2 Inco Superstack
International Nickel Company,
Copper Hill, Sudbury,
Ontario, Canada, 1971
1,250 / 381

3 Homer City Generating
Station Unit 3,
Minersville, Pennsylvania,
USA, 1977
1,217 / 371

4 = Kennecott Copper
Corporation, Magna,
Utah, USA, 1974
1,214 / 370

= Beryozovskaya GRES
Shaypovo, Russia, 1985
1,214 / 370

6 Mitchell Power Plant
Moundsville, West Virginia,
USA, 1971
1,207 / 368

7 Zasavje power station
Trbovlje, Slovenia, 1976
1,181 / 360

8 Endesa Termic
La Coruña, Spain, 1974
1,168 / 356

9 Phoenix Copper Smelter
Baia Mare, Romania, 1995
1,155 / 352

10 Syrdarya Power Plant
Units 5–10, Syrdarya,
Uzbekistan, 1975
1,148 / 350

TOP 10 **LARGEST STADIUMS**

STADIUM / LOCATION / YEAR BUILT / CAPACITY

1. Indianapolis Motor Speedway,
USA, 1909
250,000

2 Tokyo Racecourse*, Japan, 1933
223,000

3 Shanghai International Circuit,
China, 2004
200,000

4 Daytona International
Speedway,
USA, 1959
168,000

5 Lowe's Motor Speedway,
USA, 1959
167,000

6 Nakayama Racecourse*
Japan, 1990
165,000

7 Bristol Motor Speedway
USA, 1961
160,000

8 = Suzuka Circuit, Japan, 1962
155,000

= Istanbul Park, Turkey, 2005
155,000

10 Texas Motor Speedway
USA, 1997
154,000

* Horse racing; all others motor racing

TOP 10 **TALLEST STATUES**

STATUE / LOCATION	YEAR	HEIGHT FT	M
1 Spring Temple Buddha, Henan, China	2002	420	128
2 Laykyun Setkyar, Sagaing, Myanmar	2008	381	116
3 Ushiku Daibutsu, Ibaraki, Japan	1995	361	110
4 Nanshan Haishang Guanyin, Hainan, China	2005	354	108
5 Emperors Yan and Huang, Henan, China	2007	348	106
6 Sendai Daikannon, Miyagi, Japan	1985	328	100
7 Qianshou Qianyan Guanyin of Weishan, Hunan, China	2009	326	99
8 Peter the Great, Moscow, Russia	1997	315	96
9 Great Buddha, Ang Thong, Thailand	2008	300	92
10 Grand Buddha, Jiangsu, China	1996	289	88

▲ **Ushiku Daibutsu**
The 4,000-ton depiction of Amitabha Buddha features an 279-ft (85-m) elevator.

BRIDGES

TOP 10 LONGEST CABLE-STAYED BRIDGES

BRIDGE / LOCATION	YEAR COMPLETED	LENGTH OF MAIN SPAN FT	M
1 Russky Island Bridge, Primorsky Russia	2012*	3,622	1,104
2 Sutong Bridge, Changshu-Nantong, China	2008	3,570	1,088
3 Stonecutters Bridge, Hong Kong	2008	3,339	1,018
4 Edong Bridge, Hubei, China	2009	3,038	926
5 Tatara Bridge, Onomichi-Imabari, Japan	1999	2,920	890
6 Pont de Normandie, Le Havre, France	1994	2,808	856
7 Jingsha Bridge, Hubei, China	2009	2,677	816
8 Incheon-Yeongjong Bridge, South Korea	2009	2,625	800
9 Zolotoy Roy Bridge, Primorsky, Russia	2011*	2,418	737
10 Chongming North Bridge, Shanghai, China	2010	2,395	730

* Under construction—scheduled completion
Source: Swedish Institute of Steel Construction

▲ *Incheon-Yeongjong*
The 11-mile (18-km) bridge is designed to survive earthquakes and the impact of being hit by a ship.

▼ *Royal Gorge*
For 72 years this was the highest bridge in the world.

THE 10 LONGEST BRIDGES IN THE USA

BRIDGE	YEAR COMPLETED
1 Verrazano Narrows, NY	1964
2 Golden Gate, CA	1937
3 Mackinac Straits, MI	1957
4 George Washington, NY	1931/62*
5 Tacoma Narrows II, WA	1950
6 Al Zampa Memorial, CA	2003
7 Transbay, CA#	1936
8 Bronx-Whitestone, NY	1939
9 Delaware Memorial, DE#	1951/68
10 Walt Whitman, PA	1957

* Lower deck added   # Twin spans

TOP 10 HIGHEST BRIDGES

BRIDGE	LOCATION	YEAR COMPLETED	HEIGHT* FT	M
1 Siduhe River	Hubei, China	2009	1,550	472
2 Baluarte	Sinaloa, Mexico	2012	1,280	390
3 Balinghe River	Guizhou, China	2009	1,214	370
4 Beipanjiang 2003	Guizhou, China	2003	1,200	366
5 = Aizhai	Guizhau, China	2012	1,083	330
= Beipanjiang 2009	Guizhou, China	2009	1,083	330
7 Liuguanghe	Guizhou, China	2001	975	297
8 Zhijinghe River	Hubei, China	2009	965	294
9 Royal Gorge	Colorado, USA	1929	955	291
10 Millau Viaduct	Millau, France	2004	909	277

* Clearance above water

▼ *Sydney Harbour Bridge*
The Harbour Bridge is the world's widest long-span bridge.

TOP 10 **LONGEST ARCH BRIDGES**

BRIDGE / LOCATION	YEAR COMPLETED	LENGTH OF MAIN SPAN FT	M
1 Sheikh Rashid bin Saeed Crossing, Dubai, UAE	2012*	1,600	667
2 Chaotianmen, Chongqing, China	2008	1,811	552
3 Lupu, Shanghai, China	2003	1,804	550
4 New River Gorge, Fayetteville, West Virginia, USA	1977	1,699	518
5 Bayonne, Kill Van Kull, New Jersey/New York, USA	1931	1,654	504
6 Sydney Harbour, Sydney, Australia	1932	1,650	503
7 Chenab, Bakkal, India	2009	1,575	480
8 Wushan, Chongqing, China	2005	1,509	460
9 Xinguang, Guangzhou, China	2008	1,405	428
10 = Wanxian, Wanxian, China	1997	1,378	420
= Caiyuanba, Chongqing, China	2007	1,378	420

* Under construction—scheduled completion

Source: Swedish Institute of Steel Construction

▶ *Lake Pontchartrain*
The two parallel bridges connect New Orleans to Mandeville.

TOP 10 **LONGEST BRIDGES**

BRIDGE / LOCATION	YEAR COMPLETED	LENGTH FT	M
1 Danyang-Kunshan Grand Bridge, China	2010	540,700	164,800
2 Tianjin Grand Bridge, China	2010	373,000	113,700
3 Weinan Weihe Grand Bridge, China	2008	261,588	79,723
4 Bang Na Expressway, Thailand	2008	177,000	54,000
5 Beijing Grand Bridge, China	2010	157,982	48,153
6 Lake Pontchartrain Causeway, USA	1956	126,122	38,442
7 Manchac Swamp Bridge, USA	1970	120,440	36,710
8 Yangcun Bridge, China	2007	117,037	35,812
9 Hangzhou Bay Bridge, China	2007	117,037	35,673
10 Runyang Bridge, China	2005	116,990	35,660

TUNNELS

TOP 10 **LONGEST SUBSEA TUNNELS**

TUNNEL / LOCATION / YEAR COMPLETED / LENGTH (FT / M)

* Road; all others rail

1 Seikan
Japan
1988
176,673 /
53,850

2 Channel Tunnel
France/England
1994
165,518 /
50,450

3 Shin-Kanmon
Japan
1975
61,404 /
18,716

4 Tokyo Bay
Aqualine
Expressway*
Japan
1997
31,440 / 9,583

5 Xiang-an
China*
2011
28,526 /
8,695

6 Great Belt
Fixed Link
(Eastern Tunnel)
Denmark
1997
26,325 / 8,024

7 Bømlafjord*
Norway
2000
26,020 /
7,931

8 Eiksund*
Norway
2008
25,581 /
7,797

9 Karmöy
Norway
2012
25,328 /
7,720

10 Oslofjord*
Norway
2000
24,245 /
7,390

Collision Path

The Large Hadron Collider, operated by CERN near Geneva, Switzerland, is housed in a tunnel with a 17-mile (27-km) circumference. It is roughly the length of the London Underground Circle Line, and required 50 million cubic feet of material to be excavated—over half the volume of the Pentagon. By accelerating and colliding particles along its path, scientists are able to study the deepest laws of nature.

TOP 10 **LONGEST TUNNELS IN THE USA***

	TUNNEL / LOCATION	TYPE	YEAR COMPLETED	FT	M
1	New Cascade, WA	Rail	1929	41,154	12,544
2	Flathead, MT	Rail	1970	37,073	11,300
3	Moffat, CO	Rail	1928	32,795	9,996
4	Hoosac, MA	Rail	1875	25,082	7,645
5	BART Transbay Tubes, CA	Rail	1974	18,996	5,790
6	Ted Williams, MA	Road	2003	13,779	4,200
7	Anton Anderson Memorial, AK	Road/rail	2000	13,727	4,184
8	Brooklyn-Battery, NY	Road	1950	9,117	2,779
9	Eisenhower-Johnson Memorial, CO	Road	1979	8,959	2,731
10	Holland Tunnel, NY	Road	1927	8,556	2,608

* In use for road or rail transportation; excluding subways

TOP 10 **LONGEST ROAD TUNNELS**

	TUNNEL / LOCATION	YEAR COMPLETED	FT	M
1	Lærdal, Norway	2000	80,413	24,510
2	Zhongnanshan, China	2007	59,186	18,040
3	St. Gotthard, Switzerland	1980	55,505	16,918
4	Arlberg, Austria	1978	45,850	13,972
5	Hsuehshan, Taiwan	2006	42,323	12,900
6	Fréjus, France/Italy	1980	42,306	12,895
7	Mont-Blanc, France/Italy	1965	38,094	11,611
8	Gudvangen, Norway	1991	37,493	11,428
9	Baojiashan, China	2009	36,745	11,200
10	Folgefonn, Norway	2001	36,417	11,100

TOP 10 **LONGEST CANAL TUNNELS**

	TUNNEL / CANAL / LOCATION	YEAR COMPLETED	FT	M
1	Le Rôve, Canal de Marseille au Rhône, France	1927	23,359	7,120
2	Bony ("Le Grand Souterrain"), Canal de St Quentin, France	1810	18,625	5,677
3	Standedge, Huddersfield Narrow, UK	1811	17,093	5,210
4	Mauvages, Canal de la Marne et Rhin, France	1853	16,305	4,970
5	Balesmes, Canal Marne à la Saône, France	1883	15,813	4,820
6	Ruyaulcourt, Canal du Nord, France	1923	14,763	4,500
7	Strood*, Thames and Medway, UK	1924	11,837	3,608
8	Lapal, Birmingham, UK	1798	11,712	3,570
9	Sapperton, Thames and Severn, UK	1789	11,443	3,488
10	Pouilly-en-Auxois, Canal de Bourgogne, France	1832	3,333	10,935

* Later converted to a rail tunnel

◄ *Underground waterway*
The UK is home to some of oldest canal tunnels in the world.

5
CULTURE & LEARNING

SISTINE CHAPEL ANNIVERSARY

2012 marks the 500th anniversary of Michelangelo completing the painting of his famous frescoes on the ceiling of the Sistine Chapel—a commission he received from Pope Julius II. Work began in 1508, finishing four years later in October 1512. The ceiling is 131 ft (40 m) long by 43 ft (13 m) wide, which means that Michelangelo painted over 5,633 sq ft (523 sq m) of frescoes in total. They are among the most famous in the world, and include nine scenes from the Book of Genesis, of which the Creation of Adam is the best known.

LANGUAGES

TOP 10 MOST COMMON WORDS IN ENGLISH

	NOUNS	VERBS	ADJECTIVES	ALL
1	time	be*	good	the
2	person	have	new	be
3	year	do	first	to
4	way	say	last	of
5	day	get	long	and
6	thing	make	great	a
7	man	go	little	in
8	world	know	own	that
9	life	take	other	have
10	hand	see	old	I

* "be" incorporates "is," "was," and "are," etc.

Source: Oxford English Corpus

◀ **Teaching English**
English is widely spoken in more than 58 countries throughout the world.

The Oxford English Corpus is a tool used by the Oxford Dictionaries to follow the development of the English language. It is a collection of texts presented in electronic format, which provides details of written or spoken language. It represents all different sources, including newspapers, magazines, novels, professional journals, chat rooms, blogs, and emails.

TOP 10 LANGUAGES MOST SPOKEN IN THE USA

	LANGUAGE / SPEAKERS
1	English 225,505,953
2	Spanish 34,547,077
3	Chinese 2,464,572
4	French 1,984,824
5	Tagalog 1,480,429
6	Vietnamese 1,207,004
7	German 1,104,354
8	Korean 1,062,337
9	Russian 851,174
10	Italian 798,801

Source: US Census Bureau

TOP 10 LANGUAGES FROM WHICH MOST BOOKS ARE TRANSLATED

	LANGUAGE	TRANSLATIONS 1979–2009
1	English	1,032,456
2	French	189,064
3	German	172,940
4	Russian	94,714
5	Italian	56,368
6	Spanish	43,883
7	Swedish	31,358
8	Latin	16,831
9	Danish	16,694
10	Dutch	16,350

Source: UNESCO, *Index Translationum* (1979–2009)

TOP 10 LANGUAGES INTO WHICH MOST BOOKS ARE TRANSLATED

	LANGUAGE	TRANSLATIONS 1979–2009
1	German	271,085
2	Spanish	207,825
3	French	203,633
4	Japanese	124,542
5	English	116,646
6	Dutch	113,964
7	Portuguese	71,287
8	Polish	64,138
9	Russian	63,009
10	Danish	59,008

▶ **Chinese voices**
Standard Mandarin is based on the Beijing dialect, and is understood throughout mainland China.

TOP 10 **MOST-SPOKEN LANGUAGES**

LANGUAGE*	SPEAKERS
1 Chinese (Mandarin)	845,456,760
2 Spanish	328,518,810
3 English	328,008,138
4 Arabic	221,002,544
5 Hindi	181,676,620
6 Bengali	181,272,900
7 Portuguese	177,981,570
8 Russian	143,553,950
9 Japanese	122,080,100
10 German	90,294,110

* Primary speakers only

Source: Ethnologue

TOP 10 **ONLINE LANGUAGES**

LANGUAGE	% OF ALL INTERNET USERS	INTERNET USERS*
1 English	27.3	536,564,837
2 Chinese (Mandarin)	22.6	444,948,013
3 Spanish	7.8	153,309,074
4 Japanese	5.0	99,143,700
5 Portuguese	4.2	82,548,200
6 German	3.8	75,158,584
7 Arabic	3.5	65,356,400
8 French	3.0	59,779,525
9 Russian	3.0	59,700,000
10 Korean	2.0	39,440,800
Top 10 languages	*82.2*	*1,615,957,333*
Rest of world languages	*17.8*	*350,557,483*
World total	*100.0*	*1,996,514,816*

* As of June 30, 2010

SCHOOLS & UNIVERSITIES

THE 10 **COUNTRIES WITH THE MOST PRIMARY SCHOOL TEACHERS**

COUNTRY* / PUPILS PER TEACHER / TEACHERS

1 USA 14
1,775,000

2 Brazil 24
754,000

3 Nigeria 40
566,000

4 Mexico 28
523,000

5 Pakistan 40
450,000

6 Iran 19
373,000

7 Bangladesh 45
364,000

8 Italy 10
273,000

9 UK 18
250,000

10 Germany 14
243,000

World 25 27,871,000

* No data available for China, India, Indonesia, or Japan

Source: UNESCO

THE 10 **COUNTRIES WITH THE MOST SECONDARY SCHOOL TEACHERS**

COUNTRY* / PUPILS PER TEACHER / TEACHERS

1 China 16
6,221,000

2 USA 15
1,698,000

3 Indonesia 13
1,435,000

4 Russia 9
1,284,000

5 Brazil 19
1,263,000

6 Mexico 18
621,000

7 Japan 12
608,000

8 Germany 13
593,000

9 Iran 19
530,000

10 = Egypt –
491,000

= France 12
491,000

* No data for India

Source: UNESCO

▲ *Indonesia*
Despite high primary enrolment, only 75% of Indonesian children go on to senior school.

THE 10 **COUNTRIES WITH THE MOST PRIMARY SCHOOLS**

COUNTRY / PRIMARY SCHOOLS

1 China 628,840

2 India 598,354

3 Brazil 196,479

4 Indonesia 173,893

5 Mexico 95,855

6 Pakistan 77,207

7 USA 72,000

8 Russia 66,235

9 Iran 63,101

10 Colombia 48,933

Source: UNESCO

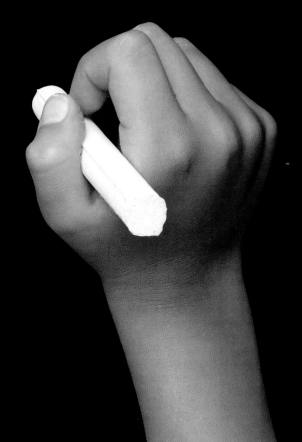

TOP 10 **COUNTRIES FOR EDUCATION**

	COUNTRY	EDUCATION INDEX*
1	= Australia	0.993
	= Finland	0.993
	= Denmark	0.993
	= New Zealand	0.993
	= Cuba	0.993
6	Canada	0.991
7	Norway	0.989
8	Republic of Korea	0.988
9	= Ireland	0.985
	= Netherlands	0.985
	USA	*0.968*

* The education index takes into account adult literacy and school enrolment rates

Source: United Nations, *Human Development Report*

▶ *Stanford celebrates*
Stanford is the world's third richest university and teaches 6,800 undergraduates and 3,800 graduate students.

TOP 10 **UNIVERSITIES**

	UNIVERSITY* / COUNTRY	SCORE
1	Harvard University, USA	96.1
2	California Institute of Technology, USA	96.0
3	Massachusetts Institute of Technology, USA	95.6
4	Stanford University, USA	94.3
5	Princeton University, USA	94.2
6	= University of Cambridge, UK	91.2
	= University of Oxford, UK	91.2
8	University of California Berkeley, USA	91.1
9	Imperial College London, UK	90.6
10	Yale University, USA	89.5

* Includes only universities that provided profiling data

Source: *Times Higher Education World University Rankings 2010–11*

The Times Higher Education World University Rankings is compiled with the help of 13,000 academics from all around the world. It gathers opinion on research and teaching, and factual data from the universities themselves.

TOP 10 **LARGEST UNIVERSITIES* IN THE USA**

	UNIVERSITY	ENROLMENT (2010)
1	Arizona State University	58,374
2	University of Central Florida	56,235
3	Ohio State University	56,064
4	University of Minnesota Twin Cities	51,721
5	University of Texas at Austin	51,195
6	University of Florida	49,827
7	Texas A&M University– College Station	49,129
8	University of South Florida	47,576
9	Michigan State University	47,131
10	Pennsylvania State University	44,832

* Public universities with individual campuses that have one physical location for four-year courses

LIBRARIES & LOANS

TOP 10 **MOST-BORROWED FICTION TITLES IN THE USA**

Source: *Library Journal 2010*

AUTHOR / TITLE

Jonathan Franzen
Freedom

Stieg Larsson
The Girl Who Kicked the
Hornets' Nest

Kathryn Stockett
The Help

Suzanne Collins
Catching Fire

**James Patterson and
Liza Marklund**
The Postcard Killers

Stieg Larsson
The Girl with the
Dragon Tattoo

Suzanne Collins
The Hunger Games

Janet Evanovich
Sizzling Sixteen

Janet Evanovich
Wicked Appetite

**James Patterson and
Maxine Paetro**
Private

TOP 10 **MOST-BORROWED NONFICTION TITLES IN THE USA**

AUTHOR / TITLE

1 **Elizabeth Gilbert**, Eat, Pray, Love
2 **Geneen Roth**, Women Food and God: An Unexpected Path to Almost Everything
3 **Michael Lewis,** The Big Short: Inside the Doomsday Machine
4 **Justin Halpern**, Sh*t My Dad Says
5 **Malcolm Gladwell**, Outliers: The Story of Success
6 **Chelsea Handler**, Chelsea Chelsea Bang Bang
7 **Stephen Hawking and Leonard Mlodinow**, The Grand Design
8 **Rebecca Skloot**, The Immortal Life of Henrietta Lacks
9 **Elizabeth Gilbert**, Committed: A Skeptic Makes Peace with Marriage
10 **Bob Woodward,** Obama's Wars

Source: *Library Journal 2010*

THE 10 **FIRST PUBLIC LIBRARIES IN THE USA**

LIBRARY / FOUNDED

1 **Peterborough Public Library,** NH 1833
2 **Buffalo and Erie County Public Library,** NY 1836
3 **New Orleans Public Library,** LA 1843
4 **Boston Public Library,** MA 1848
5 **Public Library of Cincinnati and Hamilton County,** OH 1853
6 **Springfield City Library,** MA 1857
7 **Worcester Public Library,** MA 1859
8 **Multnomah County Library,** OR 1864
9 **Detroit Public Library,** MI 1865
10 **Atlanta-Fulton Public Library,** GA 1867

Although Medford Public Library in Massachusetts, claims to have been founded as early as 1825, evidence exists that Peterborough Public Library, founded on April 9, 1833, was the first public library (the first supported by local taxes) in the USA.

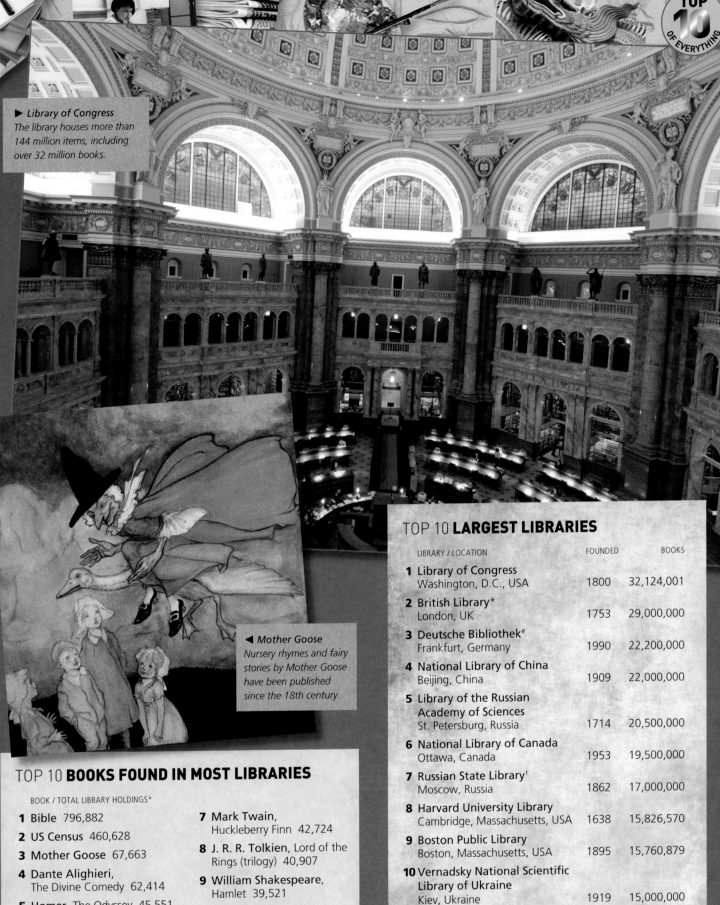

▶ **Library of Congress**
The library houses more than 144 million items, including over 32 million books.

◀ **Mother Goose**
Nursery rhymes and fairy stories by Mother Goose have been published since the 18th century.

TOP 10 **LARGEST LIBRARIES**

LIBRARY / LOCATION	FOUNDED	BOOKS
1 Library of Congress Washington, D.C., USA	1800	32,124,001
2 British Library* London, UK	1753	29,000,000
3 Deutsche Bibliothek# Frankfurt, Germany	1990	22,200,000
4 National Library of China Beijing, China	1909	22,000,000
5 Library of the Russian Academy of Sciences St. Petersburg, Russia	1714	20,500,000
6 National Library of Canada Ottawa, Canada	1953	19,500,000
7 Russian State Library† Moscow, Russia	1862	17,000,000
8 Harvard University Library Cambridge, Massachusetts, USA	1638	15,826,570
9 Boston Public Library Boston, Massachusetts, USA	1895	15,760,879
10 Vernadsky National Scientific Library of Ukraine Kiev, Ukraine	1919	15,000,000

* Founded as part of the British Museum, 1753; became an independent body in 1973
\# Formed in 1990 through the unification of the Deutsche Bibliothek, Frankfurt (founded 1947) and the Deutsche Bucherei, Leipzig
† Founded 1862 as Rumyantsev Library, formerly State V. I. Lenin Library

TOP 10 **BOOKS FOUND IN MOST LIBRARIES**

BOOK / TOTAL LIBRARY HOLDINGS*

1 Bible 796,882

2 US Census 460,628

3 Mother Goose 67,663

4 Dante Alighieri, The Divine Comedy 62,414

5 Homer, The Odyssey 45,551

6 Homer, The Iliad 44,093

7 Mark Twain, Huckleberry Finn 42,724

8 J. R. R. Tolkien, Lord of the Rings (trilogy) 40,907

9 William Shakespeare, Hamlet 39,521

10 Lewis Carroll, Alice's Adventures in Wonderland 39,277

* Based on WorldCat listings of all editions of books held in 53,000 libraries in 96 countries

Source: Online Computer Library Center (OCLC)

BOOK AWARDS

THE 10 **LATEST CARNEGIE MEDAL WINNERS**

YEAR*	AUTHOR / TITLE
2010	Neil Gaiman, The Graveyard Book
2009	Siobhan Dowd, Bog Child
2008	Philip Reeve, Here Lies Arthur
2007	Meg Rosoff, Just in Case
2005	Mal Peet, Tamar
2004	Frank Cottrell Boyce, Millions
2003	Jennifer Donnelly, A Gathering Light
2002	Sharon Creech, Ruby Holler
2001	Terry Pratchett, Amazing Maurice and his Educated Rodents
2000	Beverley Naidoo, The Other Side of Truth

* Prior to 2007, publication year; since 2007, award year—hence there was no 2006 award

Established in 1937, the Carnegie Medal is named in honor of Scots-born millionaire Andrew Carnegie, who was a notable library benefactor. In its early years, winners included such distinguished authors as Arthur Ransome, Noel Streatfeild, Walter de la Mare, and C. S. Lewis, while among notable post-war winners are books such as *Watership Down* by Richard Adams.

◀ *Neil Gaiman*
Gaiman won both the Hugo Award and the Carnegie Medal for the same work.

2010
Jerry Pinkney
The Lion &
the Mouse

2009
Beth Krommes
The House in the Night

2008
Brian Selznick
The Invention
of Hugo
Cabret

2007
David Wiesner
Flotsam

2006
Chris Raschka
The Hello,
Goodbye
Window

THE 10 **LATEST CALDECOTT MEDAL WINNERS**

YEAR* / AUTHOR / TITLE

The Caldecott Medal has been awarded annually since 1938 "to the artist of the most distinguished American picture book for children published in the US during the preceding year."

THE 10 **LATEST PULITZER PRIZE WINNERS**

YEAR	AUTHOR	TITLE
2010	Paul Harding	Tinkers
2009	Elizabeth Strout	Olive Kitteridge
2008	Junot Diaz	The Brief Wondrous Life of Oscar Wao
2007	Cormac McCarthy	The Road
2006	Geraldine Brooks	March
2005	Marilynne Robinson	Gilead
2004	Edward P. Jones	The Known World
2003	Jeffrey Eugenides	Middlesex
2002	Richard Russo	Empire Falls
2001	Michael Chabon	The Amazing Adventures of Kavalier & Clay

THE 10 **LATEST WINNERS OF HUGO AWARDS FOR BEST SCIENCE-FICTION NOVEL**

YEAR	AUTHOR / TITLE
2010	China Miéville, The City & The City / Paolo Bacigalupi, The Windup Girl
2009	Neil Gaiman, The Graveyard Book
2008	Michael Chabon, The Yiddish Policemen's Union
2007	Vernor Vinge, Rainbows End
2006	Robert Charles Wilson, Spin
2005	Susanna Clarke, Jonathan Strange & Mr Norrell
2004	Lois McMaster Bujold, Paladin of Souls
2003	Robert J. Sawyer, Hominids
2002	Neil Gaiman, American Gods
2001	J. K. Rowling, Harry Potter and the Goblet of Fire

THE 10 **LATEST WINNERS OF THE NOBEL PRIZE FOR LITERATURE**

YEAR / WINNER / COUNTRY

2010 Mario Vargas Llosa, Peru **2009** Herta Müller, Romania **2008** J. M. G. Le Clézio, France

2007 Doris Lessing, UK **2006** Orhan Pamuk, Turkey **2005** Harold Pinter, UK **2004** Elfriede Jelinek, Austria

2003 J. M. Coetzee, South Africa **2002** Imre Kertész, Hungary **2001** Sir V. S. Naipaul, UK

2005 Kevin Henkes
Kitten's First Full Moon

2004 Mordicai Gerstein
The Man Who Walked Between the Towers

2003 Eric Rohmann
My Friend Rabbit

2002 David Wiesner
The Three Pigs

2001 Judith St. George (illustrator David Small)
So You Want to be President?

2000

Bestselling Books

TOP 10 BESTSELLING NOVELS*

	AUTHOR / TITLE / FIRST PUBLISHED	ESTIMATED SALES#
1	**Charles Dickens** A Tale of Two Cities, 1859	>200,000,000
2	**J. R. R. Tolkien** The Lord of the Rings†, 1954–55	150,000,000
3	= **J. R. R. Tolkien** The Hobbit, 1937	>100,000,000
	= **Cao Xueqin** Dream of the Red Chamber, 18th century	>100,000,000
5	**Agatha Christie** And Then There Were None, 1939	100,000,000
6	**C. S. Lewis** The Lion, the Witch and the Wardrobe, 1950	85,000,000
7	**H. Rider Haggard** She, 1887	83,000,000
8	= **Antoine de Saint-Exupery** Le Petit Prince, 1943	80,000,000
	= **Dan Brown** The Da Vinci Code, 2003	80,000,000
10	**J. D. Salinger** The Catcher in the Rye, 1951	65,000,000

* Single-volume novels
\# Including translations
† Written as a single book—figure is an estimate of copies of the full story sold, whether published as one volume or three

▲ **The Hobbit**
A two-part film adaptation of the classic novel is currently in production.

CHARLES DICKENS

2012 marks the 200th anniversary of Charles Dickens' birth, so it is fitting that his most famous work should top the list of bestselling novels, with well over 200 million copies sold. There have been at least five feature films based on the book, and numerous recreations in the form of television miniseries, musicals, and even a Monty Python sketch. While first published in Dickens' own weekly literary magazine, *All the Year Round*, in 32 instalments between April 30 and November 25, 1859, *A Tale of Two Cities* has become the bestselling book in the history of fictional literature.

From 1833, when his first story was published, to his death in 1870, Dickens published more than a dozen novels—including *Oliver Twist*, *David Copperfield*, *Bleak House*, *Little Dorrit*, and *Great Expectations*—many short stories, and some plays and works of nonfiction. His books and short stories are still so popular that they have never gone out of print.

FICTIONAL FIGURES

True long-term sales figures are difficult to gauge. Although modern sales monitoring has made assessing book sales figures more accurate, it is often jokingly suggested that publishers' claims should be classified as "fiction," while all-time cumulative sales and those of multiple editions of any book make such assessments round-figure estimates at best.

THE MILLENNIUM TRILOGY

A Swedish journalist and writer, Stieg Larsson became a bestselling author after his sudden death from a heart attack in 2004. Larsson left behind three completed but unpublished manuscripts—*The Girl With the Dragon Tattoo*, *The Girl Who Played with Fire*, and *The Girl Who Kicked the Hornets' Nest*—the first of which was published just months after his death. This series of crime novels, *The Millennium Trilogy*, has sold more than 20 million copies worldwide and has spawned three popular Swedish movies.

▼ Lisbeth Salander
The heroine of Larsson's books was played by Noomi Rapace in the films.

▲ The Bard of Avon
Shakespeare is attributed with writing at least 37 plays and over 150 sonnets.

TOP 10 **BESTSELLING ENGLISH-LANGUAGE AUTHORS**

AUTHOR / COUNTRY / DATES / MAX. ESTIMATED SALES

1 = Agatha Christie (UK; 1890–1976)
4,000,000,000

= William Shakespeare (UK; 1564–16)
4,000,000,000

3 Barbara Cartland (UK; 1901–2000)
1,000,000,000

4 Harold Robbins (USA; 1916–97)
750,000,000

5 = Enid Blyton (UK; 1897–1968)
600,000,000

= Sidney Sheldon (USA; 1917–2007)
600,000,000

= Danielle Steel (USA; b. 1947)
600,000,000

8 = Gilbert Patten (USA; 1866–1945)
500,000,000

= Dr. Seuss (Theodor Seuss Geisel, USA; 1904–91)
500,000,000

10 J. K. Rowling (UK; b. 1965)
450,000,000

WIZARD WOMAN

Although J. K. Rowling ranks only 10th in the list of English-language authors, her success is extraordinary when one considers the number of works produced—in a book-by-book comparison, she would easily top the list. Her massive sales figure is based on a grand total of only seven books over a relatively short expanse of time. The huge popularity of the Harry Potter series has put Rowling at the very top of the world's richest authors list, and the brand continues to expand. Several of the Harry Potter books would also appear on the Top 10 bestselling novels list if series were included.

▲ J. K. Rowling
Rowling has received seven honorary degrees from universities in the UK and US.

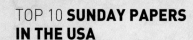

TOP 10 **DAILY NEWSPAPERS IN THE USA**

NEWSPAPER	AVERAGE CIRCULATION*
1 The Wall Street Journal	2,092,523
2 USA Today	1,862,622
3 The New York Times	951,063
4 Los Angeles Times	616,606
5 The Washington Post	578,482
6 New York Daily News	535,059
7 New York Post	525,004
8 San Jose Mercury News	516,701
9 Chicago Tribune	452,145
10 Detroit Free Press	401,889

* Average for six months to March 31, 2010

Source: Audit Bureau of Circulations Ltd

TOP 10 **SUNDAY PAPERS IN THE USA**

NEWSPAPER / AVERAGE SUNDAY CIRCULATION, 2010

1 The New York Times
1,376,230

2 Los Angeles Times
941,914

3 The Washington Post
797,679

4 Chicago Tribune
794,350

5 New York News
600,118

6 San Jose Mercury News
549,024

7 Houston Chronicle
526,440

8 Philadelphia Inquirer
517,807

9 Detroit Free Press
511,742

10 The Arizona Republic
510,500

Source: Audit Bureau of Circulations/ Newspaper Association of America

Top Newspapers

An estimated 1.7 billion people read a newspaper every day. Including non-dailies, newspapers reach a much greater audience than the Internet. The newspaper with the world's highest circulation is the Japanese *Yomiuri Shinbun*, selling 10,020,000 copies a day. Japan, China, and India each have 13, 12 and 11 newspapers respectively that have over one million readers.

TOP 10 **OLDEST NEWSPAPERS**

NEWSPAPER / COUNTRY / FOUNDED

This list includes only newspapers that have been published continuously since their founding. The former No. 1 on this list, the Swedish *Post-och Inrikes Tidningar*, founded in 1645, ceased publication on paper on January 1, 2007, and is now available only online.

Haarlems Dagblad	Gazzetta di Mantova	The London Gazette	Wiener Zeitung	Hildesheimer Allgemeine Zeitung
Netherlands	Italy	UK	Austria	Germany 1705
1656	1664	1665	1703	

TOP 10 **MAGAZINES IN THE USA**

MAGAZINE / TOTAL CIRCULATION, 2010

1 AARP The Magazine
24,371,637

2 AARP Bulletin
24,042,603

3 Better Homes and Gardens
7,621,786

4 Reader's Digest
7,114,955

5 Good Housekeeping
4,652,904

6 National Geographic
4,495,931

7 Woman's Day
3,966,414

8 Ladies' Home Journal
3,858,773

9 Family Circle
3,823,253

10 Game Informer
3,805,038

Source: Audit Bureau of Circulations/Magazine
Publishers of America

TOP 10 **COUNTRIES WHERE MOST REPORTERS HAVE DIED**

COUNTRY		DEATHS (2010)
1	Mexico	10
2	=Honduras	8
	=Pakistan	8
4	Iraq	6
5	=Nigeria	3
	=Philippines	3
7	=Angola	2
	=Indonesia	2
	=Nepal	2
	=Somalia	2
	=Thailand	2
	=Uganda	2

▲ *Mexican war zone*
In 2010, some 15,273 deaths were attributed to Mexico's drug wars. After incidents of reporters being kidnapped and murdered, many newspapers stopped coverage.

errow's Worcester
Journal
K
709

Newcastle Journal
UK
1711

Stamford Mercury
UK
1712

Northampton
Mercury
UK
1720

Hanauer Anzeiger
Germany
1725

MUSEUMS & GALLERIES

TOP 10 BEST-ATTENDED ART EXHIBITIONS, 2010

	EXHIBITION*	VENUE / CITY / DATES	ATTENDANCE# DAILY AVERAGE	TOTAL
1	Texture of Night: James McNeill Whistler	Freer and Sackler Galleries, Washington D.C., Jun 6, 2009–Jul 25, 2010	2,514	1,043,246
2	Rising Currents: Projects for NY's Waterfront	Museum of Modern Art, New York, Mar 24–Oct 11, 2010	4,358	881,520
3	Abstract America: New Painting and Sculpture	Saatchi Gallery, London, May 29–Jan 17, 2010	4,006	837,200
4	Tim Burton	Museum of Modern Art, New York, Nov 22, 2009–Apr 26, 2010	5,200	810,511
5	Post-Impressionism: from the Musée d'Orsay	National Art Center, Tokyo, May 26–Aug 16, 2010	10,757	777,551
6	The Original Copy: Photography of Sculpture	Museum of Modern Art, New York, Aug 1–Nov 1, 2010	8,073	749,638
7	Picasso in the Metropolitan Museum of Art	Metropolitan Museum of Art, New York, Apr 27–Aug 15, 2010	7,380	703,256
8	India: the Art of the Temple	Shanghai Museum, Shanghai, Aug 5–Nov 15, 2010	6,630	682,867
9	Doug & Mike Starn on the Roof: Big Bambú	Metropolitan Museum of Art, New York, Apr 27–Oct 31, 2010	3,913	631,064
10	Hans Memling	Galleria degli Uffizi, Florence, Jun 22–Oct 10, 2010	6,469	616,411

* With longest part of run in 2010
# Approximate totals provided by museums

Source: *The Art Newspaper*

▲ The Louvre
One of the largest museums in the world, the Louvre has over 35,000 exhibits.

TOP 10 MOST-VISITED GALLERIES AND MUSEUMS, 2010

	GALLERY / LOCATION	TOTAL ATTENDANCE
1	Louvre Museum, Paris, France	8,500,000
2	British Museum, London, UK	5,842,138
3	Metropolitan Museum of Art, New York, USA	5,216,988
4	Tate Modern, London, UK	5,061,172
5	National Gallery, London, UK	4,954,914
6	National Gallery of Art, Washington, DC, USA	4,775,114
7	Museum of Modern Art, New York, USA	3,131,238
8	Centre Pompidou, Paris, France	3,130,000
9	National Museum of Korea, Seoul, South Korea	3,067,909
10	Musée d'Orsay, Paris, France	2,985,510

Source: *The Art Newspaper*

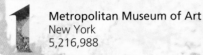

TOP 10 MOST-VISITED ART GALLERIES AND MUSEUMS IN THE USA, 2010

GALLERY / LOCATION / VISITORS

1 Metropolitan Museum of Art
New York
5,216,988

2 National Gallery of Art
Washington, D.C.
4,775,114

3 Museum of Modern Art
New York
3,131,238

4 De Young Museum
San Francisco
2,043,854

5 Art Institute of Chicago
Chicago
1,612,780

6 Getty Center (Getty Museum)
Los Angeles
1,205,685

7 National Portrait Gallery
Washington, D.C.
1,144,494

8 Museum of Fine Arts
Houston
1,125,000

9 Guggenheim
New York
1,105,352

10 Smithsonian American Art
Museum Washington, D.C.
1,100,000

TOP 10 BEST-ATTENDED EXHIBITIONS AT THE TATE MODERN, LONDON

EXHIBITION / YEAR / ATTENDANCE

1 Matisse/Picasso
2002
467,166

2 Edward Hopper
2004–05
429,909

3 Frida Kahlo
2005
369,249

4 Rothko
2008–09
327,244

5 Kandinsky: The Path to
Abstraction
2006
282,439

6 Andy Warhol
2002
218,801

7 Between Cinema and
a Hard Place
2000
200,937

8 Pop Life: Art in a Material World
2009–10
192,754

9 Henri Rousseau: Jungles in Paris
2005–06
190,795

10 Surrealism: Desire Unbound
2001–02
168,825

▶ Paul Gauguin
Beginning in 2010, the Paul Gauguin exhibition at Tate Modern proved one of the year's most popular art attractions.

TOP 10 BEST-ATTENDED EXHIBITIONS AT THE MUSEUM OF MODERN ART, NEW YORK*

EXHIBITION / YEAR / ATTENDANCE

1 Rising Currents: Projects
for NY's Waterfront
2010 / 881,520

2 Tim Burton
2010 / 810,511

3 The Original Copy:
Photography of Sculpture
2010 / 749,638

4 Richard Serra Sculpture:
40 Years
2007 / 737,074

5 Matisse: Radical Invention,
1913–17
2010 / 602,524

6 Superheroes: Fashion and
Fantasy
2008 / 576,901

7 Marina Abramovic:
The Artist is Present
2010 / 561,471

8 Home Delivery
2008 / 521,871

9 William Kentridge: Five Themes
2010 / 492,196

10 Dalí: Painting and Film
2008 / 449,483

* 20th century only

◀ The Starry Night
Since 1941, Van Gogh's best-loved work has hung in the Museum of Modern Art, New York.

ART AT AUCTION

▲ Bal au Moulin de la Galette
Renoir's 1876 masterpiece was bought at auction in May 1990 by the same Japanese businessman who bought Portrait du Dr. Gachet.

TOP 10 MOST EXPENSIVE PAINTINGS EVER SOLD AT AUCTION

PAINTING / ARTIST / SALE	PRICE ($)
1 Nude, Green Leaves, and Bust, Pablo Picasso (Spanish; 1881–1973) Christie's, New York, May 4, 2010	106,482,500
2 Garçon à la pipe, Pablo Picasso Sotheby's, New York, May 5, 2004	104,168,000
3 Dora Maar au chat, Pablo Picasso Sotheby's, New York, May 3, 2006	95,216,000
4 Portrait of Adele Bloch-Bauer II, Gustav Klimt (Austrian; 1862–1918) Christie's, New York, Nov 8, 2006	87,936,000
5 Triptych, Francis Bacon (Irish; 1909–92) Sotheby's, New York, May 14, 2008	86,281,000
6 Portrait du Dr. Gachet, Vincent van Gogh (Dutch; 1853–90) Christie's, New York, May 15, 1990	82,500,000
7 Le Bassin aux Nymphéas, Claude Monet (French; 1840–1926) Christie's, London, Jun 24, 2008	80,643,507 (£40,921,250)
8 Bal au Moulin de la Galette, Montmartre Pierre-Auguste Renoir (French; 1841–1919) Sotheby's, New York, May 17, 1990	78,100,000
9 The Massacre of the Innocents, Sir Peter Paul Rubens (Flemish; 1577-1640) Sotheby's, London, Jul 10, 2002	75,930,440 (£49,506,648)
10 White Center (Yellow, pink, and lavender on rose), Mark Rothko (American; 1903–70) Sotheby's, New York, May 15, 2007	72,840,000

Old Masters at auction

A previously unknown painting by Sir Peter Paul Rubens, "The Massacre of the Innocents," made history when it sold at Sotheby's, London, for $76,000,000. Painted between 1609 and 1611, the work had been incorrectly attributed to an assistant of Rubens, Jan van den Hoeck, and had hung unnoticed in an Austrian monastery for many years, until it was brought to the attention of Sotheby's just a few months before the sale. The record-breaking sale is still more than double the amount paid for the second most expensive Old Master painting. That title goes to Raphael's "Portrait of Lorenzo de' Medici, Duke of Urbino," which was sold by Christie's in London for $37,000,000 in 2007.

▼ *Record-breaking Rembrandt*
Portrait of a Man with Arms Akimbo *sold for $33,210,855 in 2009.*

TOP 10 **MOST EXPENSIVE WORKS OF ART BY LIVING ARTISTS**

PAINTING / ARTIST / SALE	PRICE ($)
1 Benefits Supervisor Sleeping, Lucian Freud (British; b.1922) Christie's, New York, May 13, 2008	33,641,000
2 Flag, Jasper Johns (American; b.1930) Christie's, New York, May 11, 2010	28,642,500
3 Balloon Flower—Magenta, Jeff Koons (American; b.1955) Christie's, London, Jun 30, 2008	25,765,204 (£12,921,250)
4 Hanging Heart—Magenta/Gold, Jeff Koons Sotheby's, New York, Nov 14, 2007	23,561,000
5 Naked Portrait with Reflection, Lucian Freud Christie's, London, Jun 30, 2008	23,531,904 (£11,801,250)
6 IB and Her Husband, Lucian Freud Christie's, New York, Nov 13, 2007	19,361,000
7 Lullaby Spring, Damien Hirst (British; b.1965) Sotheby's, London, Jun 21, 2007	19,230,922 (£9,652,000)
8 The Golden Calf, Damien Hirst Sotheby's, London, Sep 15, 2008	18,603,218 (£10,345,250)
9 Figure 4, Jasper Johns Christie's, New York, May 16, 2007	17,400,000
10 The Kingdom, Damien Hirst Sotheby's, London, Sep 15, 2008	17,193,400 (£9,561,250)

▶ *Jeff Koons*
Koons is especially known for his works of objects such as balloon animals in metal.

TOP 10 **MOST EXPENSIVE PHOTOGRAPHS**

PHOTOGRAPH* / PHOTOGRAPHER / SALE	PRICE ($)
1 Untitled (Cowboy)# (2001–02) Richard Prince (American; b.1949), Sotheby's, New York, Nov 14, 2007	3,401,000
2 99 Cent II# (2001), Andreas Gursky (German; b.1955), Sotheby's, London, Feb 7, 2007	3,346,456 (£1,700,000)
3 Los Angeles (1998), Andreas Gursky, Sotheby's, London, Feb 27, 2008	2,941,483 (£1,476,500)
4 The Pond—Moonlight (1904), Edward Steichen (American; 1879–1973), Sotheby's, New York, Feb 14, 2006	2,928,000
5 Untitled No. 153 (1985), Cindy Sherman (American; b. 1954), Phillips de Pury & Company, New York, Nov 8, 2010	2,770,500
6 Pyongyang IV (2007), Andreas Gursky, Sotheby's, London, Oct 15, 2010	2,125,736 (£1,329,250)
7 Untitled, No. 92 (1981), Cindy Sherman, Christie's, New York, May 16, 2007	2,112,000
8 Frankfurt (2007), Andreas Gursky, Sotheby's, New York, Nov 9, 2010	2,098,500
9 Black Sea. Ozuluce, Yellow Sea. Cheju, Red Sea (1991), Hiroshi Sugimoto (Japanese, b.1948), Christie's, New York, May 16, 2007	1,888,000
10 Madonna I (2001), Andreas Gursky, Sotheby's, London, Feb 10, 2010	1,684,280 (£1,077,250)

* Single prints only
# Other versions of same photograph also sold for lesser amounts

6
MUSIC

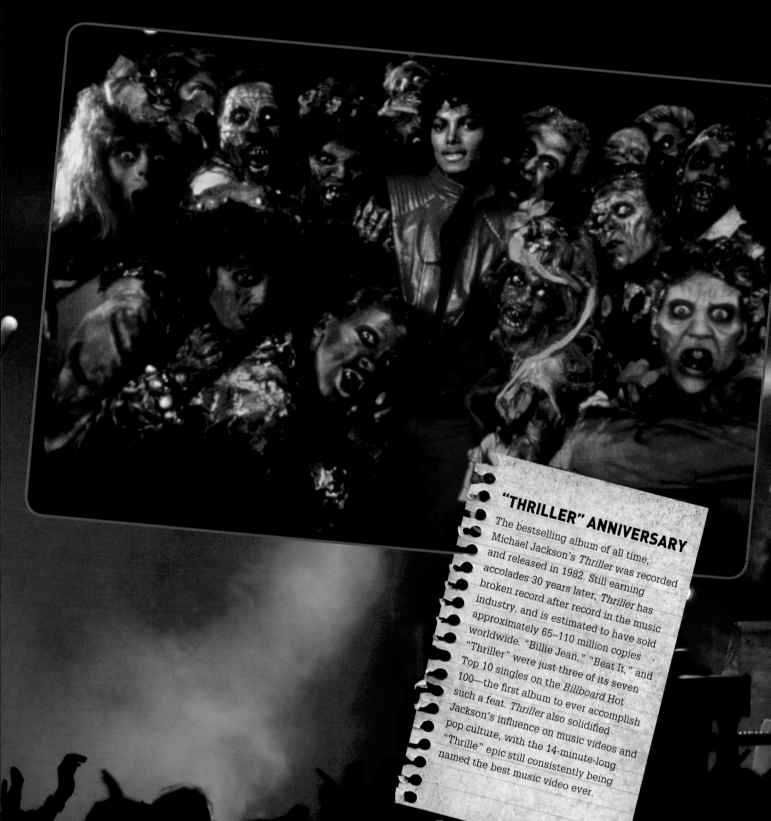

"THRILLER" ANNIVERSARY

The bestselling album of all time, Michael Jackson's *Thriller* was recorded and released in 1982. Still earning accolades 30 years later, *Thriller* has broken record after record in the music industry, and is estimated to have sold approximately 65–110 million copies worldwide. "Billie Jean," "Beat It," and "Thriller" were just three of its seven Top 10 singles on the *Billboard Hot 100*—the first album to ever accomplish such a feat. *Thriller* also solidified Jackson's influence on music videos and pop culture, with the 14-minute-long "Thrille" epic still consistently being named the best music video ever.

SINGLES

TOP 10 SINGLES OF ALL TIME

TITLE / ARTIST		YEAR OF ENTRY	SALES EXCEED
1	"White Christmas" Bing Crosby	1942	50,000,000
2	"Candle in the Wind (1997)"/ "Something About the Way You Look Tonight" Elton John	1997	33,000,000
3	"Rock Around the Clock" Bill Haley and His Comets	1954	25,000,000
=	"Little Drummer Boy" The Harry Simeone Chorale	1958	25,000,000
5	= "It's Now or Never" Elvis Presley	1960	20,000,000
=	"We Are the World" USA for Africa	1985	20,000,000
7	"Yes Sir, I Can Boogie" Baccara	1977	18,000,000
8	"Wind of Change" The Scorpions	1991	14,000,000
9	"Sukiyaki" Kyu Sakamoto	1963	13,000,000
10	= "I Want to Hold Your Hand" The Beatles	1963	12,000,000
=	"I Will Always Love You" Whitney Houston	1992	12,000,000

Source: Music Information Database

TOP 10 SINGLES THAT STAYED LONGEST IN THE US CHARTS

TITLE / ARTIST		CHART ENTRY	WEEKS IN IN CHART
1	"I'm Yours" Jason Mraz (76)	2008	76
2	"How Do I Live" LeAnn Rimes (69)	1997	69
3	"Foolish Games" Jewel (41)	1996	65
4	"Before He Cheats" Carrie Underwood (64)	2006	64
5	"You and Me" Lifehouse (62)	2005	62
6	= "Macarena" Los Del Rio (60)	1996	60
=	"Need You Know" Lady Antebellum (60)	2009	60
8	"Smooth" Santana feat. Rob Thomas (58)	1999	58
9	"Higher" Creed (57)	1999	57
10	= "I Don't Want to Wait" Paula Cole (56)	1997	56
10	= "The Way You Love Me" Faith Hill (56)	2000	56
10	= "Use Somebody" Kings Of Leon (56)	2009	56
10	= "I Got a Feeling" Black Eyed Peas (56)	2009	56

Source: Music Information Database

Numbers in parentheses denote the longest consecutive run on the charts.

TOP 10 ARTISTS WITH THE MOST NO. 1 SINGLES IN THE USA

ARTIST (TOTAL CHART HITS) / NO. 1 SINGLES	
1	Elvis Presley (131) 22
2	The Beatles (72) 20
3	Mariah Carey (35) 18
4	Michael Jackson (47) 13
5	= Madonna (52) 12
	= The Supremes (45) 12
7	Whitney Houston (38) 11
8	Janet Jackson (36) 10
9	= Stevie Wonder (61) 9
	= The Bee Gees (43) 9
	= Paul McCartney/Wings (46) 9

Source: Music Information Database

◄ King of the charts
Although Elvis died 35 years ago, he has continued to enjoy chart success in the USA.

TOP 10 SINGLES IN THE USA IN 2010

TITLE / ARTIST

1 "California Gurls"
Katy Perry feat. Snoop Dogg

2 "Hey, Soul Sister"
Train

3 "Love the Way You Lie"
Eminem feat. Rihanna

4 "Dynamite"
Taio Cruz

5 "Airplanes"
B.o.B feat. Hayley Williams

6 "OMG"
Usher feat. will.i.am

7 "Not Afraid"
Eminem

8 "Just the Way You Are"
Bruno Mars

9 "Break Your Heart"
Taio Cruz feat. Ludacris

10 "Need You Now"
Lady Antebellum

Source: Nielsen SoundScan

▲ *Black Eyed Peas*
"I Gotta Feeling" ranks No. 3 in the list of bestselling singles of all time in the USA.

▼ *Katy Perry*
Katy Perry became the ninth artist to have four No. 1 Hot 100 singles from one album.

TOP 10 SINGLES IN THE USA IN THE PAST 10 YEARS

YEAR / TITLE / ARTIST

2010 "California Gurls"
Katy Perry feat. Snoop Dogg

2009 "Boom Boom Pow"
Black Eyed Peas

2008 "Bleeding Love"
Leona Lewis

2007 "Crank That"
Soulja Boy Tell 'Em

2006 "Bad Day"
Daniel Powter

2005 "Hollaback Girl"
Gwen Stefani

2004 "I Believe"
Fantasia

2003 "Bridge Over Troubled Water"
Clay Aiken

2002 "Before Your Love"/ "A Moment Like This"
Kelly Clarkson

2001 "Loverboy"
Mariah Carey

Source: Music Information Database

ALBUMS

TOP 10 ALBUMS OF ALL TIME IN THE USA

TITLE / ARTIST	YEAR
1 = Their Greatest Hits, 1971–1975, The Eagles	1976
= Thriller, Michael Jackson	1982
3 Led Zeppelin IV, Led Zeppelin	1971
4 Back in Black, AC/DC	1980
5 Come on Over, Shania Twain	1997
6 Rumours, Fleetwood Mac	1977
7 Appetite for Destruction, Guns N' Roses	1987
8 = No Fences, Garth Brooks	1990
= The Bodyguard, Soundtrack	1992
= Boston, Boston	1976

TOP 10 ALBUMS OF ALL TIME

TITLE / ARTIST / YEAR OF ENTRY

1 Thriller
Michael Jackson 1982

2 Back in Black
AC/DC 1980

3 The Dark Side of the Moon
Pink Floyd 1973

4 The Bodyguard
Soundtrack 1992

5 Bat Out of Hell
Meat Loaf 1977

6 Their Greatest Hits 1971–1975
The Eagles 1976

7 Dirty Dancing
Soundtrack 1987

8 Millennium
The Backstreet Boys 1999

9 Saturday Night Fever
Soundtrack 1977

10 Rumours
Fleetwood Mac 1977

▲ *Rock school*
Angus Young, founding member of AC/DC, is famous for his stage antics, which include wearing a schoolboy uniform and the "duck walk."

▼ *In the pink*
Founded in 1965, Pink Floyd have sold more than 200 million albums worldwide.

TOP 10 ALBUMS THAT STAYED LONGEST IN THE US CHARTS

TITLE / ARTIST	FIRST CHART ENTRY	WEEKS IN CHART
1 The Dark Side of the Moon, Pink Floyd (593)	1973	772
2 Johnny's Greatest Hits, Johnny Mathis (208)	1958	490
3 My Fair Lady, Original Cast (192)	1956	480
4 Highlights from the Phantom of the Opera, Original Cast (331)	1990	331
5 Oklahoma!, Soundtrack (95)	1955	305
6 Tapestry, Carole King (302)	1971	302
7 Heavenly, Johnny Mathis (155)	1959	295
8 MCMXC A.D., Enigma (252)	1991	282
9 Metallica, Metallica (281)	1991	281
10 The King and I, Soundtrack (96)	1956	277

Source: Music Information Database

Numbers in parentheses denote the longest consecutive run on the charts.

Total worldwide sales of albums have traditionally been notoriously hard to gauge, but even with the huge expansion of the album market during the 1980s, and multiple million sales of many major releases, this Top 10 is still élite territory.

TOP 10 **ALBUMS IN THE USA IN 2010**

TITLE / ARTIST

1 Recovery
Eminem

2 Need You Now
Lady Antebellum

3 Speak Now
Taylor Swift

4 My World 2.0
Justin Bieber

5 The Gift
Susan Boyle

6 The Fame
Lady Gaga

7 Soldier of Love
Sade

8 Thank Me Later
Drake

9 Raymond V. Raymond
Usher

10 Animal
Ke$ha

Source: Nielsen SoundScan

TOP 10 **ALBUMS IN THE USA IN THE PAST 10 YEARS**

YEAR / TITLE / ARTIST

2010 Recovery
Eminem

2009 Fearless
Taylor Swift

2008 Tha Carter III
Lil Wayne

2007 Noel
Josh Groban

2006 High School Musical
Soundtrack

2005 The Emancipation
of Mimi
Mariah Carey

2004 Confessions
Usher

2003 Get Rich or
Die Tryin'
50 Cent

2002 The Eminem Show
Eminem

2001 Hybrid Theory
Linkin Park

Source: Nielsen SoundScan

▶ *Going Gaga*
*The Fame was the
debut studio album for
the singer/songwriter,
whose real name is
Stefani Germanotta.*

MALE SINGERS

◄ *Elton John*
Sir Elton John has had more than 50 Top 40 hits and has won 6 Grammy Awards, an Academy Award, and a Golden Globe.

TOP 10 BESTSELLING SINGLES BY MALE SOLO SINGERS IN THE USA

	TITLE / ARTIST	YEAR
1	"Candle in the Wind (1997)"/"Something About the Way You Look Tonight" Elton John	1997
2	"White Christmas" Bing Crosby	1942
3	"Low" Flo Rida (feat. T-Pain)	2007
4	"I'm Yours" Jason Mraz	2008
5	"Right Round" Flo Rida	2009
6	"Crank That" Soulja Boy Tell 'Em	2007
7	"Stronger" Kanye West	2007
8	"Hound Dog/Don't Be Cruel" Elvis Presley	1956
9	"Live Your Life" T.I. (feat. Rihanna)	2008
10	"Lollipop" Lil Wayne (feat. Static Major)	2008

TOP 10 OLDEST MALE SOLO SINGERS TO HAVE A NO. 1 SINGLE IN THE USA

	ARTIST / TITLE	YEAR	YRS	AGE MTHS	DAYS
1	Louis Armstrong, "Hello Dolly!"	1964	63	9	5
2	Lawrence Welk, "Calcutta"	1961	57	11	14
3	Morris Stoloff, "Moonglow" & "Theme from Picnic"	1956	57	10	8
4	Lorne Greene, "Ringo"	1964	50	9	23
5	Elton John, "Candle in the Wind (1997)"/"Something About the Way You Look Tonight"	1997	50	9	21
6	Frank Sinatra, "Strangers in the Night"	1967	50	6	28
7	Rod Stewart, "All for Love"	1994	49	0	12
8	Dean Martin, "Everybody Loves Somebody"	1964	47	2	8
9	Sammy Davis, Jr., "The Candy Man"	1972	46	6	16
10	Meat Loaf, "I'd Do Anything For Love (But I Won't Do That)"	1993	46	2	7

Source: Music Information Database

Carlos Santana, as leader of Santana, had two No. 1s in 2000 at the age of 53, but strictly speaking Santana is a group and not a solo artist, so is not included here.

Youngest No. 1 Male Achievers

Stevie Wonder tops the list of young achievers in the USA. He was just 13 years, 2 months, and 28 days old when he had his first No. 1 single, "Fingertips," in 1963. In second and third place are Donny Osmond (13 years, 9 months, 2 days; "Go Away Little Girl," 1971) and Michael Jackson (14 years, 1 month, 15 days; "Ben," 1972). After 33 years with no new names on the list, four new entrants were added to the Top 10 in a three-year period, 2005–07: Chris Brown, Mario, Soulja Boy, and Sean Kingston, who were all aged between 15 and 17 when they secured their first No. 1 singles.

TOP 10 BESTSELLING ALBUMS BY MALE SOLO ARTISTS IN THE USA IN THE PAST 10 YEARS

YEAR / TITLE / ARTIST

2010 Recovery
Eminem

2009 Number Ones
Michael Jackson

2008 Tha Carter III
Lil Wayne

2007 Noel
Josh Groban

2006 Futuresex/Love Sounds
Justin Timberlake

2005 The Massacre
50 Cent

2004 Confessions
Usher

2003 Get Rich Or Die Tryin'
50 Cent

2002 The Eminem Show
Eminem

2001 Hotshot
Shaggy

Source: Nielsen Soundscan

TOP 10 MALE ARTISTS WITH THE MOST PLATINUM ALBUMS IN THE USA

	ARTIST / GOLD TOTAL	PLATINUM ALBUMS
1	Garth Brooks (16)	145
2	Elvis Presley (19)	100
3	Billy Joel (18)	79
4	Elton John (38)	65
5	George Strait (38)	61
6	Bruce Springsteen (21)	52
7	Kenny Rogers (31)	45
8	Eric Clapton (25)	41
9 =	Neil Diamond (40)	40
=	Alan Jackson (17)	40

Source: RIAA

Within two years of its release, Michael Jackson's *Thriller* album had sold a record total of 20 million copies, but its success continued, being certified for sales of 29 million copies in August 2009, two months after his death.

TOP 10 BESTSELLING ALBUMS BY A MALE SOLO ARTIST IN THE USA

TITLE / ARTIST / YEAR

1 Thriller, Michael Jackson 1982
2 No Fences, Garth Brooks 1990
3 Greatest Hits, Elton John 1974
4 Born in the USA,
  Bruce Springsteen 1984
5 Bat Out of Hell, Meat Loaf 1977
6 Ropin' the Wind, Garth Brooks 1991
7 Breathless, Kenny G 1993
8 Kenny Rogers' Greatest Hits,
  Kenny Rogers 1980
9 No Jacket Required, Phil Collins 1985
10 Devil Without a Cause,
   Kid Rock 2000

Source: RIAA

◀ **Eminem**
*Eminem released his seventh studio album,
Recovery, in June 2010.*

FEMALE SINGERS

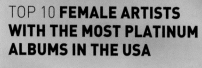

TOP 10 **FEMALE ARTISTS WITH THE MOST PLATINUM ALBUMS IN THE USA**

ARTIST / PLATINUM ALBUMS

	ARTIST	PLATINUM ALBUMS
1	Madonna (18)*	65
2	Mariah Carey (15)	61
3	Barbra Streisand (46)	59
4	Whitney Houston (9)	55
5	Celine Dion (13)	49
6	Shania Twain (4)	47
7	Reba McEntire (27)	37
8	Britney Spears (5)	31
9	Linda Ronstadt (17)	28
10	Janet Jackson (8)	26

* Gold totals listed in brackets

Source: RIAA

▶ *Queen of reinvention*
Madonna was inducted into
the Rock and Roll Hall of Fame
in 2008.

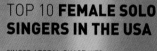

TOP 10 **BESTSELLING ALBUMS BY A FEMALE ARTIST IN THE USA**

TITLE / ARTIST / YEAR

1 **Come on Over**, Shania Twain 1997

2 **The Bodyguard**,
Whitney Houston 1992

3 **Jagged Little Pill**,
Alanis Morissette 1995

4 **... Baby One More Time**,
Britney Spears 1999

5 **Whitney Houston**,
Whitney Houston 1986

6 **Pieces of You**, Jewel 1996

7 **The Woman in Me**, Shania Twain 1995

8 **Up!**, Shania Twain 2002

9 **Falling Into You**,
Celine Dion 1996

10 **The Immaculate Collection**,
Madonna 1991

Source: RIAA

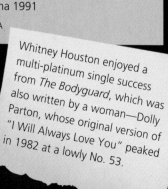

Whitney Houston enjoyed a
multi-platinum single success
from *The Bodyguard*, which was
also written by a woman—Dolly
Parton, whose original version of
"I Will Always Love You" peaked
in 1982 at a lowly No. 53.

TOP 10 **FEMALE SOLO SINGERS IN THE USA**

SINGER / TOTAL CHART HITS

	SINGER	TOTAL CHART HITS
1	Aretha Franklin	73
2	= Madonna	55
	= Dionne Warwick	55
4	Connie Francis	53
5	Brenda Lee	48
6	= Diana Ross	41
	= Barbra Streisand	41
8	Taylor Swift	40
9	Whitney Houston	39
10	Olivia Newton-John	36

Source: Music Information Database

TOP 10 **BESTSELLING SINGLES BY FEMALE SOLO SINGERS IN THE USA**

TITLE / ARTIST / YEAR

1 "Just Dance" Lady Gaga (feat. Colby O'Donis) 2009
2 "Poker Face" Lady Gaga 2009
3 "Tik-Tok" Ke$ha 2010
4 "I Will Always Love You" Whitney Houston 1992
5 "Love Story" Taylor Swift 2009
6 "Hot N Cold" Katy Perry 2008
7 "Single Ladies (Put A Ring On It)" Beyonce 2008
8 "Bad Romance" Lady Gaga 2009
9 "Party in the USA" Miley Cyrus 2009
10 "Bleeding Love" Leona Lewis 2008

Source: Music Information Database

TOP 10 **OLDEST FEMALE SOLO SINGERS TO HAVE A NO. 1 SINGLE IN THE USA**

ARTIST / TITLE	YEAR	YRS	AGE MTHS	DAYS
1 Cher "Believe"	1999	52	9	15
2 Tina Turner "What's Love Got to do with It"	1984	45	9	5
3 Aretha Franklin "I Knew You Were Waiting (For Me)"	1987	45	0	24
4 Bette Midler "The Wind Beneath My Wings"	1999	44	8	24
5 Madonna "Music"	2000	42	1	0
6 Mariah Carey "Touch My Body"	2008	38	0	16
7 Kim Carnes "Bette Davis Eyes"	1981	35	9	26
8 Mariah Carey "Don't Forget About Us"	2005	35	9	4
9 Gwen Stefani "Hollaback Girl"	2005	35	7	4
10 Dolly Parton "9 to 5"	1981	35	1	2

Source: Music Information Database

Youngest Female No. 1 Solo Artists in the USA

At 15 years, 1 month, and 20 days, Little Peggy March tops the list of youngest female singers to hit No. 1, with 1963's "I Will Follow Him," a translation of a French hit song, "Chariot." March's real name was Margaret Annemarie Battivio, her stage name deriving from her diminutive height (4 ft 10 in) and birth month. While Britney Spears, Rihanna, and other teen singers also place in the Top 10, it is notable more than half of them scored their No. 1 hits in the 1960s, including Brenda Lee, Lesley Gore, and Little Eva.

▲ Celine Dion
The French-Canadian singer performs 70 shows a year at Caesar's Palace in Las Vegas.

GROUPS & DUOS

TOP 10 **ALBUMS BY GROUPS AND DUOS IN THE USA**

TITLE / ARTIST / YEAR

1 Their Greatest Hits, 1971–1975
The Eagles 1976

2 Led Zeppelin IV
Led Zeppelin 1971

3 Back in Black
AC/DC 1980

4 Rumours
Fleetwood Mac 1977

5 Appetite for Destruction
Guns N' Roses 1987

6 Boston
Boston 1976

7 = Hotel California
The Eagles 1977

= Cracked Rear View
Hootie and the Blowfish 1995

= Physical Graffiti
Led Zeppelin 1975

10 = Supernatural
Santana 1999

= The Dark Side of the Moon
Pink Floyd 1973

= Greatest Hits
Journey 1989

= Metallica
Metallica 1991

▲ *Fleetwood Mac*
A year after Stevie Nicks joined, the band found success with its eponymous 1975 album.

TOP 10 **GROUPS AND DUOS WITH THE MOST NO. 1 ALBUMS IN THE USA**

ARTIST / NO. 1 ALBUMS

1 The Beatles 19

2 The Rolling Stones 9

3 = Led Zeppelin 7

= U2 7

5 The Eagles 6

6 = Paul McCartney & Wings 5

= Herb Alpert &
the Tijuana Brass 5

= Chicago 5

= The Kingston Trio 5

= Pink Floyd 5

= Van Halen 5

= Metallica 5

Source: Music Information Database

▼ *Luck of the Irish*
Originally from Dublin, Ireland, U2 have been together for more than three and a half decades.

TOP 10 GROUPS AND DUOS WITH THE MOST NO. 1 SINGLES IN THE USA

ARTIST / NO. 1 SINGLES

1 The Beatles 20

2 The Supremes 12

3 The Bee Gees 9

4 The Rolling Stones 8

5 = Daryl Hall & John Oates 6
= Paul McCartney & Wings 6

7 = Boyz II Men* 5
= The Eagles 5
= The Four Seasons 5
= KC & the Sunshine Band 5

* Including one with Mariah Carey

Source: Music Information Database

▲ *The Fab Four*
The bestselling Beatles' single is 1963's "She Loves You."

The top four records on this list all date from the past four years. This and the other singles from the 2000s have all benefited from the phenomenal popularity of downloading.

TOP 10 SINGLES OF ALL TIME BY GROUPS AND DUOS IN THE USA

TITLE / ARTIST / YEAR

1 "I Gotta Feeling" Black Eyed Peas 2009

2 "Boom Boom Pow" Black Eyed Peas 2009

3 "Hey, Soul Sister" Train 2010

4 "Apologize" Timbaland feat. OneRepublic 2007

5 "We Are the World" USA for Africa 1985

6 "Hey Jude" The Beatles 1968

7 "Viva La Vida" Coldplay 2008

8 "Whoomp! (There it Is)" Tag Team 1993

9 "Macarena" Los Del Rio 1996

10 "Come Together"/"Something" The Beatles 1969

TOP 10 GROUPS AND DUOS WITH THE LONGEST SINGLES CHART CAREERS IN THE USA

	ARTIST	CHART SPAN	YRS	MTHS	DAYS
1	The Isley Brothers	Sep 26, 1959–Aug 16, 2003	43	10	21
2	The Rolling Stones	May 2, 1964–Oct 4, 2003	39	5	2
3	Santana	Oct 25, 1969–Nov 19, 2005	36	0	24
4	Fleetwood Mac	Jan 31, 1970–Jun 7, 2003	33	4	7
5	The Beatles	Jan 18, 1964–May 4, 1996	32	3	16
6	The Eagles	Jun 3, 1972–Nov 1, 2003	31	5	29
7	Daryl Hall & John Oates	Feb 9, 1974–Feb 5, 2005	30	11	27
8	The Bee Gees	May 27, 1967–Feb 7, 1998	30	8	11
9	The Righteous Brothers	May 11, 1963–Mar 23, 1991	27	10	12
10	Aerosmith	Oct 20, 1973–Jun 9, 2001	27	7	20

Source: Music Information Database

This is a constantly changing list, as just one release of a classic single will move the positions around. After not being on this list for some years, the Beatles go back in at No. 5 on the strength of their catalog being issued through iTunes.

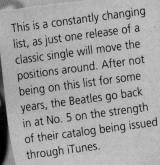

TOP 10 OF EVERYTHING FEATURE

Rolling Stones at 50

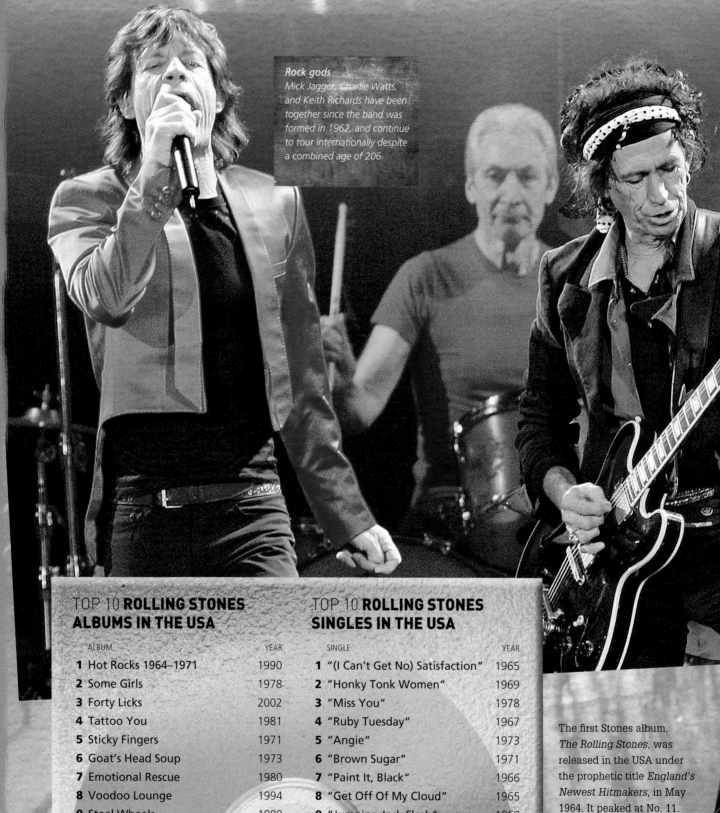

Rock gods
Mick Jagger, Charlie Watts, and Keith Richards have been together since the band was formed in 1962, and continue to tour internationally despite a combined age of 206.

TOP 10 ROLLING STONES ALBUMS IN THE USA

ALBUM	YEAR
1 Hot Rocks 1964–1971	1990
2 Some Girls	1978
3 Forty Licks	2002
4 Tattoo You	1981
5 Sticky Fingers	1971
6 Goat's Head Soup	1973
7 Emotional Rescue	1980
8 Voodoo Lounge	1994
9 Steel Wheels	1989
10 Big Hits (High Tide and Green Grass)	1966

Source: Music Information Database

TOP 10 ROLLING STONES SINGLES IN THE USA

SINGLE	YEAR
1 "(I Can't Get No) Satisfaction"	1965
2 "Honky Tonk Women"	1969
3 "Miss You"	1978
4 "Ruby Tuesday"	1967
5 "Angie"	1973
6 "Brown Sugar"	1971
7 "Paint It, Black"	1966
8 "Get Off Of My Cloud"	1965
9 "Jumping Jack Flash"	1968
10 "Start Me Up"	1981

Source: Music Information Database

The first Stones album, *The Rolling Stones*, was released in the USA under the prophetic title *England's Newest Hitmakers*, in May 1964. It peaked at No. 11. It wasn't until the following year's *Out of Our Heads*, however, that the group gained their first US No. 1 album.

▶ **Bill Wyman**
Wyman was bass player for the first 30 years but left in 1992 to play with his own band, Bill Wyman's Rhythm Kings.

◀ **Brian Jones**
A founding member of the Rolling Stones, Jones left the group in June 1969 and soon afterward drowned in his own swimming pool.

THE CHANGING FACE OF THE ROLLING STONES

There have been 10 members of the Rolling Stones over the past 50 years—some more enduring than others. Jagger, Richards, and Watts are the only ones to claim a full half-century's membership.

Name	Dates	Instrument
Mick Jagger	1962–2012	Vocals
Keith Richards	1962–2012	Guitar
Charlie Watts	1962–2012	Drums
Bill Wyman	1962–92	Bass
Brian Jones	1962–69	Guitar
Ian Stewart	1962–63	Keyboards
Dick Taylor	1962	Bass
Tony Chapman	1962	Drums
Mick Taylor	1969–74	Guitar
Ronnie Wood	1975–2012	Guitar

ROLLING STONES TIMELINE

Apr 1962 Rolling Stones form

Jul 1962 First official gig at the Marquee, London

Jun 1963 First single released in the UK: "Come On"

May 1963 Stewart leaves the line-up to become the band's manager

Sep–Nov 1963 First UK tour

April 1964 First album released in the UK: *The Rolling Stones*

Jun 1964 First UK No. 1 single "It's All Over Now"

Jun 1964 First US tour

May 1965 First US No.1 single "(I Can't Get No) Satisfaction"

Feb–Mar 1966 First tour of Australasia

Jul 1969 Brian Jones dies; Stones perform free concert in Hyde Park, London

Apr 1971 Stones sign with Atlantic Records

Jun–Jul 1972 Tour of North America

Dec 1974 Mick Taylor leaves the group

Mar 1975 Wood joins for *Black and Blue* recording sessions

Jun–Aug 1975 46-show tour of the Americas

Apr–June 1976 Nine-country tour of Europe

Jan 1989 Stones inducted into the Rock & Roll Hall of Fame

Aug 1989–Aug 1990 Steel Wheels/Urban Jungle tour

Dec 1992 Wyman leaves the band

Aug 1994–Aug 1995 Voodoo Lounge tour

Sep 1997–Sep 1998 Bridges to Babylon tour

Jan-Apr 1999 No Security tour

Sep 2002–Nov 2003 Licks tour

Aug 2005–Aug 2007 Bigger Bang tour

Apr 2012 Stones celebrate 50 years of rock 'n' roll success

◀ **Ronnie Wood**
Beginning his career as a guitarist with The Birds, Wood joined the Stones in 1975, and still plays with the band as its fourth member.

MUSIC AWARDS

THE 10 ARTISTS WITH MOST MTV AWARDS

	ARTIST	AWARDS
1	Madonna	20
2	Peter Gabriel	13
3	= R.E.M.	12
	= Eminem	12
5	= Green Day	11
	= Aerosmith	11
	= Lady Gaga	11
8	Beyonce	10
9	= Fatboy Slim	9
	= Janet Jackson	9

THE 10 LATEST RECIPIENTS OF THE MERCURY MUSIC PRIZE

YEAR	ARTIST / ALBUM
2010	The xx, xx
2009	Speech Debelle, Speech Therapy
2008	Elbow, The Seldom Seen Kid
2007	Klaxons, Myths of the Near Future
2006	Arctic Monkeys, Whatever People Say I Am, That's What I'm Not
2005	Antony & the Johnsons, I Am a Bird Now
2004	Franz Ferdinand, Franz Ferdinand
2003	Dizzee Rascal, Boy In Da Corner
2002	Ms Dynamite, A Little Deeper
2001	PJ Harvey, Stories from the City, Stories from the Sea

Source: Barclaycard Mercury Prize

▶ **Green Day**
The punk rockers' third album, Dookie, achieved diamond status after selling over 16 million copies worldwide.

TOP 10 COUNTRY MUSIC ASSOCIATION AWARD WINNERS

	ARTIST	AWARDS*
1	Brooks & Dunn	15
2	George Strait	14
3	Garth Brooks	11
4	= Chet Atkins	10
	= Vince Gill	10
6	= Dixie Chicks	9
	= Alan Jackson	9
	= The Judds	9
	= The Statler Brothers	9
10	Johnny Cash	8

* For lyrics, excluding shared, merit, and other awards

Source: Country Music Association

THE 10 **LATEST GRAMMY RECORDS OF THE YEAR**

YEAR / RECORD / ARTIST

2011
"Need You Now" Lady Antebellum

2010
"Use Somebody" Kings of Leon

2009
"Please Read the Letter"
Alison Krauss & Robert Plant

2008
"Rehab" Amy Winehouse

2007
"Not Ready to Make Nice" Dixie Chicks

2006
"Boulevard of Broken Dreams" Green Day

2005
"Here We Go Again" Ray Charles & Norah Jones

2004
"Clocks" Coldplay

2003
"Don't Know Why" Norah Jones

2002
"Walk On" U2

Source: NARAS

▶ *Georg Solti*
The conductor of the Chicago Symphony Orchestra for 22 years, Solti was nominated for 74 Grammy Awards.

TOP 10 **GROUPS WITH MOST GRAMMY AWARDS**

	GROUP	AWARDS
1	U2	22
2	= Alison Krauss and Union Station	13
	= The Beatles	13
	= Dixie Chicks	13
5	Pat Metheny Group	10
6	Metallica	9
7	= Santana	8
	= Take 6	8
9	= Coldplay	7
	= Simon and Garfunkel	7

Source: NARAS

TOP 10 **ARTISTS WITH MOST GRAMMY AWARDS**

	ARTIST	AWARDS
1	Georg Solti	31
2	Quincy Jones	27
3	= Pierre Boulez	26
	= Alison Krauss	26
5	Vladimir Horowitz	25
6	= Stevie Wonder	22
	= U2	22
8	John Williams	21
9	= Vince Gill	20
	= Henry Mancini	20
	= Bruce Springsteen	20

Source: NARAS

◀ *Alison Krauss*
The multiplatinum selling musician first picked up a fiddle at the age of five.

CLASSICAL & OPERA

TOP 10 CLASSICAL ALBUMS IN THE USA

	TITLE	PERFORMER/ORCHESTRA	YEAR
1	The Three Tenors in Concert	José Carreras, Placido Domingo, Luciano Pavarotti	1990
2	Romanza	Andrea Bocelli	1997
3	Sogno	Andrea Bocelli	1999
4	Voice of an Angel	Charlotte Church	1999
5	Chant	Benedictine Monks of Santo Domingo De Silos	1994
6	The Three Tenors in Concert 1994	José Carreras, Placido Domingo, Luciano Pavarotti	1994
7	Sacred Arias	Andrea Bocelli	1999
8	Tchaikovsky: Piano Concerto No. 1	Van Cliburn	1958
9	Amore	Andrea Bocelli	2006
10	Cieli Di Toscana Collection	Andrea Bocelli	2001

Source: Music Information Database

The 1990s saw a huge increase in sales of classical and opera music, a change that owes much to the influence of tenors such as Placido Domingo and Luciano Pavarotti, whose amazing rise to international stardom led to opera music becoming a far more accessible genre.

TOP 10 OPERAS MOST FREQUENTLY PERFORMED AT THE METROPOLITAN OPERA HOUSE, NEW YORK

	OPERA	COMPOSER	PERFORMANCES*
1	La Bohème	Giacomo Puccini	1,234
2	Aïda	Giuseppi Verdi	1,115
3	La Traviata	Giuseppi Verdi	977
4	Carmen	Georges Bizet	970
5	Tosca	Giacomo Puccini	919
6	Rigoletto	Giuseppi Verdi	841
7	Madama Butterfly	Giacomo Puccini	830
8	Faust	Charles Gounod	733
9	Pagliacci	Ruggero Leoncavallo	712
10	Cavalleria Rusticana	Pietro Mascagni	671

* As of end of 2010–11 season

Source: Metropolitan Opera

▼ *Andrea Bocelli*
Blind since childhood, Bocelli is one of the world's most popular opera singers.

▶ *Alan Gilbert*
Gilbert was the first native New Yorker to be made music director of the New York Philharmonic.

TOP 10 BESTSELLING CLASSICAL ARTISTS IN THE USA

1 Andrea Bocelli

2 Luciano Pavarotti

3 Placido Domingo

4 José Carreras

5 Charlotte Church

6 Mario Lanza

7 Van Cliburn

8 Benedictine Monks of Santo Domingo de Silos

9 Royal Philharmonic Orchestra

10 Neville Marriner

Source: Music Information Database

THE 10 LATEST BEST CLASSICAL ALBUM GRAMMY WINNERS

YEAR	COMPOSER / TITLE
2010	Giuseppe Verdi — Requiem
2009	Gustav Mahler — Symphony No. 8/Adagio from Symphony No. 10
2008	Kurt Weill — Rise and Fall of the City of Mahagonny
2007	Joan Tower — Made in America
2006	Gustav Mahler — Symphony No. 7
2005	William Bolcom — Songs of Innocence and of Experience
2004	John Adams — On the Transmigration of Souls
2003	Gustav Mahler — Symphony No. 3/ Kindertotenlieder
2002	Ralph Vaughan Williams — A Sea Symphony (Symphony No. 1)
2001	Hector Berlioz — Les Troyens

Source: NARAS

THE 10 LATEST CONDUCTORS OF THE NEW YORK PHILHARMONIC ORCHESTRA

	CONDUCTOR	YEARS
1	Alan Gilbert	2009–
2	Lorin Maazel	2002–09
3	Kurt Masur	1991–2002
4	Zubin Mehta	1978–91
5	Pierre Boulez	1971–77
6	George Szell*	1969–70
7	Leonard Bernstein	1958–69
8	Dimitri Mitropoulos	1949–58
9	Leopold Stokowski#	1949–50
10	Bruno Walter*	1947–49

* Music advisor
# Co-principal conductor

The New York Philharmonic Orchestra was founded in 1842 by conductor Ureli Corelli Hill, giving its first performance—Beethoven's Symphony No. 5—at the Apollo Rooms. In 1909, Gustav Mahler was appointed the orchestra's principal conductor. During the 1930s the orchestra, under the baton of Arturo Toscanini, began Sunday afternoon concerts from Carnegie Hall, which were broadcast on CBS radio for 38 years.

MOVIE MUSIC

▲ Mamma Mia!
Based on songs by
Abba, the film was
shot on the Greek
island of Skopelos.

Recently, animated movies with an important musical content have taken over from traditional musicals (in which the cast actually sings), with *Beauty and the Beast, Aladdin, The Lion King, Pocahontas, The Prince of Egypt, Tarzan,* and *Monsters, Inc.* all winning "Best Original Song" Oscars.

TOP 10 BESTSELLING MUSICAL ALBUMS IN THE USA

ALBUM / YEAR OF RELEASE

1 Grease
1978

2 Evita
1996

3 West Side Story
1961

4 My Fair Lady
1964

5 Beauty and the Beast
1989

6 Oklahoma!
1955

7 Mamma Mia!
2008

8 Chicago
2003

9 The Sound of Music
1965

10 South Pacific
1958

Source: Music Information Database

TOP 10 MUSICAL MOVIES

MOVIE / YEAR

1 Mamma Mia!
2008

2 Grease
1978

3 Chicago
2002

4 The Sound of Music
1965

5 The Rocky Horror Picture Show
1975

6 High School Musical 3: Senior Year
2008

7 Saturday Night Fever
1977

8 Hairspray
2007

9 Moulin Rouge!
2001

10 Dreamgirls
2006

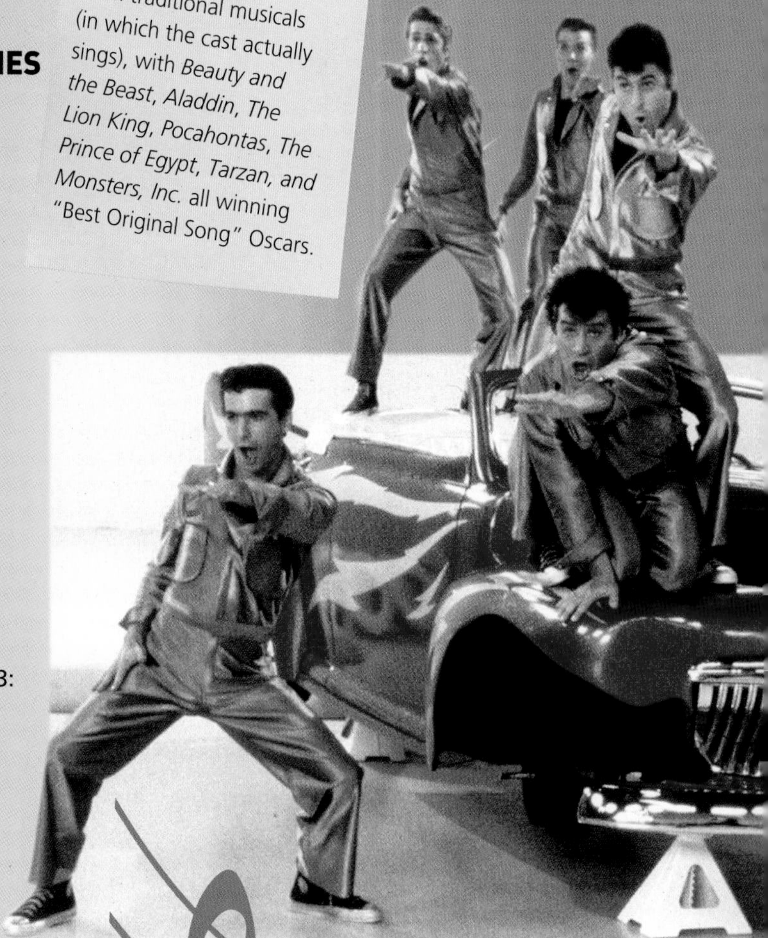

TOP 10 ORIGINAL SOUNDTRACK ALBUMS IN THE USA

	ALBUM	YEAR OF RELEASE
1	The Bodyguard	1992
2	Purple Rain	1984
3	Forrest Gump	1994
4 =	Titanic	1997
=	Dirty Dancing	1987
6	The Lion King	1994
7 =	Footloose	1984
=	Top Gun	1986
9 =	Grease	1978
=	O Brother Where Art Thou?	2000

Source: RIAA

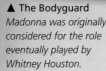

▲ The Bodyguard
Madonna was originally considered for the role eventually played by Whitney Houston.

▼ Grease
Set in a high school in the 1950s, the movie shot John Travolta and Olivia Newton-John to stardom.

TOP 10 BESTSELLING "BEST SONG" OSCAR-WINNING SINGLES IN THE USA

	ARTIST / SONG / MOVIE (IF DIFFERENT)	YEAR
1	Debby Boone, "You Light Up My Life"	1977
2	Joe Cocker & Jennifer Warnes, "Up Where We Belong" (An Officer and a Gentleman)	1982
3	Barbra Streisand, "Evergreen" (A Star is Born)	1976
4	Celine Dion, "My Heart Will Go On" (Titanic)	1997
5	Stevie Wonder, "I Just Called to Say I Love You" (The Woman in Red)	1984
6	Christopher Cross, "Arthur's Theme" (Arthur)	1981
7	Barbra Streisand, "The Way We Were"	1973
8	Eminem, "Lose Yourself" (8 Mile)	2002
9	B.J. Thomas, "Raindrops Keep Falling on My Head" (Butch Cassidy and the Sundance Kid)	1969
10	Bill Medley & Jennifer Warnes, "The Time of My Life" (Dirty Dancing)	1987

THE 10 LATEST WINNERS OF THE OSCAR FOR BEST ORIGINAL SONG

YEAR*	TITLE	MOVIE
2010	"We Belong Together"	Toy Story 3
2009	"The Weary Kind"	Crazy Heart
2008	"Jai Ho"	Slumdog Millionaire
2007	"Falling Slowly"	Once
2006	"I Need To Wake Up"	An Inconvenient Truth
2005	"It's Hard Out Here for a Pimp"	Hustle & Flow
2004	"Al Otro Lado Del Rio"	The Motorcycle Diaries
2003	"Into the West"	The Lord of the Rings: The Return of the King
2002	"Lose Yourself"	8 Mile
2001	"If I Didn't Have You"	Monsters, Inc.

* Of release; awards made the following year

7 ENTERTAINMENT

50 YEARS OF JAMES BOND

Sixty years ago, whilst at his Jamaican estate Goldeneye, Ian Fleming started work on the first of his 12 James Bond novels. Published in 1953, *Casino Royale* gained widespread popularity, and was adapted for the screen three times. In 1962, EON Productions produced its first Bond movie, *Dr. No*, starring Sean Connery. Despite not being Fleming's first choice of actor, Connery went on to star in six of the James Bond movies. Since then, George Lazenby, Roger Moore, Timothy Dalton, Pierce Brosnan, and, most recently, Daniel Craig have portrayed 007 in one of the longest-running film franchises of all time.

◄ *Hakuna Matata*
Based on the 1994 Disney film, The Lion King *musical features songs by Elton John and Tim Rice.*

THE 10 LATEST TONY AWARDS FOR A MUSICAL

YEAR	MUSICAL
2010	Memphis
2009	Billy Elliot—The Musical
2008	In the Heights
2007	Spring Awakening
2006	Jersey Boys
2005	Monthy Python's Spamalot
2004	Avenue Q
2003	Hairspray
2002	Thoroughly Modern Millie
2001	The Producers

Named for the actress and director Antoinette Perry (1888–1946), who headed the American Theater Wing during World War II, the Tony Awards, established in 1947, honor outstanding Broadway plays and musicals, actors and actresses, music, costume, and other contributions.

TOP 10 LONGEST-RUNNING MUSICALS ON BROADWAY

	SHOW	RUN	PERFORMANCES
1	The Phantom of the Opera	Jan 26, 1988–	9,547*
2	Cats	Oct 7, 1982–Sep 10, 2000	7,485
3	Les Misérables	Mar 12, 1987–May 18, 2003	6,680
4	A Chorus Line	Jul 25, 1975–Apr 28, 1990	6,137
5	Chicago	Nov 14, 1996–	5,876*
6	=Beauty and the Beast	Apr 18, 1994–Jul 29, 2007	5,461
	=The Lion King	Nov 13, 1997–	5,461*
8	Rent	Apr 26, 1996–Sep 7, 2008	5,123
9	Miss Saigon	Apr 11, 1991–Jan 28, 2001	4,092
10	Mamma Mia!	Oct 18, 2001–	3,824*

* Still running, total as of January 17, 2011

All the longest-running musicals date from the past 40 years. Prior to these record-breakers, the longest runner of the 1940s was *Oklahoma!*, which debuted in 1943 and ran for 2,212 performances up to 1948, and from the 1950s *My Fair Lady*, which opened in 1956 and closed in 1962 after 2,717 performances.

TOP 10 MOST PRODUCED PLAYS BY SHAKESPEARE, 1878–2010

	PLAY	PRODUCTIONS
1	As You Like It	83
2	=Hamlet	81
	=Twelfth Night	81
4	The Taming of the Shrew	80
5	A Midsummer Night's Dream	77
6	Much Ado About Nothing	72
7	The Merchant of Venice	70
8	Macbeth	67
9	=The Merry Wives of Windsor	62
	=Romeo and Juliet	62

Source: Shakespeare Centre

This list is based on an analysis of Shakespearean productions (rather than individual performances) from December 31, 1878 to December 31, 2010 at Stratford-upon-Avon and by the Royal Shakespeare Company in London and on tour.

TOP 10 **LONGEST SHAKESPEAREAN ROLES**

	ROLE	PLAY	LINES
1	Hamlet	Hamlet	1,422
2	Falstaff	Henry IV, Parts I and II	1,178
3	Richard III	Richard III	1,124
4	Iago	Othello	1,097
5	Henry V	Henry V	1,025
6	Othello	Othello	860
7	Vincentio	Measure for Measure	820
8	Coriolanus	Coriolanus	809
9	Timon	Timon of Athens	795
10	Antony	Antony and Cleopatra	766

If more than one play (or parts of a play) are taken into account, some would increase their tallies, among them Richard III, who appears (as Richard, Duke of Gloucester) in *Henry VI*, Part III, and Henry V who appears (as Prince Hal) in *Henry IV*, where he speaks 117 lines, making his total 1,142. Rosalind's 668-line role in *As You Like It* is the longest female part in the works of Shakespeare.

▼ Hamlet
British actor David Tennant played Hamlet in a critically acclaimed 2008–09 production.

THE 10 **LATEST WINNERS OF THE PULITZER PRIZE FOR DRAMA**

YEAR / PLAY / PLAYWRIGHT

2011 Clybourne Park / Bruce Norris

2010 Next to Normal / Brian Yorkey

2009 Ruined / Lynn Nottage

2008 August: Osage County / Tracy Letts

2007 Rabbit Hole / David Lindsay-Abaire

2006 No prize awarded*

2005 Doubt, a Parable / John Patrick Shanley

2004 I Am My Own Wife / Nilo Cruz

2003 Anna in the Tropics / Martin McDonagh

2002 Topdog/Underdog / Suzan-Lori Parks

* Changes to the running season limited eligible plays and no winner was decided on

MOVIE WORLD

TOP 10 MOVIES OF THE SILENT ERA

MOVIE / YEAR

1   The Birth of a Nation 1915
2   The Big Parade 1925
3   Ben-Hur 1926
4   The Ten Commandments 1923
5 = The Covered Wagon 1923
  = What Price Glory? 1926
7 = Hearts of the World 1918
  = Way Down East 1921
9 = The Four Horsemen of
    the Apocalypse 1921
  = Wings 1927

★ ★ ★ ★ ★
▲ Ben-Hur
The most expensive silent movie
ever made changed director and
location in the middle of filming.

TOP 10 FILM FRANCHISES OF ALL TIME

FRANCHISE / NO. OF MOVIES / YEARS	WORLD GROSS ($)
1 Harry Potter 7 / 2001–10	6,361,655,490
2 James Bond 23 / 1963–2008	5,074,402,453
3 Star Wars 6 / 1977–2005	4,441,410,761
4 Shrek 4 / 2001–10	2,955,741,576
5 The Lord of the Rings 3 / 2001–03	2,913,933,388
6 Pirates of the Caribbean 3 / 2003–07	2,681,667,528
7 Batman 6 / 1989–2008	2,648,834,002
8 Spider-Man 3 / 2002–07	2,496,285,178
9 Indiana Jones 4 / 1981–2008	1,980,610,580
10 Toy Story 3 / 1995–2020	1,946,968,297

★ ★ ★ ★ ★
▲ Harry Potter and friends
The three young Harry Potter
stars top the list of average
takings per movie starred in.

TOP 10 BLACK AND WHITE MOVIES

MOVIE / YEAR

1 Young Frankenstein (1974)
2 Schindler's List (1993)
3 Paper Moon (1973)
4 Manhattan (1979)
5 Mom and Dad (1944)
6 Who's Afraid of Virginia Woolf? (1966)
7 Easy Money (1983)
8 The Last Picture Show (1971)
9 From Here to Eternity (1953)
10 Dead Men Don't Wear Plaid (1982)

★ ★ ★ ★ ★
▲ Young Frankenstein
The affectionate parody used many of the same props from the original Frankenstein.

TOP 10 MOVIES OF ALL TIME

MOVIE / YEAR	USA	GROSS INCOME ($) OVERSEAS	WORLD TOTAL
1 Avatar 2009	760,307,594	2,009,924,355	2,770,231,949
2 Titanic* 1997	600,788,188	1,242,413,080	1,843,201,268
3 The Lord of the Rings: The Return of the King* 2003	377,027,325	742,083,616	1,119,110,941
4 Pirates of the Caribbean: Dead Man's Chest 2006	423,315,812	642,863,913	1,066,179,725
5 Toy Story 3 2010	412,031,733	644,400,000	1,056,431,733
6 Alice in Wonderland 2010	334,191,110	690,108,181	1,024,299,291
7 The Dark Knight 2008	533,345,358	468,576,467	1,001,921,825
8 Harry Potter and the Sorcerer's Stone 2001	317,575,550	657,158,000	974,733,550
9 Pirates of the Caribbean: At World's End 2007	309,420,425	651,576,067	960,996,492
10 Harry Potter and the Deathly Hallows: Part I 2010	295,001,070	657,240,000	952,241,070

* Won Best Picture Oscar

TOP 10 COUNTRIES WITH THE MOST CINEMA SCREENS

	COUNTRY	NO. OF CINEMA SCREENS *
1	USA	39,476
2	China	36,112
3	India	10,189
4	France	5,426
5	Germany	4,810
6	Spain	4,140
7	Mexico	3,920
8	UK	3,661
9	Italy	3,410
10	Japan	3,359

* Latest available year for which data available; excluding drive-in screens

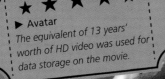

★ ★ ★ ★ ★
► Avatar
The equivalent of 13 years' worth of HD video was used for data storage on the movie.

145

OPENING WEEKENDS

TOP 10 CHRISTMAS OPENING WEEKENDS*

	MOVIE	YEAR	OPENING WEEKEND GROSS ($)
1	Sherlock Holmes	2009	24,608,941
2	Marley and Me	2008	14,380,980
3	The Curious Case of Benjamin Button	2008	11,871,831
4	Bedtime Stories	2008	10,578,817
5	Ali	2001	10,216,625
6	Catch Me if You Can	2002	9,882,063
7	Aliens Vs. Predator—Requiem	2007	9,515,615
8	Dreamgirls	2006	8,726,095
9	Valkyrie	2008	8,493,972
10	Patch Adams	1998	8,081,760

* First release anywhere in the world on Christmas weekend

TOP 10 BIGGEST SECOND-WEEKEND DROPS

	MOVIE* / YEAR	SECOND WEEKEND DROP (%)
1	Friday the 13th 2009	80.4
2	Jonas Brothers: The 3D Concert Experience 2009	77.4
3	Star Trek: Nemesis 2002	76.2
4	George A. Romero's Land of the Dead 2005	73.4
5	Bruno 2009	72.8
6	Doom 2005	72.7
7	A Nightmare on Elm Street 2010	72.3
8	Notorious 2009	71.8
9	Predators 2010	71.7
10	Hellboy II: The Golden Army 2008	70.7

* Earning over $10 million in opening weekend

TOP 10 HALLOWEEN OPENERS

	MOVIE / YEAR	OPENING WEEKEND GROSS ($)
1	Saw III 2006	33,610,391
2	Saw IV 2007	32,110,000
3	Saw II 2005	31,725,652
4	Jackass: The Movie 2002	22,763,437
5	Ray 2004	20,039,730
6	Brother Bear 2003	19,404,492
7	Saw 2004	18,276,468
8	K-PAX 2001	17,215,275
9	Stargate 1994	16,651,018
10	The Legend of Zorro 2005	16,328,506

TOP 10 G-RATED OPENING WEEKENDS

	MOVIE / YEAR	OPENING WEEKEND GROSS ($)
1	Toy Story 3 2010	110,307,189
2	Finding Nemo 2003	70,251,710
3	WALL-E 2008	63,087,526
4	Monsters, Inc. 2001	62,577,067
5	Cars 2006	60,119,509
6	Toy Story 2 1999	57,388,839
7	Ratatouille 2007	47,027,395
8	Horton Hears a Who! 2008	45,012,998
9	High School Musical 3: Senior Year 2008	42,030,184
10	The Lion King 1994	40,888,194

A G rating denotes a film that is suitable for everyone, even young children.

TOP 10 MOVIES THAT SPENT THE LONGEST AT NO. 1

	MOVIE / YEAR	CONSECUTIVE NO. 1 WEEKENDS
1	Titanic 1997	15
2	= Beverly Hills Cop 1984	13
	= Tootsie 1982	13
4	Home Alone 1990	12
5	= Crocodile Dundee 1986	9
	= Good Morning, Vietnam 1987	9
7	= Back to the Future 1985	8
	= Fatal Attraction 1987	8
	= Porky's 1982	8
10	= Avatar 2009	7
	= Ghostbusters 1984	7
	= On Golden Pond 1981	7

▲ Home Alone
Earning $477 million worldwide, Home Alone is the highest-grossing live-action comedy of all time.

TOP 10 R-RATED OPENING WEEKENDS

	MOVIE / YEAR	OPENING WEEKEND GROSS ($)
1	The Matrix Reloaded 2003	91,774,413
2	The Passion of the Christ 2004	83,848,082
3	300 2007	70,885,301
4	Hannibal 2001	58,003,121
5	Sex and the City 2008	57,038,404
6	Watchmen 2009	55,214,334
7	8 Mile 2002	51,240,555
8	Wanted 2008	50,927,641
9	Jackass 3D 2010	50,353,641
10	The Matrix Revolutions 2003	48,475,154

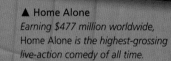
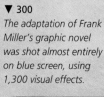

▼ 300
The adaptation of Frank Miller's graphic novel was shot almost entirely on blue screen, using 1,300 visual effects.

MOVIES OF THE DECADES

TOP 10 MOVIES OF THE 1920s

MOVIE / YEAR

1 The Big Parade 1925
2 The Four Horsemen of the Apocalypse 1921
3 Ben-Hur 1926
4 The Ten Commandments 1923
5 What Price Glory? 1926
6 The Covered Wagon 1923
7 Way Down East 1921
8 The Singing Fool 1928
9 Wings 1927
10 The Gold Rush 1925

Earnings data for early movies are unreliable, but if this list were extended back to the first decade of the 20th century, *The Birth of a Nation* (1915) would be a contender as the highest-earning film of the silent era. *The Broadway Melody* (1929), which just fails to make the list, was the first ever winner of a Best Picture Oscar.

TOP 10 MOVIES OF THE 1930s

MOVIE / YEAR

1 Gone With the Wind* 1939
2 Snow White and the Seven Dwarfs 1937
3 The Wizard of Oz 1939
4 Frankenstein 1931
5 King Kong 1933
6 San Francisco 1936
7 = Hell's Angels 1930
  = Lost Horizon 1937
  = Mr. Smith Goes to Washington 1939
10 Maytime 1937

* Winner of Best Picture Academy Award

If the income of *Gone With the Wind* is adjusted to allow for inflation in the period since its release, it could be regarded as the most successful movie ever.

TOP 10 MOVIES OF THE 1940s

MOVIE / YEAR

1 Bambi* 1942
2 Pinocchio* 1940
3 Fantasia* 1940
4 Song of the South# 1946
5 Mom and Dad 1944
6 Samson and Delilah 1949
7 The Best Years of Our Lives† 1946
8 The Bells of St. Mary's 1945
9 Duel in the Sun 1946
10 This Is the Army 1943

* Animated
# Part animated/part live-action
† Winner of Best Picture Academy Award

▶ Bambi
The feature lost money on its first run, but was rereleased six times.

▼ The Wizard of Oz
Toto, Dorothy's dog, was paid more than twice the weekly wage of the actors portraying the Munchkins.

TOP 10 MOVIES OF THE 1970s

MOVIE / YEAR

1 Star Wars* 1977
2 Jaws 1975
3 Grease 1978
4 Close Encounters of the Third Kind 1977
5 The Exorcist 1973
6 Superman 1978
7 Saturday Night Fever 1977
8 Jaws 2 1978
9 Moonraker 1979
10 The Spy Who Loved Me 1977

* Later retitled *Star Wars: Episode IV – A New Hope*

The first nine films in the list exemplify the upward trend of box-office blockbusters, each earning in excess of $200 million worldwide, with *Star Wars* reaping a total global take approaching $800 million.

TOP 10 **MOVIES OF THE**
1950s

MOVIE / YEAR

1 Lady and the Tramp* 1955
2 Peter Pan* 1953
3 Cinderella* 1950
4 The Ten Commandments 1956
5 Ben-Hur# 1959
6 Sleeping Beauty* 1959
7 Around the World in
   80 Days 1956
8 This is Cinerama 1952
9 South Pacific 1958
10 The Robe 1953

* Animated
\# Winner of Best Picture Academy Award

While the popularity of animated movies continued, the 1950s was outstanding as the decade of the "big" picture: many of the most successful films were enormous in terms of cast numbers.

TOP 10 **MOVIES OF THE**
1960s

MOVIE / YEAR

1 One Hundred and
   One Dalmatians* 1961
2 The Jungle Book* 1967
3 The Sound of Music# 1965
4 Thunderball 1965
5 Goldfinger 1964
6 Doctor Zhivago 1965
7 You Only Live Twice 1967
8 The Graduate 1968
9 Butch Cassidy and the
   Sundance Kid 1969
10 Mary Poppins 1964

* Animated
\# Winner of Best Picture Academy Award

▶ *Bond begins*
Fifty years of Bond has seen seven actors in the leading role, 14 directors, 114 drinks, and 240 kills.

TOP 10 **MOVIES OF THE**
1980s

MOVIE / YEAR

1 E.T.: The Extra-Terrestrial 1982
2 Return of the Jedi* 1983
3 The Empire Strikes Back# 1980
4 Indiana Jones and
   the Last Crusade 1989
5 Rain Man† 1988
6 Raiders of the Lost Ark 1981
7 Batman 1989
8 Back to the Future 1985
9 Who Framed Roger Rabbit 1988
10 Top Gun 1986

* Later retitled Star Wars: Episode VI—
Return of the Jedi
\# Later retitled Star Wars: Episode V—
The Empire Strikes Back
† Winner of Best Picture Academy Award

The 1980s was clearly the decade of the adventure movie, with George Lucas and Steven Spielberg

TOP 10 **MOVIES OF THE**
1990s

MOVIE / YEAR

1 Titanic* 1997
2 Star Wars: Episode I—
   The Phantom Menace 1999
3 Jurassic Park 1993
4 Independence Day 1996
5 The Lion King# 1994
6 Forrest Gump* 1994
7 The Sixth Sense 1999
8 The Lost World:
   Jurassic Park 1997
9 Men in Black 1997
10 Armageddon 1998

* Winner of Best Picture Academy Award
\# Animated

Each of the Top 10 movies of the 1990s has earned more than $550 million around the world, a total of more than $8.4 billion between them.

TOP 10 **MOVIES OF THE**
2000s

MOVIE / YEAR

1 Avatar 2009*
2 The Lord of the Rings:
   The Return of the King 2003
3 Pirates of the Caribbean:
   Dead Man's Chest 2006
4 Toy Story 3 2010
5 Alice in Wonderland 2010
6 The Dark Knight 2008
7 Harry Potter and the
   Sorcerer's Stone 2001
8 Pirates of the Caribbean:
   At World's End 2007
9 Harry Potter and the
   Deathly Hallows: Part I 2010
10 Harry Potter and the
   Order of the Phoenix 2007

* Multiple releases

MOVIE GENRES

TOP 10 **GANGSTER MOVIES**

MOVIE / YEAR

1 The Departed
2006

2 American Gangster
2007

3 The Godfather
1972

4 Public Enemies
2009

5 Pulp Fiction
1994

6 Gangs of New York
2002

7 The Godfather Part II
1974

8 Heat
1995

9 Road to Perdition
2002

10 Analyze This
1999

▲ **Public Enemy**
*Johnny Depp trained
with the FBI for his
role as Depression Era
gangster John Dillinger.*

TOP 10 **HORROR MOVIES**

MOVIE / YEAR

The Exorcist
1973

What Lies Beneath
2000

The Blair Witch Project
1999

The Ring
2002

The Grudge
2004

Paranormal Activity
2009

Scream
1996

Scream 2
1997

The Haunting
1999

Scream 3
2000

This list encompasses class[?]
supernatural and "slasher"
horror movies, but not thos[e]
featuring monster creature[s]
or historical horror flicks.

TOP 10 **SUPERHERO MOVIES***

	MOVIE	YEAR
1	The Dark Knight	2008
2	Spider-Man 3	2007
3	Spider-Man	2002
4	Spider-Man 2	2004
5	The Incredibles	2004
6	Hancock	2008
7	Iron Man 2	2010
8	Iron Man	2008
9	X-Men: The Last Stand	2006
10	Batman	1989

* Based on US gross box office

Source: IMDB-Pro

▲ **The Dark Knight**
*Heath Ledger's final film was
the fastest to earn $400 million,
doing so in just 18 days.*

▲ How the Grinch Stole Christmas
Three hours of makeup transformed Jim Carrey into Dr. Seuss's Grinch.

TOP 10 **CHRISTMAS MOVIES**

	MOVIE	YEAR	US GROSS ($)
1	How the Grinch Stole Christmas	2000	260,044,825
2	The Polar Express	2004	181,320,482
3	Elf	2003	173,398,518
4	The Santa Clause	1994	144,833,357
5	The Santa Clause 2: The Mrs. Clause	2002	139,236,327
6	A Christmas Carol	2009	137,855,863
7	Four Christmases	2008	120,146,040
8	The Santa Clause 3: The Escape Clause	2006	84,500,112
9	Tim Burton's The Nightmare before Christmas	1993	75,082,668
10	Christmas with the Kranks	2004	73,780,539

This list only includes films in which Christmas and/or Santa Claus provide the principal theme, rather than those containing Christmas or holiday scenes.

TOP 10 **SPORT MOVIES** *

MOVIE / YEAR / SPORT

1 The Blind Side 2009
American Football

2 Cars 2006
Car racing

3 The Karate Kid 2010
Martial arts

4 The Waterboy 1998
American football

5 The Longest Yard 2005
American football

6 Jerry Maguire 1996
American football

7 Talladega Nights 2006
Car racing

8 Rocky IV 1985
Boxing

9 Rocky III 1982
Boxing

10 Seabiscuit 2003
Horse racing

* Based on US gross box office

TOP 10 **3D MOVIES IN THE USA**

MOVIE / YEAR / GROSS INCOME USA ($)*

1 Avatar
2009
$760,507,624

2 Toy Story 3
2010
$415,004,880

3 Alice in Wonderland
2010
$334,191,110

4 Up
2009
$293,004,164

5 Despicable Me
2010
$251,513,985

6 Shrek Forever After
2010
$238,395,990

7 How to Train Your Dragon
2010
$217,581,231

8 Tangled
2010
$199,441,791

9 Monsters Vs. Aliens
2009
$198,351,526

10 Ice Age: Dawn of the Dinosaurs
2009
$196,573,705

* Includes box-office takings from non-3D screenings

Animated Hits

◀ Toy Story 3
Fifteen years after the original, Toy Story 3—the first feature film created entirely in CGI—was the highest-grossing film of 2010.

TOP 10 ANIMATED MOVIES OF ALL TIME

MOVIE / YEAR / WORLD GROSS

1 Toy Story 3
2010
$1,058,144,168

2 Ice Age: Dawn of the Dinosaurs
2009
$887,773,705

3 Shrek 2
2004
$880,871,036

4 Finding Nemo
2003
$864,625,978

5 Shrek the Third
2007
$791,106,665

6 The Lion King
1994
$783,841,776

7 Shrek Forever After
2010
$731,071,987

8 Up
2009
$727,079,556

9 Kung Fu Panda
2008
$633,395,021

10 The Incredibles
2004
$624,037,578

Source: IMDB-Pro

THE 10 FIRST MICKEY MOUSE CARTOONS

MOVIE	DISNEY DELIVERY DATE
1 Plane Crazy	May 15, 1928
2 Steamboat Willie	Jul 29, 1928
3 Gallopin' Gaucho	Aug 2, 1928
4 The Barn Dance	Mar 14, 1929
5 The Opry House	Mar 20, 1929
6 When the Cat's Away	May 3, 1929
7 The Plow Boy	Jun 28, 1929
8 The Barnyard Battle	Jul 2, 1929
9 The Karnival Kid	Jul 31, 1929
10 Mickey's Follies	Aug 28, 1929

Walt Disney's iconic Mickey Mouse first appeared in *Plane Crazy*, a silent film in which he copies the exploits of aviator Charles Lindbergh in an attempt to impress Minnie Mouse. *Steamboat Willie* was the first Mickey Mouse cartoon with sound. He went on to appear in some 130 movies, including a starring role in *Fantasia* (1940), while *Lend a Paw* won an Oscar in 1941. He made only occasional appearances after the 1950s, but guested in *Who Framed Roger Rabbit* (1988), *A Goofy Movie* (1995), and *Fantasia/2000* (2000).

JAPANESE SPIRIT

Japanese anime *Spirited Away* (2001) is the only non-English speaking animated movie ever to have won an Oscar. More than a decade after its release, it remains the top-grossing film in its native country's history. Global bestseller *Avatar* racked up only half of *Spirited Away*'s takings at the Japanese box office. The movie was only the second recipient of the Best Animated Feature award, which was introduced to the Oscars in 2001, when it was won by the first *Shrek* movie.

▲ *Hanks gets animated*
Motion-capture technology revolutionized the realism in animated features.

CAPTIVATING PERFORMANCE

Holiday favorite *The Polar Express* (2004) was the first fully animated feature to use motion (or performance) capture technology, a process in which the movements of live actors are recorded and then turned into an animated image. The technique has its roots in rotoscoping, in which animators traced individual frames from live-action sequences by hand. Performance capture is now a common movie technique, especially in films that combine CGI with live-action sequences, such as *The Lord of the Rings* trilogy and *Avatar*.

ANNIE ANNIVERSARY

The Annie Awards have been presented by the International Animated Film Society since 1972, and celebrate their 40th birthday in 2012. Since its inaugural year, the Winsor McKay award has been given to honor individual contributions to animation. The first of these awards went to animation pioneer brothers Max and Dave Fleischer, who brought characters such as Betty Boop and Popeye the Sailor to the big screen. More recent winners of the award have included Tim Burton, Nick Park, and Matt Groening.

▶ *Wallace and Gromit*
Three tons of plasticine were used in Nick Park's The Curse of the Were-Rabbit.

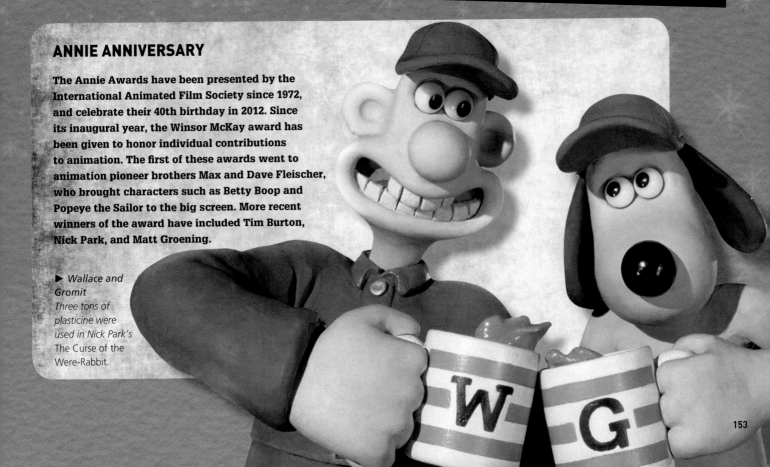

ACTORS

TOP 10 GEORGE CLOONEY MOVIES

MOVIE / YEAR

1 Ocean's Eleven 2001
2 Ocean's Twelve 2004
3 The Perfect Storm 2000
4 Ocean's Thirteen 2007
5 Batman & Robin 1997
6 Up in the Air 2009
7 Burn After Reading 2008
8 Spy Kids 2001
9 Intolerable Cruelty 2003
10 The Peacemaker 1997

TOP 10 MATT DAMON MOVIES

MOVIE / YEAR

1 The Bourne Ultimatum 2007
2 Saving Private Ryan 1998
3 Ocean's Eleven 2001
4 The Bourne Supremacy 2004
5 True Grit 2010
6 Good Will Hunting 1997
7 The Departed 2006
8 Ocean's Twelve 2004
9 The Bourne Identity 2002
10 Ocean's Thirteen 2007

▲ Matt Damon
The third movie starring Damon as Jason Bourne won all three of its Oscar nominations.

▶ Johnny Depp
Depp based his characterization of Jack Sparrow on Stones' guitarist Keith Richards.

TOP 10 JOHNNY DEPP MOVIES

MOVIE / YEAR

1 Pirates of the Caribbean: Dead Man's Chest 2006
2 Alice in Wonderland 2010
3 Pirates of the Caribbean: At World's End 2007
4 Pirates of the Caribbean: The Curse of the Black Pearl 2003
5 Charlie and the Chocolate Factory 2004
6 The Tourist 2010
7 Rango 2011
8 Public Enemies 2009
9 Sleepy Hollow 1999
10 Platoon 1986

TOP 10 **WILL SMITH MOVIES**

MOVIE / YEAR

1 Independence Day 1996
2 I Am Legend 2007
3 Men in Black 1997
4 Hancock 2008
5 Men in Black II 2002
6 Hitch 2005
7 The Pursuit of Happyness 2006
8 Shark Tale* 2004
9 I, Robot 2004
10 Bad Boys II 2003

* Voice

TOP 10 **LEONARDO DICAPRIO MOVIES**

MOVIE / YEAR

1 Titanic 1997
2 Inception 2010
3 Catch Me if You Can 2002
4 The Departed 2006
5 Shutter Island 2010
6 The Aviator 2004
7 Gangs of New York 2002
8 The Man in the Iron Mask 1998
9 Blood Diamond 2006
10 The Beach 2000

TOP 10 **BEN STILLER MOVIES**

MOVIE / YEAR

1 Meet the Fockers 2004
2 Night at the Museum 2006
3 Night at the Museum: Battle of the Smithsonian 2009
4 There's something about Mary 2000
5 Little Fokkers 2010
6 Meet the Parents 2000
7 Dodgeball: A True Underdog Story 2004
8 Tropic Thunder 2008
9 Starsky & Hutch 2004
10 Along Came Polly 2004

► *Leonardo di Caprio*
DiCaprio was the first actor that director Christopher Nolan cast in Inception.

◄ *Ben Stiller*
Visitor numbers rose 20% at the Museum of Natural History after the release of the Night at the Museum.

ACTRESSES

TOP 10 JULIA ROBERTS MOVIES

MOVIE / YEAR

1 Ocean's Eleven 2001
2 Pretty Woman 1990
3 Runaway Bride 1999
4 My Best Friend's Wedding 1997
5 Erin Brockovich 2000
6 Ocean's Twelve 2004
7 Hook 1991
8 Notting Hill 1999
9 Valentine's Day 2010
10 Sleeping with the Enemy 1991

▲ *Julia Roberts*
Roberts was the first actress to command a $20 million paycheck for a single movie.

TOP 10 CATE BLANCHETT MOVIES

MOVIE / YEAR

1 The Lord of the Rings: The Return of the King 2003
2 The Lord of the Rings: The Two Towers 2002
3 The Lord of the Rings: The Fellowship of the Ring 2001
4 Indiana Jones and the Kingdom of the Crystal Skull 2008
5 The Curious Case of Benjamin Button 2008
6 Robin Hood 2010
7 The Aviator 2004
8 The Talented Mr. Ripley 1999
9 Babel 2006
10 Elizabeth 1998

TOP 10 RACHEL WEISZ MOVIES

MOVIE / YEAR

1 The Mummy Returns 2001
2 The Mummy 1999
3 Constantine 2005
4 About a Boy 2002
5 Fred Claus 2007
6 The Lovely Bones 2009
7 Chain Reaction 1996
8 Definitely, Maybe 2008
9 Enemy at the Gates 2001
10 Runaway Jury 2003

▶ *Rachel Weisz*
The former model founded a theatrical group while a student at Cambridge, UK.

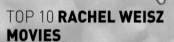

TOP 10 **CAMERON DIAZ MOVIES**

MOVIE / YEAR

1 Shrek 2* 2004
2 Shrek the Third* 2007
3 Shrek Forever After* 2010
4 Shrek* 2001
5 There's Something About Mary 1998
6 The Mask 1994
7 My Best Friend's Wedding 1997
8 Charlie's Angels 2000
9 Charlie's Angels: Full Throttle 2003
10 The Green Hornet 2011

* Voice

◄ *Cameron Diaz*
The actress's movies have earned a combined $2.6 billion in the US alone.

TOP 10 **ANGELINA JOLIE MOVIES**

MOVIE / YEAR

1 Kung Fu Panda* 2008
2 Mr. & Mrs. Smith 2005
3 Wanted 2008
4 Shark Tale* 2004
5 Salt 2010
6 The Tourist 2010
7 Lara Croft: Tomb Raider 2001
8 Gone in 60 Seconds 2000
9 Beowulf 2007
10 Alexander 2004

* Voice

TOP 10 **KEIRA KNIGHTLEY MOVIES**

MOVIE / YEAR

1 Pirates of the Caribbean: Dead Man's Chest 2006
2 Pirates of the Caribbean: At World's End 2007
3 Star Wars: Episode I – The Phantom Menace 1999
4 Pirates of the Caribbean: The Curse of the Black Pearl 2003
5 Love Actually 2003
6 King Arthur 2004
7 Atonement 2007
8 Pride and Prejudice 2005
9 Bend it Like Beckham 2003
10 The Duchess 2008

► *Keira Knightley*
Atonement featured all eight surviving World War II ambulances, and Knightley and the rest of the cast wore genuine uniforms.

DIRECTORS

▲ **Explosive success**
With The Hurt Locker, *Kathryn Bigelow became the first woman to take the Best Director Oscar.*

THE 10 LATEST BEST DIRECTOR OSCAR-WINNERS

YEAR / DIRECTOR / MOVIE

2011 Tom Hooper
The King's Speech*

2010 Kathryn Bigelow
The Hurt Locker*

2009 Danny Boyle
Slumdog Millionaire*

2008 Joel and Ethan Coen
No Country for Old Men*

2007 Martin Scorsese
The Departed*

2006 Ang Lee
Brokeback Mountain

2005 Clint Eastwood
Million Dollar Baby*

2004 Peter Jackson
The Lord of the Rings:
The Return of the King*

2003 Roman Polanski
The Pianist

2002 Ron Howard
A Beautiful Mind*

* Won Best Picture Oscar

TOP 10 MOST BANKABLE DIRECTORS

DIRECTOR / MOVIES / TOP GROSSING / AVERAGE PER MOVIE ($)

1 Lee Unkrich 4
Toy Story 3
$313,700,000

2 David Yates 3
Harry Potter 6
$296,300,000

3 Andrew Adamson 4
Shrek 2
$285,600,000

4 George Lucas 6
Star Wars
$283,400,000

5 Andrew Stanton 2
Finding Nemo
$281,800,000

6 Pete Docter 2
Up
$274,400,000

7 Kelly Asbury 2
Shrek 2
$257,300,000

8 James Cameron 9
Avatar
$212,900,000

9 John Lasseter 4
Toy Story 2
$211,100,000

10 J. J. Abrams 2
Star Trek
$195,900,000

▶ Spider-Man 3
One visual effect in the film—the birth of Sandman—took almost three years to create.

TOP 10 **DIRECTORS BY TOTAL**

	DIRECTOR	MOVIES	US BOX OFFICE ($)
1	Steven Spielberg	25	3,824,973,778
2	Robert Zemeckis	15	1,939,038,112
3	James Cameron	9	1,915,765,570
4	Ron Howard	19	1,747,233,886
5	George Lucas	6	1,698,038,621
6	Chris Columbus	14	1,670,878,041
7	Tim Burton	15	1,634,284,737
8	Michael Bay	8	1,495,552,807
9	Gore Verbinski	8	1,426,086,704
10	Peter Jackson	8	1,315,538,479

TOP 10 **DIRECTORS BY BIGGEST BUDGET**

	DIRECTOR	MOVIE	BUDGET ($)
1	Gore Verbinski	Pirates of the Caribbean: At Worlds End	300,000,000
2 =	Nathan Greno	Tangled	260,000,000
=	Byron Howard	Tangled	260,000,000
4	Sam Raimi	Spider-Man 3	258,000,000
5	David Yates	Harry Potter and the Half-Blood Prince	250,000,000
6	James Cameron	Avatar	237,000,000
7	Bryan Singer	Superman Returns	232,000,000
8	Marc Forster	Quantum of Solace	230,000,000
9	Andrew Adamson	The Chronicles of Narnia: Prince Caspian	225,000,000
10 =	Ridley Scott	Robin Hood	210,000,000
=	Michael Bay	Transformers: Revenge of the Fallen	210,000,000

Prolific Producer

Already a self-made billionaire before he started producing, Arnon Milchan has been involved in 104 movies. He has collaborated with many celebrated directors including Sergio Leone, Martin Scorsese, Ridley Scott, and Oliver Stone, and produced hits such as JFK, Pretty Woman, Free Willy, Heat, and Fight Club. His net worth is estimated at around $3.6 billion and he owns an extensive art collection.

◀ Mr. and Mrs. Smith
Arnon Milchan's top-grossing movie starred Angelina Jolie and Brad Pitt as married assassins.

ACADEMY AWARDS

TOP 10 **MOST NOMINATED MOVIES WITH NO WINS**

	MOVIE	YEAR*	NOMINATIONS
1	=The Turning Point	1977	11
	=The Colour Purple	1985	11
3	=Gangs of New York	2002	10
	=True Grit	2010	10
5	=The Little Foxes	1941	9
	=Peyton Place	1957	9
7	=Quo Vadis	1951	8
	=The Nun's Story	1959	8
	=The Sand Pebbles	1966	8
	=The Elephant Man	1980	8
	=Ragtime	1981	8
	=The Remains of the Day	1993	8

* Of release; awards made the following year

TOP 10 **MOVIES WINNING MOST AWARDS WITHOUT THE BEST PICTURE AWARD**

	MOVIE	YEAR*	AWARDS
1	Cabaret	1972	8
2	=A Place in the Sun	1951	6
	=Star Wars	1977	6
4	=Wilson	1944	5
	=The Bad and the Beautiful	1952	5
	=The King and I	1956	5
	=Mary Poppins	1964	5
	=Doctor Zhivago	1965	5
	=Who's Afraid of Virginia Woolf?	1966	5
	=Saving Private Ryan	1998	5
	=The Aviator	2004	5

* Of release; awards made the following year

▶ Million Dollar Baby
Clint Eastwood became the oldest recipient of the Best Director Oscar, at 74 years of age.

TOP 10 **BEST PICTURE WIN BOX-OFFICE BOOSTS***

	MOVIE	YEAR#	BOX-OFFICE RECEIPTS POST NOMINATION (%)
1	Million Dollar Baby	2004	56.1
2	Gandhi	1982	51.2
3	The King's Speech	2010	49.4
4	Platoon	1986	46.7
5	Chicago	2002	40.7
6	Driving Miss Daisy	1989	39.0
7	Slumdog Millionaire	2008	38.0
8	Shakespeare in Love	1998	36.5
9	Rain Man	1988	35.2
10	Schindler's List	1993	31.9

* Since 1982
# Of release; awards made the following year

THE 10 **LATEST MOVIES TO WIN THE "BIG THREE"***

MOVIE / YEAR#

1 The King's Speech 2010
2 The Hurt Locker 2009
3 Slumdog Millionaire 2008
4 No Country for Old Men 2007
5 The Departed 2006
6 The Lord of the Rings:
  The Return of the King 2003
7 A Beautiful Mind 2001
8 American Beauty 1999
9 Forrest Gump 1994
10 Schindler's List 1993

* Best Picture, Director, and Screenplay
# Of release; awards made the following year

▲ The King's Speech
*Writer David Seidler, who suffered
from a stammer in his youth, is the
oldest winner of the Best Original
Screenplay Oscar.*

THE 10 **LATEST STARS NOMINATED IN TWO ACTING CATEGORIES IN THE SAME YEAR**

ACTOR / ACTRESS	YEAR*	LEADING ROLE	SUPPORTING ROLE
1 Cate Blanchett	2007	Elizabeth: The Golden Age	I'm Not There
2 Jamie Foxx	2004	Ray#	Collateral
3 Julianne Moore	2002	Far From Heaven	The Hours
4 Emma Thompson	1993	The Remains of the Day	In the Name of the Father
5 Holly Hunter	1992	The Piano#	The Firm
6 Al Pacino	1992	Scent of a Woman#	Glengarry Glen Ross
7 Sigourney Weaver	1988	Gorillas in the Mist	Working Girl
8 Jessica Lange	1982	Frances	Tootsie#
9 Barry Fitzgerald	1944	Going My Way	Going My Way#†
10 Teresa Wright	1942	The Pride of the Yankees	Mrs. Miniver#

* Of release; awards made the following year
# Winner
† Rules have since been changed to disallow double nomination for the same performance

► Cate Blanchett
*Blanchett is the only actress to be
nominated for an Oscar for the same
role in two separate films, as Elizabeth I.*

▲ Early broadcast
NBC's first regularly scheduled broadcast featured the opening of the 1939 New York World's Fair.

THE 10 **FIRST COUNTRIES TO HAVE TELEVISION** *

COUNTRY / FIRST BROADCAST

1 UK
Nov 2, 1936

2 USSR
Dec 31, 1938

3 USA
Apr 30, 1939

4 France
Jun 29, 1949

5 Mexico
Aug 31, 1950

6 Brazil
Sep 18, 1950

7 Cuba
Oct 24, 1950

8 = Denmark
Oct 2, 1951

  = Netherlands
Oct 2, 1951

10 Argentina
Oct 17, 1951

* High-definition regular public broadcasting service

TOP 10 **TV-BUYING COUNTRIES**

COUNTRY / TVS BOUGHT PER HOUSEHOLD*

1 United Arab Emirates 4.14

2 Singapore 3.34

3 UK 2.96

4 USA 2.74

5 Australia 2.64

6 Japan 2.60

7 France 2.58

8 Chile 2.49

9 Spain 2.48

10 Greece 2.14

* In last decade   *World average 1.44*

Source: Euromonitor International

THE 10 **TOP-EARNING TV STARS**

NAME / PAY ($)

1 Oprah Winfrey
$315,000,000

2 = Dr Phil McGraw
$80,000,000

= Simon Cowell
$80,000,000

4 Ellen DeGeneres
$55,000,000

5 Ryan Seacrest
$51,000,000

6 = Judge Judy Sheindlin
$45,000,000

= David Letterman
$45,000,000

8 Conan O'Brien
$38,000,000

10 = Jay Leno
$35,000,000

= Ray Romano
$35,000,000

Source: Forbes

► Oprah
The first black billionaire's talk show has been broadcast in 140 countries over 25 seasons..

TOP 10 **TV COUNTRIES**

	COUNTRY	TV HOUSEHOLDS*
1	China	401,264,000
2	India	233,029,000
3	USA	122,463,000
4	Indonesia	72,581,000
5	Brazil	57,503,000
6	Russia	52,432,000
7	Japan	51,328,000
8	Germany	40,017,000
9	Mexico	29,770,000
10	UK	27,854,000
	Top 10 total	1,088,241,000
	World total	1,884,509,000

* 2012 forecast

Source: Euromonitor International

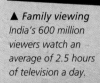

▲ **Family viewing**
India's 600 million viewers watch an average of 2.5 hours of television a day.

TOP 10 **REALITY TV SHOWS**

	SHOW	PEAK VIEWERS (%)
1	American Idol	15.1
2	Dancing with the Stars	12.9
3	The Bachelor	11.7
4	America's Got Talent	8.5
5	Survivor: Gabon	8.2
6	Amazing Race 13	6.7
7	Superstars of Dance	6.5
8	I Get That a Lot	6.4
9	Biggest Loser 7	6.3
10	Extreme Makeover	5.9

Source: Television Bureau of Advertising

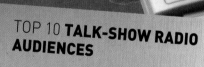

TOP 10 **TALK-SHOW RADIO AUDIENCES**

	HOST	WEEKLY LISTENERS
1	Rush Limbaugh	15,000,000
2	Sean Hannity	14,000,000
3	Glenn Beck	10,000,000
4 =	Mark Levin	8,500,000
=	Michael Savage	8,500,000
6 =	Dave Ramsey	8,000,000
=	Dr. Laura Schlessinger	8,000,000
8 =	Neal Boortz	6,000,000
=	Laura Ingraham	6,000,000
10 =	Jim Bohannon	3,750,000
=	Jerry Doyle	3,750,000
=	Mike Gallagher	3,750,000
=	Michael Medved	3,750,000
=	Doug Stephan	3,750,000

Source: *Talkers* Magazine

DVDS & GAMING

TOP 10 **DVDS, 2010**

	DVD	SALES
1	Avatar	10,156,458
2	Toy Story 3	9,935,368
3	The Twilight Saga: New Moon	7,829,939
4	The Blind Side	7,266,726
5	The Twilight Saga: Eclipse	7,133,878
6	How to Train Your Dragon	5,344,798
7	Despicable Me	5,167,066
8	Iron Man 2	5,065,079
9	The Princess and the Frog	4,514,936
10	The Hangover	4,356,314

◄ *How to Train Your Dragon*
Elephants, tigers, horses, and chihuahuas were used to record the noises of dragons.

TOP 10 **BESTSELLING DVDS OF ALL TIME**

	DVD / YEAR	SALES
1	Finding Nemo, 2003	18,500,000
2	Shrek 2, 2004	18,200,000
3	The Incredibles, 2004	15,600,000
4	Star Wars: Episode III—Revenge of the Sith, 2005	15,100,000
5	The Lord of the Rings: The Two Towers, 2002	14,750,000
6	Pirates of the Caribbean: Dead Man's Chest, 2006	14,450,000
7	Pirates of the Caribbean: At World's End, 2007	13,700,000
8	Pirates of the Caribbean: The Curse of the Black Pearl, 2003	13,300,000
9	Transformers, 2007	13,250,000
10	Cars, 2006	13,200,000

TOP 10 **VIDEO PIRACY COUNTRIES**

	COUNTRY / LOSS TO FILM INDUSTRY* ($)
1	USA $2,724,000,000
2	China $2,689,000,000
3	France $1,547,000,000
4	Mexico $1,115,000,000
5	UK $1,007,000,000
6	Russia $900,000,000
7	Japan $742,000,000
8	Spain $670,000,000
9	Germany $490,000,000
10	Thailand $465,000,000

TOP 10 **CONSOLES OF ALL TIME**

CONSOLE / RELEASE YEAR / UNITS SOLD

1 PlayStation 2
2000
141,706,748

6 Wii
2006
75,900,000

2 Nintendo DS
2004
135,580,000

7 PlayStation Portable 2004
65,660,000

3 Game Boy
1989
118,690,000

8 Nintendo Entertainment System 1983
61,910,000

4 PlayStation
1994
102,500,000

9 Xbox 360
2005
51,275,500

5 Game Boy Advance 2001
81,510,000

10 Super Nintendo Entertainment System
1990
49,100,000

▲ Call of Duty
The latest instalment of the franchise made $360 million in its first 24 hours of release.

TOP 10 **FASTEST-SELLING VIDEO GAMES**

GAME / PLATFORM	WEEKS TO REACH 5 MILLION SALES
1 Call of Duty: Black Ops — Xbox 360	1
2 = Call of Duty: Modern Warfare 2 — Xbox 360	2
= Grand Theft Auto: San Andreas — PlayStation 2	2
= Call of Duty: Black Ops — PlayStation 3	2
5 = Pokémon Diamond / Pearl — Nintendo DS	3
= Halo: Reach — Xbox 360	3
= New Super Mario Bros. — Wii	3
8 = Pokémon Heart Gold / Soul Silver — Nintendo DS	4
= Halo 3 — Xbox 360	4
= Grand Theft Auto IV — Xbox 360	4

TOP 10 **PC GAMES**

	TITLE	YEAR	SALES
1	The Sims	2000	16,080,000
2	World of Warcraft	2004	11,990,000
3	Starcraft	1998	11,320,000
4	Myst	1993	8,030,000
5	Half-Life	1998	7,850,000
6	World of Warcraft: The Burning Crusade	2007	7,420,000
7	World of Warcraft: Wrath of the Lich King	2008	6,940,000
8	RollerCoaster Tycoon	1999	5,340,000
9	Diablo II	2000	5,330,000
10	The Sims 2	2004	5,210,000

▶ Followers of Warcraft
Blizzard Entertainment's annual convention, Blizzcon, is attended by nearly 30,000 fans (of the Warcraft, Starcraft, and Diablo series).

DOWNLOADS

TOP 10 **COUNTRIES WITH THE FASTEST BROADBAND**

	COUNTRY	AVERAGE MBPS*
1	South Korea	14.0
2	Japan	8.5
3	Romania	7.0
4	Netherlands	6.3
5	Latvia	6.0
6	Czech Republic	5.4
7	Switzerland	5.3
8	= Denmark	5.0
	= Sweden	5.0
	= Canada	5.0
	= USA	5.0
	World average	*1.9*

* Megabytes per second

▲ South Korea
The top 11 fastest cities for broadband are all in South Korea, with an average peak speed of 39 megabytes per second.

TOP 10 **MOST DOWNLOADED PAID APPS***

1 Crash Bandicoot Nitro Kart 3D

2 Moto Chaser

3 Virtual Pool Online

5 Cro-Mag Rally

4 Koi Pond

6 Flick Fishing

7 Monopoly: World Edition

8 Super Monkey Ball

9 Pocket Guitar

10 iCopter

* Since launch in July 2008; all devices

TOP 10 **MOST DOWNLOADED FREE APPS***

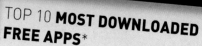

1 Facebook

2 iPint

3 Google Earth

5 PAC-MAN Lite

4 Touch Hockey: FS5

6 Labyrinth Lite

7 Lightsaber Unleashed

8 Tap Tap Revenge

9 Flashlight

10 Shazam

* Since launch in July 2008; all devices

TOP 10 **DOWNLOADED ARTISTS, 2010**

ARTIST / SALES

1 **Eminem** 15,673,000
2 **Ke$ha** 13,497,000
3 **Lady Gaga** 11,891,000
4 **Katy Perry** 11,837,000
5 **Black Eyed Peas** 11,337,000
6 **Usher** 10,717,000
7 **Glee Cast** 10,654,000
8 **Rihanna** 10,099,000
9 **Taylor Swift** 9,912,000
10 **B.o.B** 9,118,000

► *Ke$ha*
Ke$ha's debut single, "Tik Tok" reached No. 1 in 11 countries and sold nearly 13 million copies.

TOP 10 **DOWNLOADED SINGLES**

SINGLE / ARTIST / SALES*

1 **"I Gotta Feeling"** Black Eyed Peas 6,627,000
2 **"Just Dance"** Lady Gaga 5,911,000
3 **"Poker Face"** Lady Gaga 5,840,000
4 **"Low"** Flo Rider 5,781,000
5 **"Boom Boom Pow"** Black Eyed Peas 5,754,000
6 **"Tik Tok"** Ke$ha 5,483,000
7 **"I'm Yours"** Jason Mraz 5,470,000
8 **"Hey, Soul Sister"** Train 5,001,000
9 **"Apologize"** Timberland 4,880,000
10 **"Love Story"** Taylor Swift 4,853,000

* 2004–11

▲ *Kick-Ass*
After being turned down by major studios, director Matthew Vaughn independently funded the movie.

TOP 10 **PIRATED MOVIES, 2010**

MOVIE / DOWNLOADS (2010) / % OF BOX-OFFICE GROSS*

1 **Avatar** 16,580,000 / 4.5
2 **Kick-Ass** 11,400,000 / 88.9
3 **Inception** 9,720,000 / 8.8
4 **Shutter Island** 9,490,000 / 24.2
5 **Iron Man 2** 8,810,000 / 10.6
6 **Clash of the Titans** 8,040,000 / 12.2
7 **Green Zone** 7,730,000 / 61.1
8 **Sherlock Holmes** 7,160,000 / 10.3
9 **The Hurt Locker** 6,850,000 / 105.7
10 **Salt** 6,700,000 / 28.7

* Based on ticket price of $7.50

8

THE COMMERCIAL WORLD

BIRTH OF THE SUPERSTORE

Walmart Stores, Inc. was the world's largest corporation by revenue in 2010 according to the Forbes Global 2000. The chain of discount department and warehouse stores was founded by Sam Walton, who opened the first Walmart store in 1962. Ten years later, Walmart stock was offered for the first time on the New York Stock Exchange. Today—50 years after the birth of Walmart in Rogers, Arkansas—there are some 8,900 store and club locations in 15 countries, employing 2.1 million "associates," and bringing in over $400 billion in annual revenue. Thanks to Walmart, the Walton family is one of the richest in the world.

EMPLOYMENT

TOP 10 COUNTRIES WITH THE LARGEST LABOR FORCES

	COUNTRY	LABOR FORCE
1	China	776,880,961
2	India	449,888,200
3	USA	158,374,588
4	Indonesia	112,803,749
5	Brazil	99,945,055
6	Bangladesh	76,765,042
7	Russia	76,025,809
8	Japan	66,876,995
9	Pakistan	55,836,770
10	Nigeria	48,620,127

Source: World Bank

TOP 10 COUNTRIES WITH THE HIGHEST GDP PER PERSON EMPLOYED

	COUNTRY	GDP PER PERSON EMPLOYED ($)
1	USA	65,480
2	Hong Kong	58,605
3	Ireland	56,701
4	Belgium	55,448
5	France	55,052
6	Luxembourg	54,511
7	Trinidad and Tobago	53,012
8	Norway	51,736
9	UK	51,697
10	Finland	50,560
	World	16,964

Source: World Bank

▼ **China's force**
China's manufacturing workforce is twice the size of the entire G7 group of countries.

TOP 10 **US COMPANIES WITH THE MOST EMPLOYEES**

	COMPANY	EMPLOYEES
1	Wal-Mart Stores	2,100,000
2	US Postal Service	667,605
3	United Parcel Service	408,000
4	IBM	399,409
5	McDonalds	385,000
6	Target	351,000
7	Kroger	334,000
8	Sears Holdings	322,000
9	= General Electric	304,000
	= Hewlett-Packard	304,000

Source: *Fortune Global 500 2010*

THE 10 **COUNTRIES WITH THE HIGHEST PROPORTION OF CHILD WORKERS**

	COUNTRY	10–14 YEAR-OLDS AT WORK* TOTAL	%
1	Mali	726,000	51.14
2	Bhutan	136,000	51.10
3	Burundi	445,000	48.50
4	Uganda	1,343,000	43.79
5	Niger	609,000	43.62
6	Burkina Faso	686,000	43.45
7	Ethiopia	3,277,000	42.45
8	Nepal	1,154,000	42.05
9	Rwanda	413,000	41.35
10	Kenya	1,699,000	39.15
	World average	*67,444*	*11.24*

* Excludes unpaid work

Source: World Bank

TOP 10 **COMPANIES WITH THE MOST EMPLOYEES**

COMPANY* / COUNTRY / INDUSTRY / EMPLOYEES

1 **Wal-Mart Stores** / USA / Retail / 2,100,000

2 **China National Petroleum** / China / Oil and gas / 1,649,992

3 **State Grid** / China / Electricity / 1,533,800

4 **US Postal Service** / USA / Mail / 667,605

5 **Sinopec** / China / Oil and gas / 633,383

6 **Hon Hai Precision Industries** / Taiwan, China / Electronics / 611,000

7 **China Telecommunications** / China / Telecoms / 495,239

8 **Carrefour** / France / Retail / 475,976

9 **Tesco** / UK / Retail / 468,508

10 **Agricultural Bank of China** / China / Banking / 441,144

* Excludes state-owned

Source: *Financial Times FT 500 2009/Fortune Global 500 2009*

◀ *Lost childhood*
It is estimated that one in six children aged 5–14 are engaged in child labor.

TRADE

TOP 10 MOST TRADED GOODS

	CATEGORY	VALUE OF GOODS ($)	SHARE (%)
1	Fuels	1,808	14.3
2	Chemicals	1,447	11.4
3	Telecoms equipment	1,323	10.4
4	Food	987	7.8
5	Automotive products	847	6.7
6	Mining products	455	4.3
7	Iron and steel	326	2.6
8	Clothing	316	2.5
9	Textiles	211	1.7
10	Other agriculture	182	1.4

Source: World Trade Organization

TOP 10 BIGGEST PRICE INCREASES IN COMMODITIES

	COMMODITY	PRICE INCREASE* (%)
1	Iron ore	292
2	Rubber	274
3	Crude petroleum	243
4	Uranium	237
5	Copper	225
6	Natural gas	205
7	Coal	202
8	Nickel	198
9	Lead	194
10	Tin	178

* 2000–10

Source: World Trade Organization

▼ **Uranium mine**
Kazakhstan, Canada, and Australia together account for two-thirds of the world's uranium production.

TOP 10 **US IMPORTS**

PRODUCT	ANNUAL VALUE OF GOODS ($)
1 Electronics	266,612,813,477
2 Oil and gas	212,968,550,341
3 Transportation equipment	180,212,445,433
4 Chemicals	155,312,692,561
5 Heavy machinery	87,842,486,050
6 Apparel manufacturing	66,884,702,771
7 Primary metals	55,578,486,574
8 Coal	54,684,828,093
9 Fabricated metals	40,113,441,686
10 Food	36,985,946,905

Source: US Department of Commerce

TOP 10 **LEADING EXPORTERS OF COMMERCIAL SERVICES**

COUNTRY	VALUE OF SERVICES ($)	SHARE (%)
1 USA	474,000,000,000	14.1
2 UK	233,000,000,000	7.0
3 Germany	227,000,000,000	6.8
4 France	143,000,000,000	4.3
5 China	129,000,000,000	3.8
6 Japan	126,000,000,000	3.8
7 Spain	122,000,000,000	3.6
8 Italy	101,000,000,000	3.0
9 Ireland	97,000,000,000	2.9
10 Netherlands	91,000,000,000	2.7
World	*3,350,000,000,000*	*100.0*

Source: World Trade Organization

TOP 10 **LEADING IMPORTERS OF GOODS**

COUNTRY / VALUE OF GOODS ($) / SHARE (%)

1 USA
1,605,000,000,000
12.7

2 China
1,358,000,000,000
10.7

3 Germany
938,000,000,000
7.4

4 France
560,000,000,000
4.4

5 Japan
552,000,000,000
4.4

6 UK
482,000,000,000
3.8

7 Netherlands
445,000,000,000
3.5

8 Italy
413,000,000,000
3.3

9 Belgium
352,000,000,000
2.8

10 Canada
330,000,000,000
2.6

World / 12,682,000,000,000 / 100.0

Source: World Trade Organization

Personal Wealth

▶ **Mark Zuckerberg**
Dustin Moskovitz and Mark Zuckerberg are the youngest self-made billionaires in the world, having made their fortunes by establishing the social networking site Facebook. The Oscar-winning film The Social Network told the story of its formation, starring Jesse Eisenberg (background image) as Mark Zuckerberg (right).

TOP 10 **YOUNGEST AMERICAN BILLIONAIRES**

NAME / AGE / SOURCE / NET WORTH ($)*

1 Dustin Moskovitz (26)
Facebook
$2,700,000,000

2 Mark Zuckerberg (26)
Facebook
$13,500,000,000

3 Albert von Turn und Taxis (27)
Diversified
$2,000,000,000

4 Scott Duncan (28)
Pipelines
$3,100,000,000

5 Eduardo Savarin (29)
Facebook
$1,600,000,000

6 Yang Huiyan (29)
Real estate
$4,100,000,000

7 Fahd Hariri (30)
Investments
$1,600,000,000

8 Sean Parker (30)
Facebook
$1,600,000,000

9 Ayman Hariri (32)
Investments
$1,500,000,000

10 Yoshikazu Tanaka (34)
Social networking
$2,200,000,000

* Wealth calculated as of March 2011

Source: *Forbes* magazine, *The World's Billionaires 2011*

THE WORLD'S RICHEST MEN AND WOMEN

NAME / COUNTRY / COMPANY / NET WORTH ($)

MEN

1 **Carlos Slim Helu**, Mexico
Grupo Carso
$74,000,000,000

2 **William Gates III**, USA
Microsoft
$56,000,000,000

3 **Warren Buffett**, USA
Berkshire Hathaway
$50,000,000,000

4 **Bernard Arnault**, France
LVMH
$41,000,000,000

5 **Lawrence Ellison**, USA
Oracle
$39,500,000,000

WOMEN

1 **Christy Walton**, USA
Wal-Mart
$26,500,000,000

2 **Liliane Bettencourt**, France
L'Oreal
$23,500,000,000

3 **Alice L. Walton**, USA
Wal-Mart
$21,200,000,000

4 **Iris Fontbona**, Chile
Copper
$19,200,000,000

5 **Birgit Rausing**, Sweden
Tetra Laval
$14,000,000,000

Source: *Forbes* magazine, *The World's Billionaires 2011*

▲ *Liliane Bettencourt*
In 1987 the heiress established a foundation for medical, cultural, and humanitarian support.

ROCKEFELLER'S RICHES

John D. Rockefeller embodied the American dream with his rags-to-riches story. He was the founder of Standard Oil Company, which was the origin of his enormous fortune, and in 1916 he became America's first billionaire. By the time of his death his net worth had grown to $1.4 billion —an astonishing 1.53% of total American GDP. In today's terms Rockefeller's fortune is estimated to be between $400 and $600 billion, making him the wealthiest American in history.

CITIES WITH THE MOST BILLIONAIRES

The three cities in the world with most billionaires are New York (below), Moscow, and London. New York has 60 billionaires and its wealthiest resident is Michael Blomberg, who combines being mayor of the city with running his eponymous media empire, Blomberg LP. Other well-known billionaire residents include Ralph Lauren, Rupert Murdoch, and Donald Trump. Moscow is home to 50 billionaires, the wealthiest being Vladimir Lisin, chairman of Novolipetsk Steel, while London boasts 32 billionaires, including Richard Branson, Bernie Ecclestone, and Philip Green.

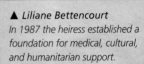

FOOD & DRINK

TOP 10 CHOCOLATE EATERS

COUNTRY / LB PER CAPITA

World average 2.4

Source (all lists):
Euromonitor International

1 UK 26.5

2 Switzerland 20.7

3 Ireland 20.5

4 Germany 17.9

5 Norway 16.5

6 Austria 16.1

7 Finland 13.0

8 Poland 12.6

9 Sweden 12.3

10 Russia 12.1

TOP 10 SEAFOOD CONSUMERS

COUNTRY / LB PER CAPITA

1 Taiwan (China) 187.2

2 Singapore 137.8

3 Malaysia 122.1

4 South Korea 110.0

5 Portugal 103.0

6 China (mainland) 76.9

7 Japan 85.1

8 Norway 81.1

9 Philippines 74.7

10 Thailand 69.9

World average 35.3

TOP 10 MEAT-EATING COUNTRIES

COUNTRY / LB PER CAPITA

1 Argentina 276.7

2 Portugal 239.4

3 Greece 237.0

4 Austria 231.7

5 Australia 224.7

6 New Zealand 214.3

7 Brazil 205.3

8 USA 186.7

9 Ireland 173.3

10 Canada 171.5

World average 83.1

TOP 10 **FRUIT JUICE DRINKERS**

COUNTRY / GALLONS PER CAPITA

1. Canada 15.9
2. Netherlands 12.7
3. UAE 12.3
4. Poland 10.0
5. Finland 9.9
6. Germany 9.2
7. Australia 8.2
8. Norway 7.9
9. USA 7.8
10. UK 7.6

World average 2.5

TOP 10 **TEA DRINKERS**

COUNTRY / CUPS PER CAPITA

1. Turkey 1,690
2. Morocco 1,160
3. Uzbekistan 998
4. Kazakhstan 924
5. Russia 888
6. Ireland 868
7. New Zealand 806
8. Iran 759
9. Egypt 689
10. UK 633

World average 191

▶ *Tea time*
Green tea with mint leaves is widely consumed throughout Morocco.

TOP 10 **TAKEOUT ORDERING COUNTRIES**

	COUNTRY	TAKEOUT ORDERS	% CHANGE IN LAST DECADE
1	Japan	2,704,738,500	-17.8
2	Italy	1,953,728,900	26.6
3	USA	1,056,722,400	4.3
4	UK	623,998,600	22.6
5	Egypt	333,837,700	29.6
6	South Korea	258,740,300	127.3
7	Thailand	185,039,000	48.8
8	Canada	157,168,800	12.9
9	Mexico	96,059,600	46.9
10	Brazil	87,498,400	11.1
	World total	7,996,500,300	10.9

TOP 10 **SPORTS AND ENERGY DRINK CONSUMERS**

COUNTRY / GALLONS PER CAPITA

1. USA 5.0
2. Denmark 4.0
3. Japan 3.2
4. Ireland 2.9
5. Australia 2.4
6. UK 2.3
7. Taiwan (China) 2.0
8. Malaysia 1.9
9. New Zealand 1.8
10. Thailand 1.7

World average 0.5

RESOURCES & ENERGY

TOP 10 ELECTRICITY-PRODUCING COUNTRIES

COUNTRY / KW/HR (2008)

1 USA
4,344,000,000,000

2 China
3,457,000,000,000

3 Japan
1,075,000,000,000

4 Russia
1,038,000,000,000

5 India
830,000,000,000

6 Canada
651,000,000,000

7 Germany
631,000,000,000

8 France
570,000,000,000

9 Brazil
463,000,000,000

10 Korea
444,000,000,000

World total 20,181,000,000,000

TOP 10 DIAMOND PRODUCERS

COUNTRY / VOLUME (CARATS)

1 Botswana
25,000,000

2 Russia
21,900,000

3 Canada
14,800,000

4 Angola
8,100,000

5 Dem. Rep. of Congo
5,400,000

6 South Africa
5,200,00

7 Guinea
2,500,000

8 Namibia
1,500,000

9 Ghana
520,000

10 Central African Republic
400,000

World total / 87,000,000

Source: The Diamond Registry

TOP 10 COAL PRODUCERS

	COUNTRY	COAL PRODUCED, 2009 (TONS)
1	China	3,275,000,000,000
2	USA	1,086,000,000,000
3	India	618,000,000,000
4	Australia	374,000,000,000
5	Indonesia	332,000,000,000
6	Russia	327,000,000,000
7	South Africa	272,000,000,000
8	Poland	149,000,000,000
9	Kazakhstan	111,000,000,000
10	Colombia	80,000,000,000
	World	*7,609,000,000,000*

Source: KWES 2010

TOP 10 GOLD-PRODUCING COUNTRIES

COUNTRY / GOLD PRODUCED, 2009 (TONS)

1 China 357.1

2 Australia 245.6

3 South Africa 242.3

4 USA 241.6

5 Russia 226.2

6 Peru 201.1

7 Indonesia 173.6

8 Canada 105.8

9 Ghana 99.5

10 Uzbekistan 82.1

World total 2,834.9

Source: Gold Fields Mineral Services Ltd, *Gold Survey 2010*

TOP 10 **COUNTRIES MOST RELIANT ON NUCLEAR ENERGY**

	COUNTRY	% NUCLEAR (2008)
1	France	77.1
2	Belgium	49.0
3	Ukraine	46.7
4	Switzerland	43.8
5	Sweden	42.6
6	Hungary	40.1
7	Korea	34.0
8	Czech Republic	30.9
9	Finland	28.8
10	Japan	24.0

Source: International Energy Agency

▶ *French power*
France is the world's largest exporter of electric power, with 58 nuclear reactors.

TOP 10 **COUNTRIES WITH THE GREATEST OIL RESERVES**

COUNTRY / PROVED RESERVES, 2009: TONS / % OF WORLD TOTAL

While world oil consumption has increased, new reserves have been progressively discovered: in 1999 the total stood at 148,500,000,000 tons, or 87% of the present level.

Saudi Arabia
40,014,000,000
19.8%

USA 4,079,000,000
2.4%

World 200,290,000,000
100.0%

Source: *BP Statistical Review of World Energy 2010*

Venezuela
27,337,000,000
12.9%

Iran
20,834,000,000
10.3%

Iraq
17,086,000,000
8.6%

Kuwait
15,432,000,000
7.6%

United Arab Emirates
14,330,000,000
7.3%

Russia
11,244,000,000
5.6%

Libya
6,393,000,000
3.3%

Kazakhstan
5,842,000,000
3.0%

Nigeria
5,512,000,000
2.8%

ENVIRONMENT

THE 10 **COUNTRIES WITH THE WORST AIR POLLUTION**

COUNTRY	PARTICULATE MATTER*
1 Uruguay	174.7
2 Sudan	165.0
3 Mali	151.9
4 Bangladesh	135.4
5 Niger	132.2
6 United Arab Emirates	127.1
7 Pakistan	120.3
8 Egypt	119.2
9 Iraq	115.2
10 Saudi Arabia	112.9

* Micrograms per cubic meter

Source: Environmental Performance Index

◀ *Pollution in Pakistan*
As urbanization in Pakistan increases, so does the level of air pollution in the cities.

THE 10 **LARGEST OIL SPILLS**

SPILL / LOCATION / YEAR / BARRELS SPILT

Source: International Tanker Owners Pollution Federation, United Nations

1
Gulf War, Persian Gulf
1991 / 5–10,000,000

2
Deepwater Horizon, Gulf of Mexico
2010 / 5,000,000

3
Ixtoc I, Gulf of Mexico
1979–80 / 3,300,000

4
Atlantic Express, Trinidad and Tobago /
1979 / 2,100,000

5
= **ABT Summer**, Angola
1991 / 1,900,000

7
Castillo de Bellver, South Africa

8
Amoco Cadiz, France
1978 / 1,600,000

9
MT Haven, Italy
1991 / 1,100,000

10
Odyssey, Canada /
1988 / 1,000,000

TOP 10 **COUNTRIES WITH THE MOST PROTECTED AREAS**

COUNTRY / TERRESTRIAL PROTECTED AREA (%)

 Venezuela / 71.3

 Brunei / 59.3

 Germany / 56.2

 Seychelles / 55.6

 Kiribati / 55.0

 Estonia / 47.8

 Belize / 44.5

Zambia / 41.1

Liechtenstein / 40.1

Tanzania / 38.8

Source: United Nations Environmental Program

TOP 10 **CAPITAL CITIES WITH THE CLEANEST AIR**

	CITY / COUNTRY	PARTICULATE MATTER*
1	Minsk, Belarus	9
2	=Paris, France	12
	=Stockholm, Sweden	12
	=Wellington, New Zealand	12
5	Cape Town, South Africa	15
6	=St. Johns, Antigua and Barbuda	16
	=Kampala, Uganda	16
8	=Luxembourg, Luxembourg	18
	=Ottawa, Canada	18
	=Caracas, Venezuela	18

* Micrograms per cubic meter

Source: World Bank

▼ *Heating Helsinki*
Around 90% of Helsinki's buildings are warmed by its district heating system, which uses excess heat from power plants, data centers, and even sewage.

TOP 10 **ECO-CITIES**

	CITY	ECO-CITY INDEX
1	Calgary, Canada	145.7
2	Honolulu, USA	145.1
3	=Ottawa, Canada	139.9
	=Helsinki, Finland	139.9
5	Wellington, New Zealand	138.9
6	Minneapolis, USA	137.8
7	Adelaide, Australia	137.5
8	Copenhagen, Denmark	137.4
9	=Kobe, Japan	135.6
	=Oslo, Norway	135.6
	=Stockholm, Sweden	135.6

Source: Mercer Quality of Living Survey

COMMUNICATIONS & NETWORKING

TOP 10 INTERNATIONAL CALLING COUNTRIES

COUNTRY / INTERNATIONAL CALL MINUTES

	COUNTRY	INTERNATIONAL CALL MINUTES
1	USA	108,879,600,000
2	Germany	13,585,600,000
3	France	11,745,400,000
4	Canada	11,665,500,000
5	UK	6,764,900,000
6	Singapore	6,077,500,000
7	Italy	5,400,200,000
8	Japan	5,305,300,000
9	United Arab Emirates	4,978,900,000
10	Spain	4,763,400,000
	World total	257,454,600,000

Source: Euromonitor International

TOP 10 CELLPHONE USERS

COUNTRY / MINUTES PER CAPITA

	COUNTRY	MINUTES PER CAPITA
1	Cyprus	3,751
2	Columbia	3,708
3	Finland	3,095
4	Austria	2,871
5	Norway	2,792
6	Iceland	2,674
7	Greece	2,618
8	UK	2,543
9	Ireland	2,461
10	South Korea	2,391

Source: Euromonitor International

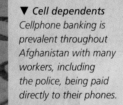

▼ **Cell dependents**
Cellphone banking is prevalent throughout Afghanistan with many workers, including the police, being paid directly to their phones.

TOP 10 CELLPHONE-DEPENDENT COUNTRIES

COUNTRY / CELLPHONE PROPORTION OF TELECOM REVENUE (%)

	COUNTRY	CELLPHONE PROPORTION OF TELECOM REVENUE (%)
1	Dem. Rep. of Congo	97.3
2	Mali	97.2
3	Mauritania	95.7
4	Sudan	93.7
5	Cameroon	93.4
6	Algeria	91.3
7	Albania	90.9
8	Afghanistan	90.7
9	Czech Republic	89.7
10	South Africa	84.8
	USA	47.9

Source: Euromonitor International

TOP 10 **YOUTUBE VIEWING COUNTRIES**

COUNTRY / AVERAGE HOURS PER MONTH

	Country	Hours			Country	Hours
1	Germany	5.2	**6**	= USA	4.3
2	Singapore	5.0		= Japan	4.3
3	Hong Kong	4.7	**8**	France	2.9
4	UK	4.5	**9**	Austria	2.7
5	Canada	4.4	**10**	Malaysia	2.3

Source: Comscore

TOP 10 **3G NETWORK COUNTRIES**

COUNTRY / % 3G

	Country	% 3G
1	South Korea	91.0
2	= Japan	75.0
	= Malaysia	75.0
4	Portugal	74.3
5	Singapore	73.5
6	Saudi Arabia	70.0
7	USA	65.0
8	= Australia	60.0
	= Canada	60.0
	= United Arab Emirates	60.0

Source: Euromonitor International

TOP 10 **COUNTRIES ON FACEBOOK**

	COUNTRY	USERS*
1	USA	146,591,880
2	Indonesia	33,920,020
3	UK	27,545,920
4	Turkey	24,788,400
5	Philippines	20,802,540
6	France	20,271,860
7	Mexico	18,830,960
8	India	18,818,720
9	Italy	17,753,040
10	Canada	16,636,880
	World total	*585,184,940*

* As of January 2011

Source: Facebook

TOP 10 **FASTEST ROLLER COASTERS**

ROLLER COASTER / THEME PARK / COUNTRY / BUILT / MAX. SPEED (MPH / KM/H)

1 **Formula Rossa**
Ferrari World Abu Dhabi, UAE, 2010
149.1 / 240.0

2 **Kingda Ka**
Six Flags Great Adventure, USA, 2005
128.0 / 206.0

3 **Top Thrill Dragster**
Cedar Point, USA, 2003
120.0 / 193.1

4 **Dodonpa**
Fiji-Q Highland, Japan, 2001
106.9 / 172.0

5 **Tower of Terror II**
Dreamworld, Australia, 1997
100.0 / 160.9

6 **Steel Dragon 2000**
Nagashima Spa Land, Japan, 2000
95.0 / 152.9

7 **Millennium Force**
Cedar Point, USA, 2000
93.0 / 149.7

8 **Intimidator 305**
Kings Dominion, USA, 2010
90.0 / 144.8

9 = **Goliath**
Six Flags Magic Mountain, USA, 2000
85.0 / 136.8

= **Phantom's Revenge**
Kennywood, USA, 1991
85.0 / 136.8

= **Titan**
Six Flags Over Texas, USA, 2001
85.0 / 136.8

Source: Roller Coaster Database

▼ *G-Force*
The Millennium Force roller coaster reaches a top speed of 93 mph (150 km/h).

TOP 10 **MOST-VISITED THEME PARKS**

	NAME	LOCATION	VISITORS
1	Magic Kingdom*	Florida, USA	17,233,000
2	Disneyland	California, USA	15,900,000
3	Tokyo Disneyland	Tokyo, Japan	13,646,000
4	Disneyland Paris	Paris, France	12,740,000
5	Tokyo Disney Sea	Tokyo, Japan	12,004,000
6	Epcot*	Florida, USA	10,990,000
7	Disney's Hollywood Studios*	Florida, USA	9,700,000
8	Disney's Animal Kingdom*	Florida, USA	9,590,000
9	Universal Studios Japan	Osaka, Japan	8,000,000
10	Everland	Gyeonggi-Do, South Korea	6,169,000

* At Walt Disney World   Source: Themed Entertainment Association

▲ *Magic Kingdom*
Based on Disneyland in Anaheim, California, the Magic Kingdom opened in 1971.

TOP 10 **COUNTRIES SPENDING THE MOST ON TOURISM**

COUNTRY / TOURISM SPENDING, 2009

1 Germany $81,200,000,000
2 USA $73,200,000,000
3 UK $50,300,000,000
4 China $43,700,000,000
5 France $38,500,000,000
6 Italy $27,900,000,000
7 Japan $25,100,000,000
8 Canada $24,200,000,000
9 Russia $20,800,000,000
10 Netherlands $20,700,000,000

Source: World Tourism Organization

TOP 10 **MOST VISITED NATIONAL PARKS IN THE USA**

	NATIONAL PARK / LOCATION	VISITORS (2010)
1	Great Smoky Mountains, North Carolina/Tennessee	9,463,538
2	Grand Canyon, Arizona	4,388,386
3	Yosemite, California	3,901,408
4	Yellowstone, Wyoming	3,640,185
5	Rocky Mountain, Colorado	2,955,821
6	Olympic, Washington	2,844,563
7	Grand Teton, Wyoming	2,669,374
8	Zion, Utah	2,665,972
9	Acadia, Maine	2,504,208
10	Cuyahoga Valley, Ohio	2,492,670

There are 58 national parks in the USA, 14 of which are also World Heritage Sites. Yellowstone was the first to be designated a national park—by President Ulysses S. Grant in 1872—and the most recent, in 2004, is Great Sand Dunes in Colorado. The most-visited, Great Smoky Mountains National Park, was established in 1934.

TOP 10 **MOST-VISITED COUNTRIES**

COUNTRY / INTERNATIONAL VISITORS*

1 France 74,200,000
2 USA 54,900,000
3 Spain 52,200,000
4 China 50,900,000
5 Italy 43,200,000
6 UK 28,000,000
7 Turkey 25,500,000
8 Germany 24,200,000
9 Malaysia 23,600,000
10 Mexico 21,500,000

* 2009 or later   Source: World Tourism Organization

9
ON THE MOVE

BLOODHOUND SSC

This year, RAF pilot Andy Green will attempt to break his current land speed record by driving *Bloodhound SSC* at over 1,000 mph (1,610 km/h). Reaching speeds faster than a bullet from a Magnum .357, the car will be powered by both a Eurofighter Typhoon jet engine and a hybrid rocket. The 18-in (46-cm) rocket will use synthetic rubber fuel with nearly a ton of concentrated hydrogen peroxide as an oxidizer. Combined, these give a total thrust of 212 kilonewtons—equivalent to the power of over 1,000 family saloon cars. Air brakes, parachutes, and friction brakes will decelerate the car, exposing Andy Green to forces similar to that of a Space Shuttle during launch and re-entry.

FASTEST ON LAND

THE 10 FIRST HOLDERS OF THE LAND SPEED RECORD

DRIVER / COUNTRY / CAR	LOCATION	DATE	SPEED* MPH	KM/H
1 Gaston de Chasseloup-Laubat (France), Jeantaud	Achères, France	Dec 18, 1898	39.24	62.78
2 Camille Jenatzy (Belgium), Jenatzy	Achères, France	Jan 17, 1899	41.42	66.27
3 Gaston de Chasseloup-Laubat, Jeantaud	Achères, France	Jan 17, 1899	43.69	69.90
4 Camille Jenatzy, Jenatzy	Achères, France	Jan 27, 1899	49.92	79.37
5 Gaston de Chasseloup-Laubat, Jeantaud	Achères, France	Mar 4, 1899	57.60	92.16
6 Camille Jenatzy, Jenatzy	Achères, France	Apr 29, 1899	65.79	105.26
7 Leon Serpollet (France), Serpollet	Nice, France	Apr 13, 1902	75.06	120.09
8 William Vanderbilt (USA), Mors	Albis, France	Aug 5, 1902	76.08	121.72
9 Henri Fournier (France), Mors	Dourdan, France	Nov 5, 1902	76.60	122.56
10 M. Augières (France), Mors	Dourdan, France	Nov 17, 1902	77.13	123.40

* Measured over 0.6 mile (1 km)

The official Land Speed Record was set and broken five times within a year. The first six holders were rival racers Comte Gaston de Chasseloup-Laubat (France) and Camille Jenatzy (Belgium). Both the *Jeantaud* and the *Jenatzy* (nicknamed *La Jamais Contente*—"Never Satisfied") were electrically powered.

THE 10 LATEST HOLDERS OF THE LAND SPEED RECORD

DRIVER / CAR / DATE / SPEED (MPH / KM/H)

1 Andy Green (UK)
ThrustSSC*
Oct 15, 1997
763.04 / 1,227.99

2 Richard Noble (UK)
Thrust2*
Oct 4, 1983
633.47 / 1,019.47

3 Gary Gabelich (USA)
The Blue Flame
Oct 23, 1970
622.41 / 995.85

4 Craig Breedlove (USA)
Spirit of America—Sonic 1
Nov 15, 1965
600.60 / 960.96

5 Art Arfons (USA)
Green Monster
Nov 7, 1965
576.55 / 922.48

6 Craig Breedlove (USA)
Spirit of America—Sonic 1
Nov 2, 1965
555.48 / 888.76

7 Art Arfons (USA)
Green Monster
Oct 27, 1964
536.71 / 858.73

8 Craig Breedlove (USA)
Spirit of America
Oct 15, 1964
526.28 / 842.04

9 Craig Breedlove (USA)
Spirit of America
Oct 13, 1964
468.7 / 749.95

10 Art Arfons (USA)
Green Monster
Oct 5, 1964
434.02 / 694.43

* Location = Black Rock Desert, Nevada, USA; all other speeds were achieved at Bonneville Salt Flats, Utah, USA; speed averaged over a measured mile in two directions

▼ **Green Monster**
Arfons' world record-holding Green Monster was actually painted red and blue.

Fastest Train Journeys

Though the Japanese JR-Maglev has achieved a speed of 361 mph (581 km/h) on a magnetic-levitation track, the fastest conventional wheeled train record goes to the French TGV. A modified TGV test unit broke the world record in April 2007 with a speed of 357.2 mph (574.8 km/h). The fastest unmodified conventional train is the Chinese CRH380A, which set a record speed of 302.0 mph (486.1 km/h) in December 2010. With an average speed of 194.2 mph (312.5 km/h), the world's fastest scheduled rail journey is the Chinese CRH Wuhan-Guangzhou High-Speed Railway.

▲ **Express service**
The China Railway High-speed (CRH) trains currently offer the fastest daily commercial train services in the world.

THE 10 LATEST HOLDERS OF THE MOTORCYCLE SPEED RECORD

	RIDER*	MOTORCYCLE	DATE	SPEED MPH	KM/H
1	Rocky Robinson	Ack Attack, dual-Suzuki-Hayabusa	Sep 25, 2010	376.36	605.70
2	Chris Carr	BUB Seven Streamliner	Sep 24, 2009	367.38	591.24
3	Rocky Robinson	Ack Attack, dual-Suzuki-Hayabusa	Sep 26, 2008	360.91	580.83
4	Chris Carr	BUB Seven Streamliner	Sep 5, 2006	350.88	564.69
5	Rocky Robinson	Ack Attack, dual-Suzuki-Hayabusa	Sep 3, 2006	342.80	551.68
6	Dave Campos	Twin 91 cu in/1,491 cc Ruxton Harley-Davidson Easyriders	Jul 14, 1990	322.15	518.45
7	Donald A. Vesco	Twin 1,016 cc Kawasaki Lightning Bolt	Aug 15, 1978	318.60	512.73
8	Donald A. Vesco	Twin 1,016 cc Kawasaki Lightning Bolt	Aug 23, 1978	315.44	507.65
9	Donald A. Vesco	1,496 cc Yamaha Silver Bird	Sep 28, 1975	302.93	487.51
10	Donald A. Vesco	Yamaha	Oct 1, 1974	281.71	453.36

* All from the USA

All the records listed here were achieved at the Bonneville Salt Flats, USA. To break a Fédération Internationale Motocycliste record, the motorcycle has to cover a measured distance, making two runs within one hour, and taking the average of the two. American Motorcycling Association records require a turnaround within two hours.

▶ **BUB Seven**
Not your everyday motorcycle, Bub Seven was driven to record-breaking speeds by Chris Carr.

AIR SPEED

THE 10 LATEST AIR SPEED RECORDS HELD BY JETS*

	PILOT(S)#	LOCATION	AIRCRAFT	DATE	SPEED† MPH	KM/H
1	Eldon W. Joersz/ George T. Morgan Jr	Beale AFB, California, USA	Lockheed SR-71A	Jul 28, 1976	2,193.167	3,529.560
2	Robert L. Stephens/ Daniel Andre	Edwards AFB, California, USA	Lockheed YF-12A	May 1, 1965	2,070.102	3,331.507
3	Georgi Mossolov, USSR	Podmoskownoe, USSR	Mikoyan E-166	Jul 7, 1962	1,665.896	2,681.000
4	Robert B. Robinson	Edwards AFB, USA	McDonnell F4H-1F Phantom II	Nov 22, 1961	1,606.509	2,585.425
5	Joseph W. Rogers	Edwards AFB, USA	Convair F-106A Delta Dart	Dec 15, 1959	1,525.924	2,455.736
6	Georgi Mossolov, USSR	Jukowski-Petrowskol, USSR	Mikoyan E-66	Oct 31, 1959	1,483.834	2,388.000
7	Walter W. Irwin	Edwards AFB, USA	Lockheed YF-104A Starfighter	May 16, 1958	1,404.012	2,259.538
8	Adrian E. Drew	Edwards AFB, USA	McDonnell F-101A Voodoo	Dec 12, 1957	1,207.635	1,943.500
9	Peter Twiss, UK	Chichester, UK	Fairey Delta Two	Mar 19, 1956	1,132.138	1,822.000
10	Horace Hanes	Palmdale, USA	F100C Super Sabre	Aug 20, 1955	822.268	1,323.312

* As of January 1, 2011
# All pilots from the USA unless otherwise stated
† Over a straight course for ground-launched only, hence excluding X-15 records

The day before Joersz and Morgan set the current world record, Adolphus Bledsoe and John T. Fuller (both USA) traveled at 2,092.294 mph (3,367.221 km/h) in their Lockheed SR-71A, but this was over a closed circuit. This record still stands today. The speed of 822.268 mph (1,323.312 km/h) achieved on August 20, 1955 by Horace A. Hanes (USA) at Palmdale, USA, in a North American F-100C Super Saber, was the first official supersonic record-holder.

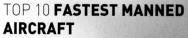

TOP 10 **FASTEST MANNED AIRCRAFT**

	AIRCRAFT	TOP SPEED (MACH)
1	X-15	6.72
2 =	SR-71 Blackbird (YF-12)	3.2
=	MiG-25R Foxbat-B	3.2
=	X-2	3.2
5	XB-70 Valkyrie	3.1
6	MiG-31 Foxhound	2.83
7	MiG-25 Foxbat (Ye-155)	2.8
8 =	F-15 Eagle	2.5
=	F-111 Aardvark	2.5
10	X-1	2.435

▲ *Ready for launch*
The X-15 was part of the USAF/NASA
X-series of experimental aircraft.

FASTEST X-15 FLIGHTS

Although some were achieved almost 50 years ago, the speeds attained by the rocket-powered X-15 and X-15A-2 aircraft in a program of 199 flights in the period 1959–68 remain the greatest ever attained by piloted vehicles in the Earth's atmosphere. They were air-launched by being released from B-52 bombers, and thus do not qualify for the official air speed record, for which aircraft must take off and land under their own power. The X-15s attained progressively greater speeds, ultimately more than double that of the now long-standing conventional air speed record, and set an unofficial altitude record during Flight No. 91 on August 22, 1963, when Joseph A. Walker piloted an X-15 to 354,200 ft (107,960 m)—some 67 miles (108 km) high.

▲ *Armstrong's X-15*
Neil Armstrong flew
over 200 different
aircraft, including seven
X-15 flights.

▲ *Flight of the Concorde*
An Anglo-French
project, Concorde
first flew in 1969 and
entered regular service
on January 21, 1976.
It was retired in 2003.

TOP 10 **FASTEST ROUTES OF CONCORDE***

	FROM	TO	DATE	SPEED MPH	KM/H
1	New York, USA	London, UK	Feb 7, 1996	1,193.08	1,920.07
2	Caracas, Venezuela	Santa Maria, Acores, Portugal	Mar 20, 1982	1,161.90	1,869.90
3	Caracas, Venezuela	Paris, France	Sep 24, 1979	1,139.46	1,833.79
4	Barbados	London, UK	Nov 24, 1977	1,134.86	1,826.38
5	Honolulu, Hawaii, USA	Guam	Oct 13, 1992	1,126.81	1,813.43
6	New York, USA	Paris, France	Oct 21, 1982	1,122.71	1,806.82
7	Rio de Janeiro, Brazil	Dakar, Senegal	Mar 29, 1982	1,114.94	1,794.32
8	Acapulco, Mexico	Honolulu, Hawaii, USA	Oct 12, 1992	1,103.41	1,775.76
9	Washington, D.C., USA	Marrakech, Morocco	Feb 12, 2000	1,100.77	1,771.52
10	Paris, France	New York, USA	Apr 1, 1981	1,095.48	1,763.00

* Based on the fastest flight made between any two cities

Source: FIA

WATER SPEED

THE 10 LATEST HOLDERS OF THE WATER SPEED RECORD—JET POWERED*

DRIVER / COUNTRY / BOAT / LOCATION / DATE	SPEED KM/H	SPEED MPH
1 Ken Warby, Australia Spirit of Australia Blowering Dam, Australia Oct 8, 1978	511.13	317.60
2 Ken Warby, Australia Spirit of Australia Blowering Dam, Australia Nov 20, 1977	463.78	288.18
3 Lee Taylor, USA Hustler Lake Guntersville, Alabama, USA Jun 30, 1967	459.02	285.22
4 Donald Campbell, UK Bluebird K7 Lake Dumbleyung, Australia Dec 31, 1964	444.71	276.33
5 Donald Campbell, UK Bluebird K7 Coniston Water, England, UK May 14, 1959	418.99	260.35
6 Donald Campbell, UK Bluebird K7 Coniston Water, England, UK Nov 10, 1958	400.12	248.62
7 Donald Campbell, UK Bluebird K7 Coniston Water, England, UK Nov 7, 1957	384.75	239.07
8 Donald Campbell, UK Bluebird K7 Coniston Water, England, UK Sep 19, 1956	363.12	225.63
9 Donald Campbell, UK Bluebird K7 Lake Mead, Nevada, USA Nov 16, 1955	347.94	216.20
10 Donald Campbell, UK Bluebird K7 Ullswater, England, UK Jul 23, 1955	325.60	202.32

* As of January 1, 2011

THE 10 **LATEST HOLDERS OF THE WATER SPEED RECORD— PROPELLER DRIVEN***

DRIVER# / BOAT / LOCATION / DATE /
SPEED (MPH / KM/H)

1 Dave Villwock,
Miss Budweiser, Lake Oroville,
California, USA / Mar 13, 2004
220.493 / 354.849

2 Russ Wicks,
Miss Freei, Lake Washington,
Washington, USA / Jun 15, 2000
205.494 / 330.711

3 Roy Duby,
Miss US1,
Lake Guntersville,
Alabama, USA
Apr 17, 1962
200.419 / 322.543

4 Bill Muncey,
Miss Thriftaway,
Lake Washington,
Washington, USA
Feb 16, 1960
192.001 / 308.996

THE 10 **LATEST HOLDERS OF THE NON-STOP ROUND THE WORLD SAILING RECORD***

SKIPPER(S) / COUNTRY	YACHT	YEAR(S)	START/FINISH	AVERAGE SPEED (KNOTS)	DAYS
1 Franck Cammas, France	Groupama 3	2010	Brest, France	18.70	48
2 Bruno Peyron, France	Orange II	2005	Brest, France	17.89	50
3 Steve Fossett, USA	Cheyenne	2004	Brest, France	15.52	58
4 Bruno Peyron, France	Orange	2002	Brest, France	13.98	64
5 Olivier De Kersauson, France	Sport Elec	1997	Brest, France	12.66	71
6 Robin Knox-Johnston, UK & Peter Blake, New Zealand	Enza	1994–95	Brest, France	12.00	74
7 Bruno Peyron, France	Commodore Explorer	1993–94	Brest, France	11.35	79
8 Titouan Lamazou, France	Ecureuil D'Aquitaine II	1989–90	Sables D'Olonnes, France	8.23	109
9 Dodge Morgan, USA	American Promise	1985–86	St. George's, Bermuda	7.07	150
10 John Ridgway, UK	English Rose V	1983–84	Ardmore, Scotland	6.48	193

* Eastbound; as of January 1, 2011

Source: World Sailing Speed Record Council

5 Jack Regas,
Hawaii Kai III,
Lake Washington,
Washington, USA
Nov 30, 1957
187.627 / 301.956

6 Art Asbury,
Canada,
Miss Supertest II,
Lake Ontario,
Canada
Nov 1, 1957
184.540 / 296.988

7 Stanley Sayres
and Elmer
Leninschmidt,
Slo-Mo-Shun IV,
Lake Washington,
Washington, USA
Jul 7, 1952
178.497 / 287.263

8 Stanley Sayres
and Ted Jones,
Slo-Mo-Shun IV,
Lake Washington,
Washington, USA
Jun 26, 1950
160.323 / 258.015

9 Malcolm
Campbell, UK,
Bluebird K4,
Coniston Water,
England, UK
Aug 19, 1939
141.740 / 228.108

10 Malcolm
Campbell, UK,
Bluebird K3,
Hallwiler See,
Switzerland
Aug 17, 1938
130.910 / 210.679

* As of January 1, 2011
# All from USA unless otherwise stated

ROAD & RAIL

VW vehicles
The 1.9 sq mile (5 sq km) Wolfsburg plant in Germany—producer of the ever-popular VWs, uses 1,500 tons of sheet metal each day.

TOP 10 **MOTOR-VEHICLE MANUFACTURERS**

MANUFACTURER	MAIN COUNTRY OF PRODUCTION	VEHICLES (2009)
1 Toyota	Japan	7,234,439
2 General Motors	China	6,459,053
3 Volkswagen	Germany	6,067,208
4 Ford	USA	4,685,394
5 Hyundai	South Korea	4,645,776
6 PSA	France	3,042,311
7 Honda	Japan	3,012,637
8 Nissan	Japan	2,744,562
9 Fiat	Italy	2,460,222
10 Suzuki	India	2,387,537

Source: International Organization of Motor Vehicle Manufacturers

TOP 10 **COUNTRIES WITH THE LONGEST ROAD NETWORKS**

COUNTRY	TOTAL ROAD NETWORK MILES	KM
1 USA	4,042,768	6,506,204
2 China	2,226,817	3,583,715
3 India	2,063,207	3,320,410
4 Brazil	1,088,560	1,751,868
5 Japan	747,992	1,203,777
6 Canada	647,655	1,042,300
7 France	638,262	1,027,183
8 Russia	584,089	940,000
9 Australia	505,157	812,972
10 Spain	423,339	681,298

Source: CIA, *The World Factbook 2010*

▶ *Driving high*
Shanghai's 7,252 miles (11,671 km) of highway include six elevated roads through the city center.

TOP 10 **LONGEST RAIL NETWORKS**

COUNTRY	LENGTH MILES	KM
1 USA	140,695	226,427
2 Russia	54,157	87,157
3 China	48,364	77,834
4 India	39,777	64,015
5 Canada	29,011	46,688
6 Germany	26,033	41,896
7 Australia	23,522	37,855
8 Argentina	19,517	31,409
9 France	18,152	29,213
10 Brazil	17,931	28,857

► **Cargo carriers**
Just 15% of the rail network in the United States is used for passenger journeys.

TOP 10 **BUSIEST UNDERGROUND RAILWAY NETWORKS**

CITY / PASSENGERS PER ANNUM (2010)*

1 Tokyo
Japan
3,160,000,000

2 Moscow
Russia
2,392,000,000

3 Seoul
South Korea
2,048,000,000

4 New York
USA
1,579,000,000

5 Paris
France
1,479,000,000

6 Beijing
China
1,457,000,000

7 Mexico City,
Mexico
1,414,000,000

8 Hong Kong
China
1,323,000,000

9 Shanghai
China
1,300,000,000

10 London
UK
1,090,000,000

* Or latest year for which figures available

TOP 10 **BUSIEST NEW YORK SUBWAY STATIONS**

STATION	PASSENGERS (2009)
1 Times Square– 42 Street	58,099,000
2 34 Street–Penn	51,378,000
3 Grand Central– 42 Street	42,003,000
4 34 Street– Herald Square	36,946,000
5 14 Street– Union Square	34,245,000
6 59 Street– Columbus Circle	20,419,000
7 Lexington Avenue	18,924,000
8 86 Street	18,892,000
9 Fulton Street Interchange	18,846,000
10 Lexington Avenue– 53 Street	18,618,000

Source: Metropolitan Transport Authority

AIR & WATER

THE 10 FIRST ROUND-THE-WORLD FLIGHTS

	PILOT(S) / AIRCRAFT	ROUTE (START/ END LOCATION)	TOTAL DISTANCE		DATES
			MILES	KM	
1	**Lt. Lowell H. Smith/Lt. Leslie P. Arnold** (USA) Douglas World Cruiser, Chicago	Seattle, Washington, USA	26,345	42,398	Apr 6–Sep 28, 1924
2	**Lt. Erik H. Nelson/Lt. John Harding Jr** (USA) Douglas World Cruiser, New Orleans	Seattle, Washington, USA	27,553	44,342	Apr 6–Sep 28, 1924
3	**Dr. Hugo Eckener, Ernst Lehmann and crew** (Germany), Airship, Graf Zeppelin	Lakehurst, New Jersey, USA	20,373	37,787	Apr 8–29, 1929
4	**Wiley Post and Harold Gatty** (USA) Lockheed Vega, Winnie Mae	Roosevelt Field, Long Island, USA	15,474	24,903	Jun 23–Jul 1, 1931
5	**Wolfgang von Gronau, Ghert von Roth, Franz Hack, Fritz Albrecht** (Germany) Dornier seaplane, Grönland-Wal D-2053	List, Germany	27,240	44,000	Jul 22–Nov 23, 1932
6	**Wiley Post** (USA) Lockheed Vega, Winnie Mae (first solo)	Floyd Bennett Field, New York, USA	15,596	25,093	Jul 15–22, 1933
7	**Howard Hughes, Lt. Thomas Thurlow, Henry P. McClean Conner, Richard Stoddart, Eddie Lund** (US), Lockheed 14, New York World's Fair 1939	Floyd Bennett Field, New York, USA	14,672	23,612	Jul 10–14, 1938
8	**= Clifford Evans** (USA) Piper PA-12, City of Washington	Teterboro, New, Jersey, USA	25,162	40,494	Aug 9–Dec 10, 1947
	= George Truman (USA) Piper PA-12, City of the Angels	Teterboro, New, Jersey, USA	25,162	40,493	Aug 9–Dec 10, 1947
10	**Capt. James Gallagher and crew of 13** (USA) Boeing B-50A, Lucky Lady II (first nonstop circumnavigation with inflight refueling)	Fort Worth, Texas, USA	23,452	37,742	Feb 26–Mar 2, 1949

TOP 10 LONGEST WINGSPAN POWERED AIRCRAFT

	AIRCRAFT / MAX. TAKEOFF WEIGHT	WINGSPAN		
		FT	IN	M
1	H-4 Hercules "Spruce Goose" 400,000 lb/180,000 kg	319	11	97.5
2	Antonov An-225 Mriya 1,322,773 lb/640,000 kg	290	2	88.4
3	Airbus A380-800F 1,300,700 lb/590,000 kg	261	8	79.8
4	Antonov An-124 Rusian 892,872 lb/405,000 kg	240	5	73.3
5	Convair B-36 Peacemaker 410,000 lb/190,000 kg	230	0	70.1
6	Bristol 167 Brabazon 290,000 lb/ 130,000 kg	229	11	70.0
7	Boeing 747-8 975,000 lb/442,000 kg	224	7	68.5
8	Lockheed C-5 Galaxy 840,000 lb/381,000 kg	222	9	67.3
9	Saunders-Roe SR45 Princess 345,025 lb/156,500 kg	219	6	66.9
10	Boeing 777-300ER 775,000 lb/351,534 kg	212	7	64.8

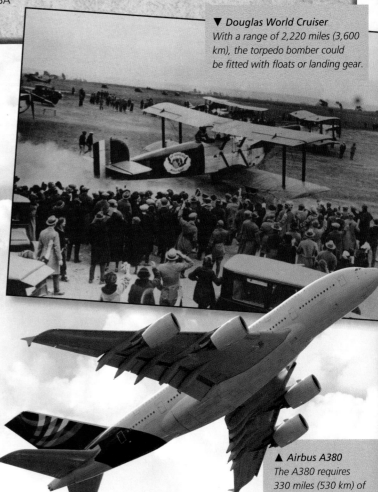

▼ **Douglas World Cruiser**
With a range of 2,220 miles (3,600 km), the torpedo bomber could be fitted with floats or landing gear.

▲ **Airbus A380**
The A380 requires 330 miles (530 km) of wiring and 950 gallons (3,600 liters) of paint.

TOP 10 BUSIEST AIRPORTS

	AIRPORT	PASSENGERS, 2008	CODE
1	ATLANTA, USA	88,032,086	ATL
2	LONDON HEATHROW, UK	66,037,578	LHR
3	BEIJING, CHINA	65,372,012	PEK
4	CHICAGO, USA	64,158,343	ORD
5	TOKYO, JAPAN	61,903,656	HND
6	PARIS, FRANCE	57,906,866	CDG
7	LOS ANGELES, USA	56,520,843	LAX
8	DALLAS/FORT WORTH, USA	56,030,457	DFW
9	FRANKFURT, GERMANY	50,932,840	FRA
10	DENVER, USA	50,167,485	DEN

Source: Airports Council International

TOP 10 LARGEST MOTOR YACHTS

	YACHT NAME	LAUNCH YEAR	FT	LENGTH IN	M
1	Eclipse	2010	557	0	169.8
2	Dubai	2006	531	5	162.0
3	Al Salamah	1999	456	10	139.2
4	Rising Sun	2004	454	1	138.4
5	Al Mirqab	2008	436	4	133.0
6	Octopus	2003	414	0	126.2
7	Savarona	1931	408	0	124.4
8	Crystal	2010	406	10	124.0
9	Alexander	1965	400	2	122.0
10	A	2008	390	4	119.0

Source: *Power & Motoryacht 2010*

▶ **Eclipse**
Roman Abramovich's fifth yacht can house 62 guests with 50 crew, and features two helicopter pads and a mini-submarine.

TOP 10 LONGEST SHIP CANALS

	CANAL / COUNTRY	OPENED	LENGTH MILES	KM
1	Grand Canal, China	AD 283*	1,114	1,795
2	Erie Canal, USA	1825	363	584
3	Göta Canal, Sweden	1832	240	386
4	St. Lawrence Seaway, Canada/USA	1959	180	290
5	Canal du Midi, France	1692	149	240
6	Main-Danube, Germany	1992	106	171
7	Suez, Egypt	1869	101	162
8 =	Albert, Belgium	1939	80	129
=	Moscow-Volga, Russia	1937	80	129
10	Volga-Don, Russia	1952	63	101

* Extended from AD 605–10 and rebuilt between 1958–72

◀ **Göta Canal**
The Göta Canal in Sweden links Gothenburg on the west coast to Söderköping on the Baltic.

Marine Disasters

THE 10 WORST PEACETIME MARINE DISASTERS

SHIP / LOCATION / DATE   ESTIMATED NO. KILLED

▲ *Doomed ships*
The Doña Paz (above left) at anchor in the Philippines, and Titanic (above) leaving port on her fateful maiden voyage.

1 MV Doña Paz
Tabias Strait, Philippines, Dec 20, 1987   >4,000
The ferry *Doña Paz* was struck by oil tanker MT *Vector*. The official death toll was 1,749, but the *Doña Paz* was overcrowded, some sources claiming a total of 4,341.

2 SS Kiangya
Off Shanghai, China, Dec 4, 1948   2,750–3,920
The overloaded passenger steamship *Kiangya*, carrying Chinese refugees, is believed to have struck a Japanese mine. An estimated 700–1,000 survivors were rescued by other vessels.

3 MV Le Joola
Off The Gambia, Sep 26, 2002   >1,863
The overcrowded Senegalese ferry capsized in a storm.

4 Tek Sing
Gaspar Strait, Indonesia, Feb 6, 1822   1,600
The large Chinese junk laden with migrant Chinese workers ran aground and sank.

5 Sultana
Mississippi River, USA, Apr 27, 1865   1,547
A boiler on the Mississippi paddleboat *Sultana* exploded and the vessel sank. As it occurred soon after the assassination of President Abraham Lincoln, it received little press coverage.

6 RMS Titanic
North Atlantic, Apr 15, 1912   1,517
The most famous marine disaster of all, the *Titanic*— the world's largest liner—sank on her maiden voyage after striking an iceberg.

7 Toya Maru   1,159
Tsugaru Strait, Japan, Sep 26, 1954
The Japanese ferry sank in a typhoon, between Hokkaido and Honshu islands, with an estimated 150 rescued.

8 SS General Slocum
New York, USA, Jun 15, 1904   1,021
The excursion steamship caught fire in the East River, New York, with many victims burned or drowned.

9 MS al-Salam Boccaccio 98
Red Sea, Feb 3, 2006   1,018
The Egyptian car ferry sank following a fire on board.

10 RMS Empress of Ireland
Saint Lawrence River, Canada, May 29, 1914   1,012
The Royal Mail ship was struck by Norwegian collier SS *Storstad*, resulting in Canada's worst-ever marine disaster.

WARTIME MARINE DISASTERS

Recent assessments of the death tolls in some World War II marine disasters means that the sinking of the *Doña Paz* would only feature at No. 10 in an overall list of marine disasters. The worst recorded wartime marine disaster—and the greatest loss of life resulting from the sinking of one vessel in maritime history—is the German liner *Wilhelm Gustloff*. The ship was torpedoed by the Soviet submarine *S-13* off Gdansk, Poland, on January 30, 1945 while laden with evacuated civilian refugees and military personnel, resulting in an estimated 9,400 dead.

"THE SHIP THAT COULDN'T SINK"

2012 marks the 100th anniversary of RMS *Titanic*'s first and last voyage. The "unsinkable" luxury cruise liner—the largest passenger ship in the world at the time—was approximately two-thirds of the way across the Atlantic when she struck an iceberg on April 14, 1912, and sank in the early hours of the next day, resulting in the deaths of 1,517 of the 2,227 people on board. The ship had received multiple iceberg warnings throughout the day.

April 14, 1912, 11.04pm Lookout Frederick Fleet telephones the ship's bridge with the news, "Iceberg, right ahead!" First Officer Murdoch gives the order to turn and stop, but the *Titanic*'s right side scrapes the iceburg and the ship begins to flood.

April 15, 12.05am Captain Smith orders his crew to prepare the lifeboats.

12.25am The captain orders that the lifeboats be loaded with "women and children first." *Titanic*'s distress signal is received by the ship *Carpathia*.

12.45am The first lifeboat is launched and the first distress rocket is fired. Over the next hour and a half, 18 lifeboats carrying just over 700 passengers are launched, but many are only partly full.

2.05am The *Titanic*'s huge bronze propellers begin to rise above the waterline.

2.20am Minutes after the electrical power fails, the *Titanic* splits in half and—two hours and 40 minutes after the initial collision—the "unsinkable" ship sinks.

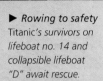

▶ *Rowing to safety*
Titanic's survivors on lifeboat no. 14 and collapsible lifeboat "D" await rescue.

THE ONES WHO SURVIVED

At approximately 4.10am on April 15, 1912, the *Carpathia* picked up the first of the *Titanic*'s lifeboats. Had the lifeboats been filled to capacity, all 534 women and children on board could have been saved, with enough room left over for an additional 644 men. From a total of 2,227 people aboard the *Titanic*, however, only 706—less than a third—survived. The last of the survivors, Millvina Dean, who was just nine weeks old at the time of the disaster, died in June 2009 at the age of 97.

TITANIC DRAMA

The sinking of the *Titanic* has been the subject of many films and TV movies, the first of which was made the very same year of the disaster. Costing approximately $200 million, James Cameron's 1997 epic love story *Titanic* is probably the most famous, and became one of the highest-grossing movies in history.

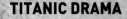

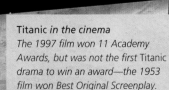

Titanic in the cinema
The 1997 film won 11 Academy Awards, but was not the first Titanic drama to win an award—the 1953 film won Best Original Screenplay.

AIR DISASTERS

THE 10 FIRST POWERED AIRCRAFT FATALITIES

	VICTIM	NATIONALITY	LOCATION	DATE
1	Lt. Thomas Etholen Selfridge	American	Fort Myer, USA	Sep 17, 1908
2	Eugène Lefèbvre	French	Juvisy, France	Sep 7, 1909
3	Ferdinand Ferber	French	Boulogne, France	Sep 22, 1909
4	Ena Rossi	Italian	Rome, Italy	Sep 22, 1909
5	Antonio Fernandez	Spanish	Nice, France	Dec 6, 1909
6	Léon Delagrange	French	Croix d'Hins, France	Jan 4, 1910
7	Hubert Le Blon	French	San Sebastián, Spain	Apr 2, 1910
8	Hauvette Michelin	French	Lyons, France	May 13, 1910
9	Aindan de Zoseley	Hungarian	Budapest, Hungary	Jun 2, 1910
10	Thaddeus Robl	German	Stettin, Germany	Jun 18, 1910

Although there had been many fatalities in the early years of ballooning and among pioneer parachutists, it was not until 1908 that anyone was killed in an airplane. On September 17, at Fort Myer, Virginia, Orville Wright was demonstrating his Type A *Flyer*. On board was a passenger, 26-year-old Lieutenant Thomas Etholen Selfridge of the Army Signal Corps. At a height of just 75 ft (23 m), one of the propellers struck a wire, sending the plane out of control. It crash-landed, injuring Wright and killing Lt. Selfridge, who thus became powered flying's first victim.

TOP 10 MOST FATAL PHASES OF COMMERCIAL FLIGHT

	PHASE	% OF FATAL ACCIDENTS*
1	Landing	21
2	= Final approach	13
	= Taxi, load and unload	13
4	Takeoff	12
5	Initial approach	11
6	Initial climb	9
7	Cruise (second half)	6
8	= Climb	4
	= Descent	4
	= Cruise (first half)	4

* 2000–09

Source: Boeing

The Worst Air Show Crashes

In front of an audience of 300,000 in Ramstein, Germany, on August 28, 1988, a midair collision occurred (pictured), which claimed the lives of 67 spectators and three pilots. Aircraft of the Italian Air Force display team, Frecce Tricolori, crashed on to the runway and tumbled into the spectator area. The deadliest incident occurred at Syknyliv airfield, Ukraine, on July 27, 2002, when a failed low-altitude rolling maneuver claimed the lives of 77 people. Both pilots ejected to safety and were sentenced to a combined 22 years in prison.

THE 10 **WORST AIR DISASTERS IN THE WORLD**

LOCATION / DATE / INCIDENT   NO. KILLED

1 New York, USA, Sep 11, 2001   c. 1,622
Following a hijacking by terrorists, an American Airlines Boeing 767 was deliberately flown into the North Tower of the World Trade Center, killing all 81 passengers (including five hijackers), 11 crew on board, and an estimated 1,530 on the ground.

2 New York, USA, Sep 11, 2001   c. 677
As part of the coordinated attack, hijackers commandeered a second Boeing 767 and crashed it into the South Tower of the World Trade Center, killing all 56 passengers and nine crew on board, and approximately 612 on the ground.

3 Tenerife, Canary Islands, Mar 27, 1977   583
Two Boeing 747s (PanAm and KLM, carrying 380 passengers and 16 crew, and 234 passengers and 14 crew respectively) collided and caught fire on the runway of Los Rodeos airport after the pilots received incorrect instructions from the control tower.

4 Mt Osutaka, Japan, Aug 12, 1985   520
A JAL Boeing 747 on an internal flight from Tokyo to Osaka crashed, killing all but four of the 509 passengers and all 15 crew.

5 Charkhi Dadri, India, Nov 12, 1996   349
A Saudi Arabian Airlines Boeing 747 collided with a Kazakh Airlines Ilyushin IL 76 cargo aircraft on its descent and exploded, killing all 312 (289 passengers and 23 crew) on the Boeing and all 37 (27 passengers and 10 crew) on the Ilyushin.

6 Paris, France, Mar 3, 1974   346
Immediately after takeoff for London, a Turkish Airlines DC-10 suffered an explosive decompression when a door burst open, and crashed at Ermenonville, north of Paris, killing all aboard.

7 Off the Irish coast, Jun 23, 1985   329
An Air India Boeing 747 on a flight from Vancouver to Delhi exploded in midair, probably as a result of a terrorist bomb, killing all 307 passengers and 22 crew.

8 Riyadh, Saudi Arabia, Aug 19, 1980   301
Following an emergency landing a Saudia (Saudi Arabian) Airlines Lockheed TriStar caught fire. The crew was unable to open the doors and all on board died from smoke inhalation.

9 Off the Iranian coast, Jul 3, 1988   290
An Iran Air A300 airbus was shot down in error by a missile fired by the USS *Vincennes*, resulting in the deaths of all 274 passengers and 16 crew.

10 Sirach Mountain, Iran, Feb 19, 2003   275
An Ilyushin 76 on a flight from Zahedan to Kerman crashed into the mountain in poor weather. It was carrying 257 Revolutionary Guards and a crew of 18, none of whom survived.

THE 10 **WORST AIRSHIP DISASTERS**

LOCATION / DATE / INCIDENT   NO. KILLED

1 Coast off New Jersey, USA, Apr 4, 1933   73
US Navy airship *Akron* crashed into the sea in a storm, leaving only three survivors.

2 Over the Mediterranean, Dec 21, 1923   52
French airship *Dixmude* is assumed to have been struck by lightning, broke up, and crashed into the sea.

3 Near Beauvais, France, Oct 5, 1930   50
British airship *R101* crashed into a hillside leaving 48 dead, with two dying later, and six survivors.

4 Coast off Hull, UK, Aug 24, 1921   44
Airship *R38* broke in half on a training and test flight.

5 Lakehurst, New Jersey, USA, May 6, 1937   36
German Zeppelin *Hindenburg* caught fire when mooring. Remarkably, 62 survived the blaze.

6 Hampton Roads, Virginia, USA, Feb 21, 1922   34
Roma, an Italian airship bought by the US Army, hit power lines and crashed, killing all but 11 men on board.

7 Berlin, Germany, Oct 17, 1913   28
The first air disaster with more than 20 fatalities, German airship *LZ18* crashed after engine failure and an explosion during a test flight at Berlin-Johannisthal.

8 Baltic Sea, Mar 30, 1917   23
German airship *SL9* was struck by lightning on a flight from Seerappen to Seddin and crashed into the sea.

9 Mouth of the River Elbe, Germany, Sep 3, 1915   19
German airship *L10* was struck by lightning and plunged into the sea.

10 Coast off Barnegat City, New Jersey, USA, Jul 6, 1960   18
Largest-ever non-rigid airship US Navy *Goodyear ZPG-3W* crashed into the sea. There were three survivors.

▼ *Charkhi Dadri*
Airborne Collision Avoidance Systems are now compulsory after the deadliest midair collision in history.

10
SPORT

100 METERS WORLD RECORD CENTENARY

On July 6, 1912, on the opening day of the men's 100 meters competition at the Stockholm Olympics, Philadelphia-born Don Lippincott became the first man to be recognized by the IAAF as the official holder of the world 100 meters record. Electronic timing was being used for the first time at the 1912 Olympic Games, and Lippincott won his heat in 10.6 seconds, a record not surpassed until 1920. The first man to run it in under 10 seconds was American Jim Hines, with a personal best of 9.95 on October 14, 1968, a record which stood for 15 years. The current holder, Usain Bolt, ran 9.58 seconds in Berlin on August 16, 2009. This beat his previous record by over a tenth of a second—the largest margin of improvement since electronic timing was introduced.

Olympics 2012

TOP 10 MOST SUCCESSFUL HOST NATIONS AT THE SUMMER OLYMPICS*

	HOST	YEAR	GOLD	SILVER	BRONZE	TOTAL
1	USA	1904	78	84	82	244
2	USSR	1980	80	69	46	195
3	USA	1984	83	60	30	173
4	Great Britain	1908	56	51	39	146
5	USA	1932	41	32	30	103
6 =	France	1900	26	41	34	101
=	USA	1996	44	32	25	101
8	China	2008	51	21	28	100
9	Germany	1936	33	26	30	89
10	Sweden	1912	24	24	17	65

* Based on total medals won

▼ *China goes gold*
China dominated the 2008 diving events, winning seven gold medals.

Canada in 1976 is the only host nation not to have won a gold medal. They won five silver and six bronze medals. Mexico in 1968 won a record low number of medals by a host nation when they took just three gold, three silver, and three bronze medals for a total of nine.

AUSTERE OLYMPICS

Because the 1948 Olympics were the first Games after World War II, and rationing was still in place in Britain, they became known as the Austerity Games.

	COUNTRY	GOLD	SILVER	BRONZE	TOTAL
1	USA	38	27	19	84
2	Sweden	17	11	18	46
3	France	11	6	15	32
4	Italy	9	12	10	31
5	Hungary	10	5	13	28
6	Great Britain	4	16	7	27

LONDON OLYMPICS 1908

Thanks to the 1908 London Olympics, the current distance of 26 miles 385 yards for the marathon was established. Scheduled for 26 miles from Windsor Park to the White City stadium, the finish line was moved back 385 yards so the race would finish in front of the royal box. And it was the marathon that produced high drama when Dorando Pietri (Italy) who, near total collapse at the end of the race, was helped over the line—only to be disqualified.

▼ *Olympic aquatics*
The 2012 Aquatics Centre at the Olympic Park in Stratford houses two 50-m pools.

LONDON OLYMPICS 2012

When it staged the 1908 and 1948 Olympics, London became the second city after Paris to host two Summer Games. In 2012 it will become the first city to host the world's greatest sporting event for a third time.

Voting for the 2012 Olympics Nine cities originally submitted applications to host the 2012 Summer Olympics: Havana (Cuba), Istanbul (Turkey), Leipzig (Germany), London (England), Madrid (Spain), Moscow (Russia), New York (USA), Paris (France), and Rio de Janeiro (Brazil). On May 18, 2004 the IOC Executive Board selected the five candidates: London, Madrid, Moscow, New York, and Paris. The final decision on who should host the Games was made at the 117th IOC Session in Singapore on July 6, 2005. The voting went as follows:

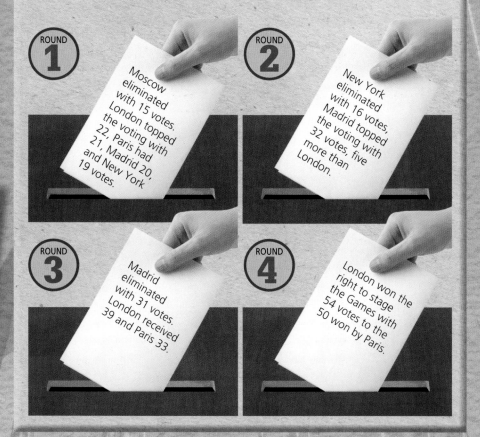

ROUND **1**
Moscow eliminated with 15 votes. London topped the voting with 22, Paris had 21, Madrid 20, and New York 19 votes.

ROUND **2**
New York eliminated with 16 votes, Madrid topped the voting with 32 votes, five more than London.

ROUND **3**
Madrid eliminated with 31 votes. London received 39 and Paris 33.

ROUND **4**
London won the right to stage the Games with 54 votes to the 50 won by Paris.

THE 10 **LATEST SUMMER OLYMPIC HOST CITIES**

2012 London, England
2008 Beijing, China **2004** Athens, Greece,
2000 Sydney, Australia **1996** Atlanta, USA
1992 Barcelona, Spain **1988** Seoul, South Korea **1984** Los Angeles, USA
1980 Moscow, Russia
1976 Montreal, Canada

LONDON 2012 FACTFILE

Costs It is estimated that it will cost between $11–13 billion to host the 2012 Games. **The site area** The new 80,000-capacity Olympic Stadium in Stratford will host the athletics events, and opening and closing ceremonies. **Competing nations** Over 10,000 athletes from 205 nations will be competing in 26 sports. **The torch** The Olympic torch arrives in Britain on May 18, 2012 and goes around the country before reaching the Olympic Stadium on July 27.

ATHLETICS

TOP 10 FASTEST MEN OVER 100 METERS*

ATHLETE / COUNTRY / VENUE / DATE

TIME (SECS)

1 **Usain Bolt**, Jamaica
Berlin, Germany
Aug 16, 2009
9.58

2 **Tyson Gay**, USA
Shanghai, China
Sep 20, 2009
9.69

3 **Asafa Powell**, Jamaica
Lausanne, Switzerland
Sep 2, 2008
9.72

4 **Nesta Carter**, Jamaica
Rieti, Italy
Aug 29, 2010
9.78

5 **Maurice Greene**, USA
Athens, Greece
Jun 16, 1999
9.79

6 = **Donovan Bailey**, Canada   = **Bruny Surin**, Canada
Atlanta, USA   Seville, Spain
Jul 27, 1996   Aug 22, 1999
9.84

8 = **Justin Gatlin**, USA   = **Olusoji A. Fasuba**, Nigeria   = **Leroy Burrell**, USA
Athens, Greece   Doha, Qatar   Lausanne, Switzerland
Aug 22, 2004   May 12, 2006   Jul 6, 1994
9.85

> When Usain Bolt set a new world record in the 100 meters final at the 2009 World Championships, he broke his own world record of 9.69 seconds, which he set in Beijing exactly one year earlier, on August 16, 2008. The first IAAF 100 meters record is credited to Don Lippincott of the USA, who ran a time of 10.6 seconds in his heat at the 1912 Stockholm Olympic Games.

* Based on the fastest time achieved by each man; as of January 1, 2011

Source: IAAF

THE 10 LATEST HOLDERS OF THE MEN'S WORLD MILE RECORD*

HOLDER / COUNTRY / WHERE SET	TIME (MIN:SEC)	DATE SET
1 Hicham El Guerrouj, Morocco Rome, Italy	3:43.13	Jul 7, 1999
2 Noureddine Morceli, Algeria Rieti, Italy	3:44.39	Sep 5, 1993
3 Steve Cram, UK Oslo, Norway	3:46.32	Jul 27, 1985
4 Sebastian Coe, UK Brussels, Belgium	3:47.33	Aug 28, 1981
5 Steve Ovett, UK Koblenz, Germany	3:48.40	Aug 26, 1981
6 Sebastian Coe, UK Zürich, Switzerland	3:48.53	Aug 19, 1981
7 Steve Ovett, UK Oslo, Norway	3:48.8	Jul 1, 1980
8 Sebastian Coe, UK Oslo, Norway	3:48.95	Jul 17, 1979
9 John Walker, New Zealand Gothenburg, Sweden	3:49.4	Aug 12, 1975
10 Filbert Bayi, Tanzania Kingston, Jamaica	3:51.0	May 17, 1975

* As of January 1, 2011

Source: IAAF

◀ *Hicham El Guerrouj*
Two-time Olympic champion Hicham El Guerrouj also broke the 1500 and 2000 m records.

Longstanding Long-jump Records

When American Bob Beamon's staggering long jump of 8.90 meters at the 1968 Olympics in Mexico City, Mexico, bettered the old world record by a mammoth margin of more than 21.5 in (55 cm), it was a record that seemed likely to stand for a long time. And in fact it was nearly 23 years before Mike Powell of the USA broke the world record in August 1991. However, going into the 2012 London Olympics, Beamon's jump still stands as an Olympic record after 44 years—and is the longest standing record in the history of the Games.

When she broke her own world record in winning the 2003 London Marathon, Paula Radcliffe knocked a staggering 1 minute 53 seconds off her previous best mark, which she set in the Chicago Marathon six months earlier. Radcliffe won the London Marathon three times.

TOP 10 FASTEST WOMEN'S MARATHONS*

	ATHLETE / COUNTRY / WHERE SET	WHEN SET	TIME (HR:MIN:SEC)
1	Paula Radcliffe, UK London, England	Apr 13, 2003	2:15:25
2	Paula Radcliffe, UK Chicago, USA	Oct 13, 2002	2:17:18
3	Paula Radcliffe, UK London, England	Apr 17, 2005	2:17:42
4	Catherine Ndereba, Kenya Chicago, USA	Oct 7, 2001	2:18:47
5	Paula Radcliffe, UK London, England	Apr 14, 2002	2:18:56
6	Mizuki Noguchi, Japan Berlin, Germany	Sep 25, 2005	2:19:12
7	Irina Mikitenko, Germany Berlin, Germany	Sep 28, 2008	2:19:19
8	Catherine Ndereba, Kenya Chicago, USA	Oct 13, 2002	2:19:26
9	Deena Kastor, USA London, England	Apr 23, 2006	2:19:36
10	Yingjie Sun, China Beijing, China	Oct 19, 2003	2:19:39

* As of January 1, 2011   Source: IAAF

TOP 10 LONGEST LONG-JUMPS*

	ATHLETE / COUNTRY / WHERE SET	WHEN SET	DISTANCE (M)
1	Mike Powell, USA Tokyo, Japan	Aug 30, 1991	8.95
2	Bob Beamon, USA Mexico City, Mexico	Oct 18, 1968	8.90
3	Carl Lewis, USA Tokyo, Japan	Aug 30, 1991	8.87
4	Robert Emmiyan, USSR Tsakhkadzor, USSR	May 22, 1987	8.86
5	Carl Lewis, USA Indianapolis, USA	Jun 19, 1983	8.79
6	=Carl Lewis, USA Indianapolis, USA	Jul 24, 1982	8.76
	=Carl Lewis, USA Indianapolis, USA	Jul 18, 1988	8.76
8	Carl Lewis, USA Indianapolis, USA	Aug 16, 1987	8.75
9	=Larry Myricks, USA Indianapolis, USA	Jul 18, 1988	8.74
	=Erick Walder, USA El Paso, USA	Apr 2, 1994	8.74
	=Dwight Phillips, USA Eugene, Oregan, USA	Jun 17, 2009	8.74

* As of 1 January 2011   Source: IAAF

At the 1991 World Championships, both Carl Lewis and Mike Powell seemed likely to beat Bob Beamon's long-standing world record. In round four, Lewis jumped 8.91 to better Beamon's distance but it was deemed to be wind-assisted. However, in the next round Powell jumped a legal 8.95 to shatter the 23-year-old world record.

CRICKET

TOP 10 **MOST RUNS IN TEST CRICKET**

	PLAYER / COUNTRY	YEARS	MATCHES	RUNS*
1	Sachin Tendulkar, India	1989–2011	176	14,532
2	Ricky Ponting, Australia	1995–2011	152	12,363
3	Rahul Dravid, India/ICC	1996–2011	149	12,027
4	Brian Lara, West Indies/ICC	1990–2006	131	11,953
6	Jacques Kallis, South Africa/ICC	1995–2011	145	11,838
5	Allan Border, Australia	1978–1994	156	11,174
7	Steve Waugh, Australia	1985–2004	168	10,927
8	Sunil Gavaskar, India	1971–1987	125	10,122
9	Mahela Jayawardene, Sri Lanka	1997–2011	116	9,527
10	Shivnarine Chanderpaul, West Indies	1994–2011	129	9,063

* As of April 1, 2011

TOP 10 **MOST RUNS IN ONE-DAY INTERNATIONALS**

	PLAYER / COUNTRY	YEARS	MATCHES	RUNS*
1	Sachin Tendulkar, India	1989–2011	452	18,093
2	Sanath Jayasuriya, Sri Lanka/Asia	1989–2009	444	13,428
3	Ricky Ponting, Australia/ICC	1995–2011	352	13,082
4	Inzamam-ul-Haq, Pakistan/Asia	1991–2007	378	11,739
5	Sourav Ganguly, India/Asia	1992–2007	311	11,363
6	Jacques Kallis, South Africa/Africa/ICC	1996–2011	307	11,002
7	Rahul Dravid, India/Asia/ICC	1996–2009	339	10,765
8	Brian Lara, West Indies/ICC	1990–2007	299	10,405
9	Mohammad Yousuf, Pakistan/Asia	1998–2011	288	9,720
10	Adam Gilchrist, Australia/ICC	1996–2008	287	9,619

* As of April 1, 2011

▲ Tandulkar's Test
Sachin Tendulkar is the first and only man to score 50 Test centuries.

Most World Cup Runs

The India v. England group game at Bangalore in the 2011 World Cup was the highest-ever scoring match in the competition, with each side scoring 338 runs in a 676-run thriller. The highest individual team total is 413-5 by India against Bermuda at Port of Spain in 2007, and the highest individual innings is 188 not out by Gary Kirsten of South Africa against UAE at Rawalpindi in 1996.

TOP 10 **HIGHEST TEAM TOTALS IN TWENTY20 CRICKET**

	TEAM / OPPONENTS	VENUE	DATE	TOTAL*
1	Sri Lanka v. Kenya	Johannesburg	Sep 14, 2007	260–6
2	Somerset v. Gloucestershire	Taunton	Jun 27, 2006	250–3
3	Chennai v. Rajasthan	Chennai	Apr 3, 2010	246–5
4	Nondescripts v. Sri Lanka Air Force Sports Club	Colombo	Oct 16, 2005	245–4
5	Karachi Dolphins v. Lahore Eagles	Lahore	Oct 14, 2010	243–2
6	Essex v. Sussex	Chelmsford	Jun 24, 2008	242–3
7	South Africa v. England	Centurion	Nov 15, 2009	241–6
8	Chennai v. Punjab	Mohali	Apr 19, 2008	240–5
9	= Easterns v. Centrals	Bulawayo	May 16, 2009	239–3
	= Sussex v. Glamorgan	Hove	Jun 23, 2010	239–5

* As of April 1, 2011

► **Scoring partners**
Sri Lanka players Mahela Jayawardene and Kumar Sangakkara after their record-breaking partnership.

◄ **Good all-rounder**
Sanath Jayasuriya was elected a member of the Sri Lankan parliament in 2010.

TOP 10 **HIGHEST PARTNERSHIPS IN TEST CRICKET**

	PARTNERS / COUNTRY / OPPONENTS / DATE	WKT	RUNS*
1	**Kumar Sangakkara, Mahela Jayawardene** Sri Lanka v. South Africa, Jul 27, 2006	3rd	624
2	**Sanath Jayasuriya, Roshan Mahanama** Sri Lanka v. India, Aug 2, 1997	2nd	576
3	**Andrew Jones, Martin Crowe** New Zealand v. Sri Lanka, Jan 31, 1991	3rd	467
4	= **Bill Ponsford, Don Bradman** Australia v. England, Aug 18, 1934	2nd	451
	= **Mudassar Nazar, Javed Miandad** Pakistan v. India, Jan 14, 1983	3rd	451
6	**Conrad Hunte, Gary Sobers** West Indies v. Pakistan, Feb 26, 1958	2nd	446
7	**Marvan Atapattu, Kumar Sangakkara** Sri Lanka v. Zimbabwe, May 14, 2004	2nd	438
8	**Mahela Jayawardene, Thilan Samaraweera** Sri Lanka v. Pakistan, Feb 21, 2009	4th	437
9	**Jacques Rudolph, Boeta Dippenaar** South Africa v. Bangladesh, Apr 24, 2003	3rd	429#
10	**Neil McKenzie, Graeme Smith** South Africa v. Bangladesh, Feb 29, 2008	1st	415

* As of April 1, 2011
\# Stand unbroken

BASEBALL

TOP 10 **MOST ALL-STAR GAME APPEARANCES**

	PLAYER	YEARS	GAMES PLAYED*
1 =	Stan Musial	1943–63	24
=	Willie Mays	1954–73	24
=	Hank Aaron	1955–75	24
4 =	Ted Williams	1940–60	18
=	Brooks Robinson	1960–74	18
=	Cal Ripken	1983–2001	18
7 =	Mickey Mantle	1953–68	16
=	Al Kaline	1955–74	16
=	Pete Rose	1965–85	16
10 =	Yogi Berra	1949–62	15
=	Rod Carew	1967–84	15

* Up to and including 2010

Source: MLB

▲ **Star player**
Hank Aaron was 41 when he appeared in his final All-Star game in 1975.

TOP 10 **TEAMS WITH THE MOST GAMES PLAYED IN MAJOR LEAGUE BASEBALL** *

	TEAM	YEARS	GAMES
1	Chicago Cubs	1876–2010	20,088
2	Atlanta Braves	1876–2010	20,053
3	St. Louis Cardinals	1882–2010	19,675
4	Cincinnati Reds	1882–2010	19,673
5	Pittsburgh Pirates	1882–2010	19,633
6	San Francisco Giants	1883–2010	19,557
7	Philadelphia Phillies	1883–2010	19,482
8	Los Angeles Dodgers	1884–2010	19,473
9	Detroit Tigers	1901–2010	17,175
10	Minnesota Twins	1901–2010	17,157

* In regular season games up to 2010

Source: MLB

The Cubs were known as the White Stockings when they formed in 1876.

The Chicago Cubs' first National League game was on April 25, 1876 when they beat the Louisville Grays 4–0.

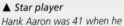

▲ **Chicago Cubs**
Despite being one of the oldest professional teams, the Cubs have not won the World Series since 1908.

▶ **Award winner**
*Steve Carlton played for
six teams, but won all his
Cy Young awards whilst at
Philadelphia Phillies.*

TOP 10 **MOST CY YOUNG AWARDS**

	PLAYER	YEARS	AWARDS*
1	Roger Clemens	1986–2004	7
2	Randy Johnson	1995–2002	5
3	= Steve Carlton	1972–82	4
	= Greg Maddux	1992–95	4
5	= Sandy Koufax	1963–66	3
	= Tom Seaver	1969–75	3
	= Jim Palmer	1973–76	3
	= Pedro Martinez	1997–2000	3
9	= Bob Gibson	1968–70	2
	= Tom Glavine	1991–98	2
	= Denny McLain	1968–69	2
	= Gaylord Perry	1972–78	2
	= Bret Saberhagen	1985–89	2
	= Johan Santana	2004–06	2
	= Tim Lincecum	2008–09	2
	= Roy Halladay	2003–10	2

The Cy Young Award is presented each year to
the best pitcher in both the American League and
National League. The award was first made in 1956
following the death the previous year of one of the
game's all-time great pitchers, Cy Young. Originally
only one award was made, but since 1967 there
has been one award for the best pitcher in each
league. The first recipient was Don Newcombe of
the Brooklyn Dodgers.

THE 10 **LATEST NO. 1 PICKS IN THE MLB DRAFT**

YEAR	PLAYER	POSITION	PICKED BY
2010	Bryce Harper	Outfielder	Washington Nationals
2009	Stephen Strasburg	Pitcher	Washington Nationals
2008	Tim Beckham	Shortstop	Tampa Bay Rays
2007	David Price	Pitcher	Tampa Bay Devil Rays
2006	Luke Hochevar	Pitcher	Kansas City Royals
2005	Justin Upton	Shortstop	Arizona Diamondbacks
2004	Matt Bush	Shortstop	San Diego Padres
2003	Delmon Young	Outfielder	Tampa Bay Devil Rays
2002	Bryan Bullington	Pitcher	Pittsburgh Pirates
2001	Joe Mauer	Catcher	Minnesota Twins

Source: MLB

▶ **Harper's home run**
*As a 17-year-old in 2010, Bryce Harper hit 31
home runs in 66 games for his college team.*

BASKETBALL

TOP 10 NBA TEAMS WITH THE MOST REGULAR SEASON WINS*

TEAM / YEARS / PLAYED / WON

1 Los Angeles Lakers
1949–2010
4,893 / 3,027

2 Boston Celtics
1947–2010
5,003 / 2,972

3 Philadelphia 76ers
1950–2010
4,828 / 2,569

4 New York Knickerbockers
1947–2010
4,999 / 2,483

5 Detroit Pistons
1949–2010
4,892 / 2,427

6 Atlanta Hawks
1950–2010
4,830 / 2,376

7 Sacramento Kings
1949–2010
4,893 / 2,300

8 Golden State Warriors
1947–2010
4,998 / 2,293

9 San Antonio Spurs
1968–2010
3,500 / 2,031

10 Phoenix Suns
1969–2010
3,412 / 1,914

* As of the end of the 2009–10 season

▲ *Leading Lakers*
The Lakers' win-loss percentage of .619 is the best of all NBA teams—past and present.

TOP 10 MOST CAREER POINTS IN NBA PLAYOFF GAMES

	PLAYER / YEARS	POINTS*
1	Michael Jordan 1985–98	5,987
2	Kareem Abdul-Jabbar 1970–89	5,762
3	Shaquille O'Neal 1994–2010	5,248
4	Kobe Bryant 1997–2010	5,052
5	Karl Malone 1986–2004	4,761
6	Jerry West 1961–74	4,457
7	Tim Duncan 1998–2010	3,914
8	Larry Bird 1980–92	3,897
9	John Havlicek 1963–77	3,776
10	Hakeem Olajuwon 1985–2002	3,755

* Up to and including the 2009–10 post season

Source: NBA

TOP 10 **MOST POINTS IN A SINGLE NBA GAME***

PLAYER / TEAM / OPPONENTS / DATE	POINTS
1 **Wilt Chamberlain**, Philadelphia Warriors New York Knicks / Mar 2, 1962	100
2 **Kobe Bryant**, Los Angeles Lakers Toronto Raptors / Jan 22, 2006	81
3 **Wilt Chamberlain**, Philadelphia Warriors Los Angeles Lakers / Dec 8, 1961#	78
4 =**Wilt Chamberlain**, Philadelphia Warriors Chicago Packers / Jan 13, 1962	73
=**Wilt Chamberlain**, San Francisco Warriors New York Knicks / Nov 16, 1962	73
=**David Thompson**, Denver Nuggets Detroit Pistons / Apr 9, 1978	73
7 **Wilt Chamberlain**, San Francisco Warriors Los Angeles Lakers / Nov 3, 1962	72
8 =**David Robinson**, San Antonio Spurs Los Angeles Clippers / Apr 24, 1994	71
=**Elgin Baylor**, Los Angeles Lakers New York Knicks / Nov 15, 1960	71
10 **Wilt Chamberlain**, San Francisco Warriors Syracuse Nationals / Mar 10, 1963	70

* As of the end of the 2009–10 season
# Including three periods of overtime

TOP 10 **MOST 3-POINT FIELD GOALS IN AN NBA SEASON***

PLAYER / TEAM / SEASON	3-PT FGS
1 **Ray Allen** Seattle Supersonics / 2005–06	269
2 **Dennis Scott** Orlando Magic / 1995–96	267
3 **George McCloud** Dallas Mavericks / 1995–96	257
4 **Jason Richardson** Charlotte Bobcats / 2007–08	243
5 **Peja Stojakovic** Sacramento Kings / 2003–04	240
6 =**Peja Stojakovic** New Orleans Hornets / 2007–08	231
=**Mookie Blaylock** Atlanta Hawks / 1995–96	231
8 =**Reggie Miller** Indiana Pacers / 1996–97	229
=**Ray Allen** Milwaukee Bucks / 2001–02	229
10 =**Quentin Richardson** Phoenix Suns / 2004–05	226
=**Kyle Korver** Philadelphia 76ers / 2004–05	226
=**Rashard Lewis** Orlando Magic / 2007–08	226

* Regular season up to and including 2009–10 season

◄ *Shaquille O'Neal*
In 2010, record breaker Shaquille O'Neal moved to his sixth NBA team, Boston Celtics.

▲ *Ray Allen*
On February 10, 2011 Ray Allen's 2,562nd 3-point field goal of his career set a new NBA record.

THE 10 LONGEST-REIGNING WORLD HEAVYWEIGHT CHAMPIONS*

BOXER#	YEARS	REIGNS	YRS	DURATION MTHS	DAYS
1 Joe Louis	1937–49	1	11	8	8
2 Muhammad Ali†	1964–79	3	8	11	15
3 Lennox Lewis, UK	1992–2004	3	8	2	18
4 Jack Dempsey	1919–26	1	7	2	20
5 Larry Holmes	1978–85	1	7	2	13
6 Wladimir Klitschko, Ukraine	2000–11	2	7	0	26
7 John L. Sullivan	1885–92	1	7	0	10
8 Jack Johnson	1908–15	1	6	3	11
9 Evander Holyfield	1990–2001	4	6	1	2
10 James J. Jeffries	1899–1903	1	5	11	5

* As of January 1, 2011
\# All boxers from the USA unless otherwise stated
† Formerly Cassius Clay

For many years boxing historians regarded the James Corbett v. John L. Sullivan bout on September 7, 1892 as the first world heavyweight contest under Queensberry Rules, but records now show that Sullivan's win over Dominick McCaffrey (USA) on August 29, 1885 was for the "Championship of the World" and fought under Queensberry Rules.

The longest World Boxing Championship fights

Before the introduction of the Queensberry Rules in 1866, which stipulated that a round should last three minutes, a round lasted until such time as a fighter was knocked down. Consequently, contests often lasted many rounds; a 276-round contest between Jack Jones and Patsy Tunney at Cheshire, England, in 1825 being the longest recorded. Under Queensberry Rules the longest world title fight was the 80-round featherweight bout that took place between Ike Weir and Frank Murphy at O'Brien's Opera House, Kouts, Indiana, in March 1889.

▶ *Wladimir Klitschko*
Both Wladimir Klitschko and his brother, Vitali, held world heavyweight titles in 2011.

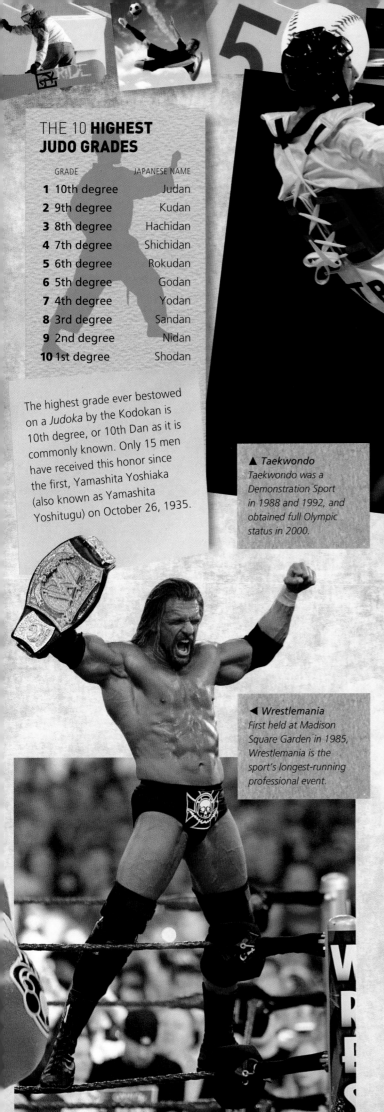

THE 10 HIGHEST JUDO GRADES

	GRADE	JAPANESE NAME
1	10th degree	Judan
2	9th degree	Kudan
3	8th degree	Hachidan
4	7th degree	Shichidan
5	6th degree	Rokudan
6	5th degree	Godan
7	4th degree	Yodan
8	3rd degree	Sandan
9	2nd degree	Nidan
10	1st degree	Shodan

The highest grade ever bestowed on a *Judoka* by the Kodokan is 10th degree, or 10th Dan as it is commonly known. Only 15 men have received this honor since the first, Yamashita Yoshiaka (also known as Yamashita Yoshitugu) on October 26, 1935.

▲ *Taekwondo*
Taekwondo was a Demonstration Sport in 1988 and 1992, and obtained full Olympic status in 2000.

◀ *Wrestlemania*
First held at Madison Square Garden in 1985, Wrestlemania is the sport's longest-running professional event.

TOP 10 OLYMPIC MEDAL-WINNING COUNTRIES AT TAEKWONDO*

	COUNTRY	GOLD	SILVER	BRONZE	TOTAL
1	South Korea	9	1	2	12
2	Chinese Taipei	2	1	4	7
3	USA	2	2	2	6
4	= China	4	0	1	5
	= Mexico	2	1	2	5
6	= Iran	2	0	2	4
	= Greece	1	3	0	4
	= Cuba	1	2	1	4
	= Turkey	0	2	2	4
	= France	0	1	3	4

* Based on total medals won up to and including the 2008 Beijing Olympics

TOP 10 ATTENDANCES AT WWE WRESTLEMANIA

	VENUE	YEAR	ATTENDANCE*
1	Pontiac Silverdome, Pontiac, Michigan	1987	93,173
2	Ford Field, Detroit, Michigan	2007	80,103
3	Citrus Bowl, Orlando, Florida	2008	74,635
4	Reliant Stadium, Houston, Texas	2009	72,744
5	University of Phoenix Stadium, Glendale, Arizona	2010	72,219
6	Georgia Dome, Atlanta, Georgia	2011	71,617
7	SkyDome, Toronto, Canada	2002	68,237
8	Reliant Astrodome, Houston, Texas	2001	67,925
9	SkyDome, Toronto, Canada	1990	67,678
10	Hoosier Dome, Indianapolis, Indiana	1992	62,167

* Up to and including Wrestlemania XXVII (2011)

HOCKEY

TOP 10 GOALIES WITH THE MOST CAREER SHUTOUTS*

PLAYER / YEARS PLAYED / SHUTOUTS

1 Martin Brodeur
1991–2011
110

2 Terry Sawchuk
1949–70
103

3 George Hainsworth
1926–37
94

4 Glenn Hall
1952–71
84

5 Jacques Plante
1952–73
82

6 = Alec Connell
1924–37
81

= Tiny Thompson
1928–40
81

= Dominik Hasek
1990–2008
81

9 = Tony Esposito
1968–84
76

= Ed Belfour
1988–2007
76

* Regular season shutouts up to and including 2009–10

Source: NHL

▲ *Martin Brodeur*
Top goalie Brodeur has spent his entire NHL career with the New Jersey Devils.

◄ *Jaromír Jágr*
Jágr was the Czech Republic's flag bearer at the 2010 Winter Olympics.

TOP 10 MOST GAME-WINNING GOALS IN A CAREER*

	PLAYER	YEARS PLAYED	GAME-WINNING GOALS
1	Phil Esposito	1963–81	118
2	Jaromír Jágr	1990–2008	112
3	Brett Hull	1986–2006	110
4	Brendan Shanahan	1987–2009	109
5	=Teemu Selänne	1992–2011	97
	=Guy Lafleur	1971–91	97
7	Mats Sundin	1990–2009	96
8	Steve Yzerman	1983–2006	94
9	=Sergei Fedorov	1990–2009	93
	=Joe Nieuwendyk	1986–2007	93

* In regular season games up to and including 2009–10   Source: NHL

TOP 10 MOST GOALS IN A SEASON*

PLAYER / TEAM / SEASON / GOALS

1 Wayne Gretzky
Edmonton Oilers
1981–82 — **92**

2 Wayne Gretzky
Edmonton Oilers
1983–84 — **87**

3 Brett Hull
St. Louis Blues
1990–91 — **86**

4 Mario Lemieux
Pittsburgh Penguins
1988–89 — **85**

5 = Phil Esposito
Boston Bruins
1970–71 — **76**

= Alexander Mogilny
Buffalo Sabres
1992–93

= Teemu Selänne
Winnipeg Jets
1992–93

8 Wayne Gretzky
Edmonton Oilers
1984–85 — **73**

9 Brett Hull
St. Louis Blues
1989–90 — **72**

10 = Wayne Gretzky
Edmonton Oilers
1982–83 — **71**

= Jari Kurri
Edmonton Oilers
1984–85

* In a regular season up to the end of 2009–10

Hart Memorial Trophy

The trophy is named after Dr. David Hart, the father of former Montreal Canadiens manager-coach Cecil Hart, who presented the trophy to the NHL in the 1923–24 season. The first recipient was Frank Nighbor of the Ottawa Senators. Wayne Gretzky won the award a record nine times between 1980 and 1989.

▲ *Wayne Gretzky*
When he retired in 1999, Gretzky held more than 50 NHL regular season and play-off records.

TOP 10 COACHES WITH THE LONGEST NHL CAREERS*

	COACH	FROM	TO	GAMES	SEASONS
1	Scotty Bowman	1968	2002	2,141	30
2	Dick Irvin	1929	1956	1,449	27
3	Al Arbour	1971	2008	1,607	23
4	= Mike Keenan	1985	2009	1,386	20
	= Jack Adams	1928	1947	964	20
	= Pat Quinn	1979	2010	1,400	20
7	Art Ross	1918	1945	758	18
8	= Bryan Murray	1982	2008	1,239	17
	= Ron Wilson	1994	2011	1,257	17
10	= Sid Abel	1953	1976	964	16
	= Billy Reay	1958	1977	1,102	16
	= Roger Neilson	1978	2002	1,000	16
	= Jacques Lemaire	1994	2010	1,213	16
	= Jacques Martin	1987	2011	1,182	16

* To the start of the 2010–11 season

SOCCER

▲ Spain triumphs
Spain's 2010 World Cup win over the Netherlands added to their Euro success in 2008.

TOP 10 **COUNTRIES IN THE 2010 FIFA WORLD CUP***

	COUNTRY
1	Spain
2	Netherlands
3	Germany
4	Uruguay
5	Argentina
6	Brazil
7	Ghana
8	Paraguay
9	Japan
10	Chile

* Final ranking as published by FIFA

Source: FIFA

TOP 10 **MOST WINS IN THE BARCLAYS PREMIER LEAGUE***

	CLUB	MATCHES PLAYED	MATCHES WON
1	Manchester United	715	460
2	Arsenal	716	387
3	Chelsea	715	372
4	Liverpool	715	356
5	Aston Villa	715	269
6	Tottenham Hotspur	716	268
7	Newcastle United	635	253
8	Blackburn Rovers	641	250
9	Everton	716	248
10	West Ham United	599	199

* From the formation of the League in 1992 to January 1, 2011

Source: Barclays Premier League

◄ Ronaldo
The World Cup's top scorer, Ronaldo retired in February 2011.

TOP 10 **WORLD CUP GOALSCORERS**

PLAYER / COUNTRY / YEARS / GOALS (FINAL STAGES 1930–2010)

1	**2**	**2**	**4**	**5**	**6**
Ronaldo	= Gerd Müller	= Miroslav Klose	Just Fontaine	Pelé	= Sándor Kocsis
Brazil	West Germany	Germany	France	Brazil	Hungary
1998–2006	1970–74	2002–10	1958	1958–70	1954
15	14	14	13	12	11

TOP 10 **RICHEST MANAGERS IN BRITISH FOOTBALL***

MANAGER / COUNTRY / TEAM / WORTH

1 Fabio Capello, Italy
England
$58,000,000

2 Roy Keane, Ireland
Ipswich Town
$45,000,000

3 Alex Ferguson, Scotland
Manchester United
$42,000,000

4 Carlo Ancelotti, Italy
Chelsea
$34,000,000

5 Arsene Wenger, France
Arsenal
$27,000,000

6 = Sven-Goran Eriksson,
Sweden
Leicester City
$24,000,000

= Roberto Mancini, Italy
Manchester City
$24,000,000

8 = Ole Gunnar Solskjaer,
Norway
Manchester United
Reserves
$16,000,000

= Mark Hughes, Wales
Fulham
$16,000,000

= Harry Redknapp, England
Tottenham Hotspur
$16,000,000

* At the start of the 2010–11 season

Source: FourFourTwo

► *Zlatan Ibrahimovic*
Before moving to Inter Milan,
Ibrahimovic played for Malmo,
Ajax, and Juventus.

TOP 10 **TRANSFERS WORLDWIDE***

PLAYER / COUNTRY	FROM	TO	YEAR	FEE ($)
1 Cristiano Ronaldo, Portugal	Manchester United	Real Madrid	2009	128,900,000
2 Zlatan Ibrahimovic, Sweden	Inter Milan	Barcelona	2009	97,800,000
3 Kaká, Brazil	AC Milan	Real Madrid	2009	90,250,000
4 Fernando Torres, Spain	Liverpool	Chelsea	2011	80,600,000
5 Zinedine Zidane, France	Juventus	Real Madrid	2001	76,850,000
6 Luis Figo, Portugal	Barcelona	Real Madrid	2000	60,250,000
7 Hernán Crespo, Argentina	Parma	Lazio	2000	57,500,000
8 Andy Carroll, England	Newcastle United	Liverpool	2011	56,400,000
9 David Villa, Spain	Valencia	Barcelona	2010	55,000,000
10 Gianluigi Buffon, Italy	Parma	Juventus	2001	53,200,000

* As of the end of the January 2011 transfer window

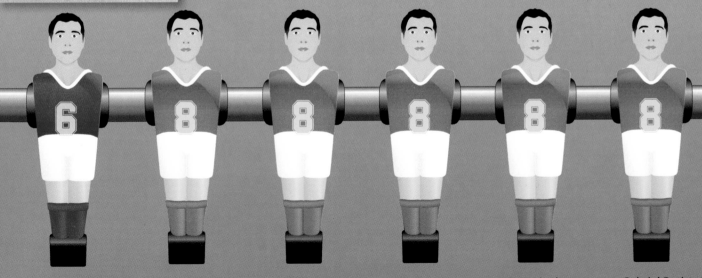

= Jürgen Klinsmann
Germany
1990–98
11

= Helmut Rahn
West Germany
1954–58
10

= Teófilo Cubillas
Peru
1970–78
10

= Grzegorz Lato
Poland
1974–82
10

= Gary Lineker
England
1986–90
10

= Gabriel Batistuta
Argentina
1994–2002
10

FOOTBALL

▲ *Cardinals v. Bears*
The Arizona Cardinals and the Chicago Bears have met 90 times in the NFL, with the Bears winning 57.

THE 10 OLDEST CURRENT NFL FRANCHISES

TEAM / NAME WHEN FRANCHISE GRANTED / FRANCHISE DATE

1. = Arizona Cardinals (Chicago Cardinals) Sep 17, 1920
   = Chicago Bears (Decatur Staleys) Sep 17, 1920
3. Green Bay Packers Aug 27, 1921
4. New York Giants Aug 1, 1925
5. Detroit Lions (Portsmouth Spartans) Jul 12, 1930
6. Washington Redskins (Boston Braves) Jul 9, 1932
7. = Philadelphia Eagles Jul 8, 1933
   = Pittsburgh Steelers (Pittsburgh Pirates) Jul 8, 1933
9. St. Louis Rams (Cleveland Rams) Feb 12, 1937
10. = Cleveland Browns* Jun 4, 1944
    = San Francisco 49ers* Jun 4, 1944

* Charter member of the All-American Football Conference (AAFC)

Source: NFL

TOP 10 SUPER BOWL ATTENDANCES

TEAMS / YEAR / VENUE	ATTENDANCE
1 Pittsburgh Steelers v. Los Angeles Rams 1980 Rose Bowl, Pasadena	103,985
2 Washington Redskins v. Miami Dolphins 1983 Rose Bowl, Pasadena	103,667
3 Oakland Raiders v. Minnesota Vikings 1977 Rose Bowl, Pasadena	103,438
4 Green Bay Packers v. Pittsburgh Steelers 2011 Cowboys Stadium, Arlington	103,219
5 New York Giants v. Denver Broncos 1987 Rose Bowl, Pasadena	101,063
6 Dallas Cowboys v. Buffalo Bills 1993 Rose Bowl, Pasadena	98,374
7 Miami Dolphins v. Washington Redskins 1973 Memorial Coliseum, Los Angeles	90,182
8 San Francisco 49ers v. Miami Dolphins 1985 Stanford Stadium, California	84,059
9 San Francisco 49ers v. Cincinnati Bengals 1982 Pontiac Silverdrome, Michigan	81,270
10 Dallas Cowboys v. Miami Dolphins 1972 Tulane Stadium, New Orleans	81,023

TOP 10 MOST WINS IN THE NFL*

	TEAM	YEARS	WINS
1	Chicago Bears	1920–2010	704
2	Green Bay Packers	1921–2010	664
3	New York Giants	1925–2010	636
4	Washington Redskins	1932–2010	547
5	Pittsburgh Steelers	1933–2010	541
6	St. Louis Rams	1937–2010	511
7	= Philadelphia Eagles	1933–2010	509
	= San Francisco 49ers	1946–2010	509
9	Detroit Lions	1930–2010	496
10	Arizona Cardinals	1920–2010	488

* Regular seasons, 1920–2010

The first of the Chicago Bears' 704 wins in the NFL was a 20–0 win over Moline Universal Tractors on Sunday, October 3, 1920. The Bears were known as the Decatur Staleys at the time and the match was in the American Professional Football Association (APFA)—the forerunner of the NFL.

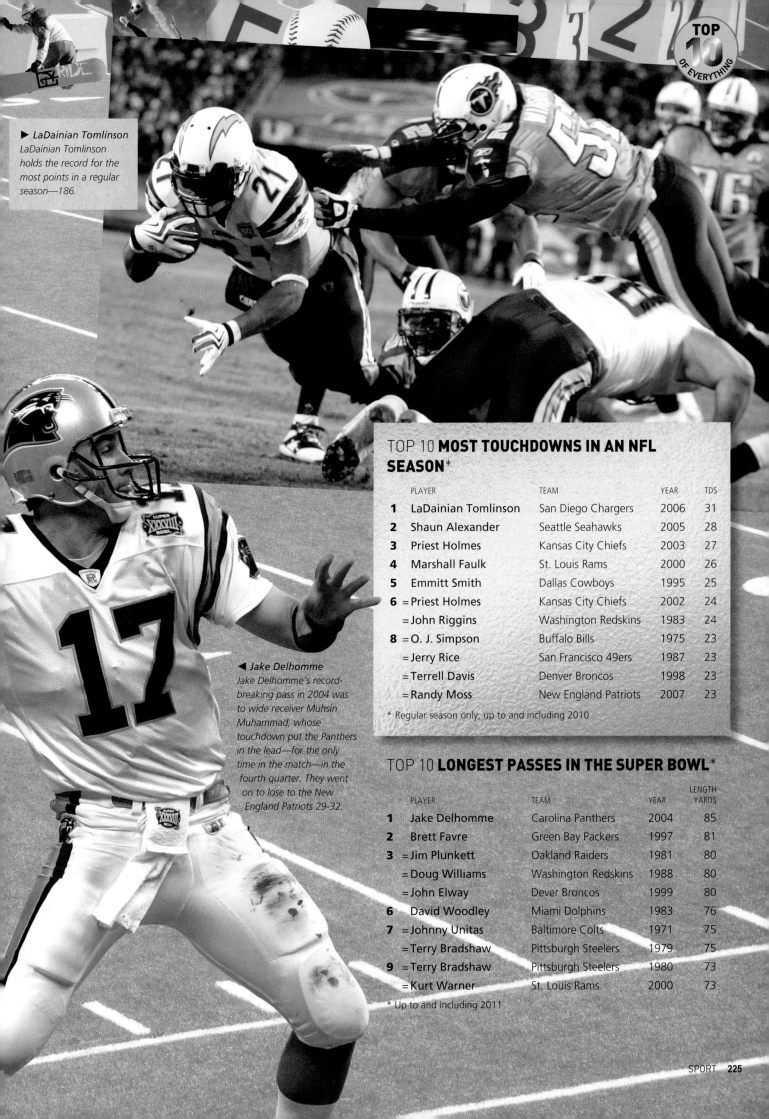

▶ **LaDainian Tomlinson**
LaDainian Tomlinson holds the record for the most points in a regular season—186.

◀ **Jake Delhomme**
Jake Delhomme's record-breaking pass in 2004 was to wide receiver Muhsin Muhammad, whose touchdown put the Panthers in the lead—for the only time in the match—in the fourth quarter. They went on to lose to the New England Patriots 29-32.

TOP 10 **MOST TOUCHDOWNS IN AN NFL SEASON***

	PLAYER	TEAM	YEAR	TDS
1	LaDainian Tomlinson	San Diego Chargers	2006	31
2	Shaun Alexander	Seattle Seahawks	2005	28
3	Priest Holmes	Kansas City Chiefs	2003	27
4	Marshall Faulk	St. Louis Rams	2000	26
5	Emmitt Smith	Dallas Cowboys	1995	25
6 =	Priest Holmes	Kansas City Chiefs	2002	24
=	John Riggins	Washington Redskins	1983	24
8 =	O. J. Simpson	Buffalo Bills	1975	23
=	Jerry Rice	San Francisco 49ers	1987	23
=	Terrell Davis	Denver Broncos	1998	23
=	Randy Moss	New England Patriots	2007	23

* Regular season only, up to and including 2010

TOP 10 **LONGEST PASSES IN THE SUPER BOWL***

	PLAYER	TEAM	YEAR	LENGTH YARDS
1	Jake Delhomme	Carolina Panthers	2004	85
2	Brett Favre	Green Bay Packers	1997	81
3 =	Jim Plunkett	Oakland Raiders	1981	80
=	Doug Williams	Washington Redskins	1988	80
=	John Elway	Dever Broncos	1999	80
6	David Woodley	Miami Dolphins	1983	76
7 =	Johnny Unitas	Baltimore Colts	1971	75
=	Terry Bradshaw	Pittsburgh Steelers	1979	75
9 =	Terry Bradshaw	Pittsburgh Steelers	1980	73
=	Kurt Warner	St. Louis Rams	2000	73

* Up to and including 2011

RUGBY

TOP 10 **MOST TRIES IN A SUPER LEAGUE REGULAR SEASON***

	PLAYER	CLUB	YEAR	TRIES
1	Lesley Vainikolo	Bradford Bulls	2004	36
2	Danny McGuire	Leeds Rhinos	2004	35
3 =	Ryan Hall	Leeds Rhinos	2009	29
=	Pat Richards	Wigan Warriors	2010	29
5	Paul Newlove	St. Helens	1996	28
6 =	Kris Radlinski	Wigan Warriors	2001	27
=	Mark Calderwood	Leeds Rhinos	2005	27
8 =	Matt Daylight	Gateshead Thunder	1999	25
=	Toa Kohe-Love	Warrington Wolves	1999	25
=	Darren Albert	St. Helens	1999	25
=	Lesley Vainikolo	Bradford Bulls	2005	25
=	Justin Murphy	Catalans Dragons	2006	25

* Up to and including 2010

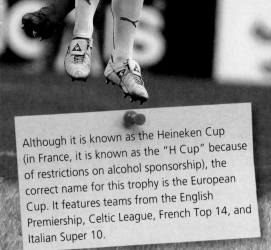

▼ *Toulouse*
The most successful French team, Toulouse have won the French Championship a record 17 times.

TOP 10 **MOST APPEARANCES IN THE HEINEKEN CUP FINAL***

	CLUB / COUNTRY	YEAR(S)	WINS	RU	APPS
1	Toulouse, France	1996–2010	4	2	6
2	Leicester Tigers, England	1997–2009	2	3	5
3	Munster, Ireland	2000–08	2	2	4
4 =	Brive, France	1997–98	1	1	2
=	London Wasps, England	2004–07	2	0	2
=	Biarritz, France	2006–10	0	2	2
=	Stade Français, France	2001–05	0	2	2
8 =	Cardiff, Wales	1996	0	1	1
=	Bath, England	1998	1	0	1
=	Ulster, Ireland	1999	1	0	1
=	Colomiers, France	1999	0	1	1
=	Northampton Saints, England	2000	1	0	1
=	Perpignan, France	2003	0	1	1
=	Leinster, Ireland	2009	1	0	1

* Up to and including 2010

Although it is known as the Heineken Cup (in France, it is known as the "H Cup" because of restrictions on alcohol sponsorship), the correct name for this trophy is the European Cup. It features teams from the English Premiership, Celtic League, French Top 14, and Italian Super 10.

TOP 10 **POINTS SCORERS IN INTERNATIONAL RUGBY**

PLAYER / COUNTRY / YEARS	TESTS	POINTS*
1 Jonny Wilkinson England/Lions 1998–2011	91 (6)	1,195 (67)
2 Dan Carter New Zealand 2003–10	79	1,188
3 Neil Jenkins Wales/Lions 1991–2003	91 (4)	1,090 (41)
4 Diego Dominguez Argentina/Italy 1989–2003	76	1,010
5 Ronan O'Gara Ireland/Lions 2000–11	110 (2)	1,006 (0)
6 Andrew Mehrtens New Zealand 1995–2004	70	967
7 Stephen Jones Wales/Lions 1998–2011	105 (6)	934 (53)
8 Michael Lynagh Australia 1984–95	72	911
9 Percy Montgomery South Africa 1997–2008	102	893
10 Matthew Burke Australia 1993–2004	81	878

* As of April 1, 2011

Figures in brackets indicate the number of appearances for the British and Irish Lions. Wilkinson lost his world record to Dan Carter in November 2010, but regained it when he converted a penalty against France at Twickenham on February 26, 2011.

TOP 10 **TRY SCORERS IN THE IRB WORLD CUP***

	PLAYER	COUNTRY	YEARS	APPS	TRIES
1	Jonah Lomu	New Zealand	1995–99	11	15
2	Doug Howlett	New Zealand	2003–07	10	13
3 =	Rory Underwood	England	1987–95	15	11
=	Joe Rokocoko	New Zealand	2003–07	8	11
=	Chris Latham	Australia	1999–2007	7	11
6 =	David Campese	Australia	1987–95	15	10
=	Brian Lima	Samoa	1991–2007	18	10
8 =	Gavin Hastings	Scotland	1987–95	13	9
=	Jeff Wilson	New Zealand	1995–99	11	9
10 =	Christophe Dominici	France	1999–2007	15	8
=	Mils Muliaina	New Zealand	2003–07	10	8
=	Bryan Habana	South Africa	2007	7	8

* In all IRB World Cups 1987–2007

Source: IRB

▼ *Jonah Lomu*
In his 63 Tests for the All Blacks between 1994 and 2002, Jonah Lomu scored 37 tries, to put him in fifth place on the all-time New Zealand list.

TENNIS

▼ *Rod Laver*
Laver is the only person to complete two Grand Slams.

TOP 10 **MOST WEEKS SPENT AT NO. 1 ON THE WTA RANKINGS**

	PLAYER / COUNTRY	FROM	TO	WEEKS*
1	Steffi Graf, Germany	Aug 17, 1987	Mar 30, 1997	377
2	Martina Navratilova, Czechoslovakia/USA	Jul 10, 1978	Aug 16, 1987	332
3	Chris Evert, USA	Nov 3, 1975	Nov 24, 1985	260
4	Martina Hingis, Switzerland	Mar 31, 1997	Oct 14, 2001	209
5	Monica Seles, Yugoslavia/USA	Mar 11, 1991	Nov 24, 1996	178
6	Serena Williams, USA	Jul 8, 2002	Oct 10, 2010	123
7	Justine Henin, Belgium	Oct 20, 2003	May 18, 2008	117
8	Lindsay Davenport, USA	Oct 12, 1998	Jan 29, 2006	98
9	Amélie Mauresmo, France	Sep 13, 2004	Nov 12, 2006	39
10	Dinara Safina, Russia	Apr 20, 2009	Nov 1, 2009	26

* As of January 1, 2011

Source: WTA

TOP 10 **MOST MEN'S SINGLES TITLES IN A CALENDAR YEAR***

	PLAYER / COUNTRY	YEAR	OUTDOOR	INDOOR	TOTAL
1	Rod Laver, Australia	1969	11	7	18
2	Guillermo Vilas, Argentina	1977	15	1	16
3	= Ilie Nastase, Romania	1973	11	4	15
	= Jimmy Connors, USA	1974	8	7	15
	= Ivan Lendl, Czechoslovakia	1982	6	9	15
6	= Björn Borg, Sweden	1979	8	5	13
	= John McEnroe, USA	1984	5	8	13
8	= Ilie Nastase, Romania	1972	7	5	12
	= Jimmy Connors, USA	1976	6	6	12
	= Thomas Muster, Austria	1995	11	1	12
	= Roger Federer, Switzerland	2006	9	3	12

* In the Open era, 1968–2010, as recognized by the ATP

Source: ATP

▼ *Steffi Graf*
Between 1986 and 1999, Graf won a total of 107 singles tournaments.

Most Grand Slam Singles Titles in a Decade

Australia's Margaret Court (née Smith) holds the record for winning the most Grand Slam titles in one decade, winning 16 in the 1960s. The men's record is held by Switzerland's Roger Federer, who won 15 titles in the 2000s. The 1960s was a formidable decade for Australian players because, in addition to Court's record, Roy Emerson won 12 titles and Rod Laver 11.

► *Rafael Nadal*
Nadal is one of two Spanish players—along with Carlos Moya from Mallorca—to top the ATP rankings.

THE 10 LAST PLAYERS TO WIN THREE OR MORE GRAND SLAM SINGLES TITLES IN A CALENDAR YEAR*

PLAYER / COUNTRY / TITLES WON	YEAR
1 Rafael Nadal, Spain French Open, Wimbledon, US Open	2010
2 Roger Federer, Switzerland Australian Open, Wimbledon, US Open	2007
3 Roger Federer, Switzerland Australian Open, Wimbledon, US Open	2006
4 Roger Federer, Switzerland Australian Open, Wimbledon, US Open	2004
5 Serena Williams, USA French Open, Wimbledon, US Open	2002
6 Martina Hingis, Switzerland Australian Open, Wimbledon, US Open	1997
7 Steffi Graf, Germany French Open, Wimbledon, US Open	1996
8 Steffi Graf, Germany French Open, Wimbledon, US Open	1995
9 Steffi Graf, Germany French Open, Wimbledon, US Open	1993
10 Monica Seles, Yugoslavia Australian Open, French Open, US Open	1992

* Up to and including 2010

TOP 10 ATP WORLD TOUR MASTERS 1000 TITLES*

	PLAYER / COUNTRY		YEARS	TITLES
1	Rafael Nadal, Spain		2005–10	18
2	= Andre Agassi, USA		1990–2004	17
	= Roger Federer, Switzerland		2002–10	17
4	Pete Sampras, USA		1992–2000	11
5	Thomas Muster, Austria		1990–97	8
6	Michael Chang, USA		1990–97	7
7	= Boris Becker, Germany		1990–96	5
	= Jim Courier, USA		1991–93	5
	= Marcelo Ríos, Chile		1997–99	5
	= Gustavo Kuerten, Brazil		1999–2001	5
	= Marat Safin, Russia		2000–05	5
	= Novak Djokovic, Serbia		2007–09	5
	= Andy Roddick, USA		2003–10	5

* Singles titles 1990–2010

Source: ATP

The ATP World Tour Masters 1000 was inaugurated in 1990, and Stefan Edberg (Sweden) won the first event at Indian Wells. It has had several name changes throughout the years, and changed to its current style in 2009. In the season-long series of nine events on the men's ATP tour, ranking points are more than for regular tour events but not as many as for Grand Slam events.

GOLF

THE 10 LAST MEN TO RECORD A ROUND OF 63 IN A MAJOR CHAMPIONSHIP*

	PLAYER / COUNTRY	MAJOR	VENUE	YEAR
1	Rory McIlroy, Northern Ireland	British Open	St. Andrews	2010
2	Tiger Woods, USA	US PGA	Southern Hills	2007
3	Thomas Bjorn, Denmark	US PGA	Baltusrol	2005
4	Vijay Singh, Fiji	US Open	Olympic Fields	2003
5	Mark O'Meara, USA	US PGA	Atlanta	2001
6	José Maria Olazabal, Spain	US PGA	Valhalla	2000
7	Greg Norman, Australia	US Masters	Augusta	1996
8	Brad Faxon, USA	US PGA#	Riviera	1995
9	Michael Bradley, USA	US PGA#	Riviera	1995
10	Vijay Singh	US PGA	Inverness	1993

* Up to and including 2010
\# Faxon scored his 63 in the final round of the 1995 US PGA Championship; Bradley's 63 was in the first round.

▼ Rory McIlroy
McIlroy led the 2010 Open after his 63, but followed it with a second round 80.

▲ Nick Faldo
On his debut in the 1977 Ryder Cup, Nick Faldo won all three matches he played.

TOP 10 MOST RYDER CUP APPEARANCES*

	PLAYER	TEAM#	YEARS	APPEARANCES
1	Nick Faldo	E	1977–97	11
2 =	Christy O'Connor, Sr.	E	1955–73	10
=	Bernhard Langer	E	1981–2002	10
4	Dai Rees	E	1937–61	9
5 =	Peter Alliss	E	1953–69	8
=	Bernard Hunt	E	1953–69	8
=	Billy Casper	USA	1961–75	8
=	Neil Coles	E	1961–77	8
=	Bernard Gallacher	E	1969–83	8
=	Ian Woosnam	E	1983–87	8
=	Ray Floyd	USA	1969–93	8
=	Lanny Wadkins	USA	1977–93	8
=	Severiano Ballesteros	E	1979–95	8
=	Sam Torrance	E	1981–95	8
=	Colin Montgomerie	E	1991–2006	8
=	Phil Mickleson	USA	1995–2010	8

* As a player, up to and including 2010
\# USA = member of the US Ryder Cup team; E = member of the European Ryder Cup team (1979–2010), Great Britain & Ireland (1973–77) and/or Great Britain (1927–71)

TOP 10 CAREER MONEY-WINNERS ON THE CHAMPIONS TOUR*

	GOLFER	YEARS	WINNINGS ($)
1	Hale Irwin	1995–2010	25,570,804
2	Gil Morgan	1996–2010	19,855,653
3	Dana Quigley	1997–2010	14,715,857
4	Bruce Fleisher	1999–2010	14,592,350
5	Tom Kite	2000–10	14,525,662
6	Larry Nelson	1997–2010	13,928,229
7	Jim Thorpe	1999–2009	13,423,156
8	Allen Doyle	1998–2010	13,285,174
9	Tom Jenkins	1998–2010	13,097,063
10	Tom Watson	1999–2010	12,584,440

* As of January 1, 2011

Source: PGA Tour

The Champions Tour is a season-long series of tournaments organized by the PGA Tour in the USA and other parts of the world for golfers over the age of 50. It started life as the Senior PGA Tour in 1980 and changed its name to the Champions Tour in 2002.

TOP 10 MOST PGA CAREER WINS*

	PLAYER	YEARS	TOTAL
1	SAM SNEAD	1936–65	82
2	JACK NICKLAUS	1962–86	73
3	TIGER WOODS	1996–2009	71
4	BEN HOGAN	1938–59	64
5	ARNOLD PALMER	1955–73	62
6	BYRON NELSON	1935–51	52
7	BILLY CASPER	1956–75	51
8	WALTER HAGEN	1916–36	44
9	CARY MIDDLECOFF	1945–61	40
10	= GENE SARAZEN	1922–41	39
	= TOM WATSON	1974–98	39

* On the PGA Tour, up to and including January 1, 2011

All golfers in the Top 10 are from the USA. The most wins by a non-American is 34 by Vijay Singh (Fiji). The record on the European Tour is 50 by Severiano Ballesteros (Spain) between 1976 and 1995.

TOP 10 MOST WINS ON THE LPGA TOUR

	PLAYER*	YEARS	WINS#
1	Kathy Whitworth	1962–85	88
2	Mickey Wright	1956–73	82
3	Annika Sörenstam, Sweden	1995–2008	72
4	Patty Berg	1937–62	60
5	Louise Suggs	1946–62	58
6	Betsy Rawls	1951–72	55
7	Nancy Lopez	1978–97	48
8	JoAnne Carner	1969–85	43
9	Sandra Haynie	1962–82	42
10	Babe Zaharias	1940–55	41

* All golfers from the USA unless otherwise stated
# As of January 1, 2011

Source: LPGA

► Jack Nicklaus
As well as 73 Tour wins, Jack Nicklaus won 10 Champions Tour events, the last in 1996.

ON FOUR WHEELS

◀ *Jimmie Johnson*
In 2010, Johnson became the first man to win five consecutive NASCAR championships.

TOP 10 **MOST NASCAR SPRINT CUP SERIES RACE WINNERS***

	DRIVER	FIRST WIN	LAST WIN	TOTAL WINS
1	Richard Petty	1960	1984	200
2	David Pearson	1961	1980	105
3 =	Bobby Allison	1966	1988	84
=	Darrell Waltrip	1975	1992	84
5	Cale Yarborough	1965	1985	83
6	Jeff Gordon	1994	2009	82
7	Dale Earnhardt	1979	2000	76
8	Rusty Wallace	1986	2004	55
9	Lee Petty	1949	1961	54
10	Jimmie Johnson	2002	2010	53

* Up to and including 2010

Source: NASCAR

TOP 10 **MOST POLE POSITIONS IN A FORMULA ONE CAREER**

DRIVER / COUNTRY / YEARS / POLES*

1 Michael Schumacher,
Germany 1994–2006
68

2 Ayrton Senna
Brazil 1985–94
65

3 = Jim Clark
UK 1962–68
33

= Alain Prost
France 1981–93
33

5 Nigel Mansell
UK 1984–94
32

6 Juan Manuel Fangio,
Argentina 1950–58
29

7 Mika Häkkinen,
Finland 1997–2000
26

8 = Niki Lauda
Austria 1974–78
24

= Nelson Piquet
Brazil 1980–87
24

10 = Damon Hill
UK 1993–96
20

= Fernando Alonso
Spain 2003–10
20

* To the end of the 2010 season

The Sprint Cup Series is the leading series of races organized by NASCAR (National Association for Stock Car Auto Racing) in the United States. It was known as the Strictly Stock Series in 1949, the Grand National Series between 1950–70, the Winston Cup Series 1971–2003, and the NEXTEL Cup Series from 2004–07 before adopting its current style, NASCAR Sprint Cup Series, in 2008.

In 1992, Nigel Mansell started in pole position a record 14 times in one season. In the other two races he started, he was in second place on the grid in the Hungarian Grand Prix and in third place in the Canadian Grand Prix.

▶ *Michael Schumacher*
Since his return to Formula One in 2010, Schumacher has been unable to add to his record 68 poles.

THE 10 **LATEST WINNERS OF THE INDIANAPOLIS 500**

YEAR	DRIVER / COUNTRY	START POSITION	CAR	SPEED MPH	SPEED KM/H
2010	Dario Franchitti, UK	3	Dallara	141.045	226.990
2009	Hélio Castroneves, Brazil	1	Dallara	139.724	224.864
2008	Scott Dixon, New Zealand	1	Dallara	140.657	226.366
2007	Dario Franchitti, UK	3	Dallara	139.927	225.191
2006	Sam Hornish, Jr., USA	1	Dallara	142.285	228.985
2005	Dan Wheldon, UK	16	Dallara	139.379	224.308
2004	Buddy Rice, USA	1	Panoz G Force	137.959	222.024
2003	Gil de Ferran, Brazil	10	Panoz G Force	142.066	228.633
2002	Hélio Castroneves, Brazil	13	Dallara	142.326	229.052
2001	Hélio Castroneves, Brazil	11	Dallara	139.275	224.142

▲ *Sebastian Vettel*
Vettel is the second German Formula One champion after Michael Schumacher.

TOP 10 **YOUNGEST FORMULA ONE CHAMPIONS***

	DRIVER / COUNTRY	SEASON	AGE# YRS	AGE# DAYS
1	Sebastian Vettel, Germany	2010	23	133
2	Lewis Hamilton, UK	2008	23	301
3	Fernando Alonso, Spain	2005	24	58
4	Emerson Fittipaldi, Brazil	1972	25	273
5	Michael Schumacher, Germany	1994	25	314
6	Niki Lauda, Austria	1975	26	197
7	Jacques Villeneuve, Canada	1997	26	200
8	Jim Clark, USA	1963	27	188
9	Kimi Räikkönen, Finland	2007	28	4
10	Jochen Rindt†, Austria	1970	28	140

* Up to and including 2010
# At first world title win
† Posthumous world champion (age at death)

ON TWO WHEELS

TOP 10 MOST CYCLING GRAND TOUR WINS*

	RIDER / COUNTRY	YEARS	TOUR	VUELTA	GIRO	TOTAL#
1	Eddy Merckx, Belgium	1968–74	5	1	5	11
2	Bernard Hinault, France	1978–85	5	2	3	10
3	Jacques Anquetil, France	1957–64	5	1	2	8
4 =	Lance Armstrong, USA	1999–2005	7	0	0	7
=	Fausto Coppi, Italy	1940–53	2	0	5	7
=	Miguel Indurain, Spain	1991–95	5	0	2	7
7 =	Gino Bartali, Italy	1936–48	2	0	3	5
=	Afredo Binda, Italy	1923–29	0	0	5	5
=	Alberto Contador, Spain	2007–10	3	1	1	5
=	Felice Gimondi, Italy	1965–76	1	1	3	5

* Aggregate wins in the three Grand Tours—Tour de France, Vuelta a España and Giro d'Italia
\# Up to and including 2010

TOP 10 MOST TOUR DE FRANCE APPEARANCES

	RIDER / COUNTRY	YEARS	RACES*
1	Joop Zoetemelk, Netherlands	1970–86	16
2 =	Lucien Van Impe, Belgium	1969–85	15
=	Guy Nulens, Belgium	1980–94	15
=	Viatcheslav Ekimov, Russia	1990–2006	15
=	George Hincapie, USA	1996–2010	15
=	Christophe Moreau, France	1996–2010	15
7 =	André Darrigade, France	1953–66	14
=	Raymond Poulidor, France	1962–74	14
=	Sean Kelly, Ireland	1978–92	14
=	Erik Zabel, Germany	1994–2008	14
=	Stuart O'Grady, Australia	1997–2010	14

* Up to and including 2010

Joop Zoetemelk won the Tour just once, in 1980. He finished second on a further six occasions, including his debut year, 1970.

TOP 10 MOST DAYS SPENT WEARING THE TOUR DE FRANCE LEADER'S JERSEY

RIDER / COUNTRY / DAYS*

1 Eddy Merckx, Belgium 111
2 Lance Armstrong, USA 83
3 Bernard Hinault, France 79
4 Miguel Indurain, Spain 60
5 Jacques Anquetil, France 52
6 Antonin Magne, France 39
7 Nicolas Frantz, Luxembourg 37
8 André Leducq, France 35
9 Louison Bobet, France 34
10 Ottavio Bottecchia, Italy 33

* Up to and including 2010

Source: Le Tour de France

▼ *Lance Armstrong*
Less than three years before his first Tour win, Lance Armstrong underwent surgery and chemotherapy for cancer.

Not surprisingly, Eddy Merckx holds the record for the most stage wins in the Tour de France—34 between 1969 and 1975.

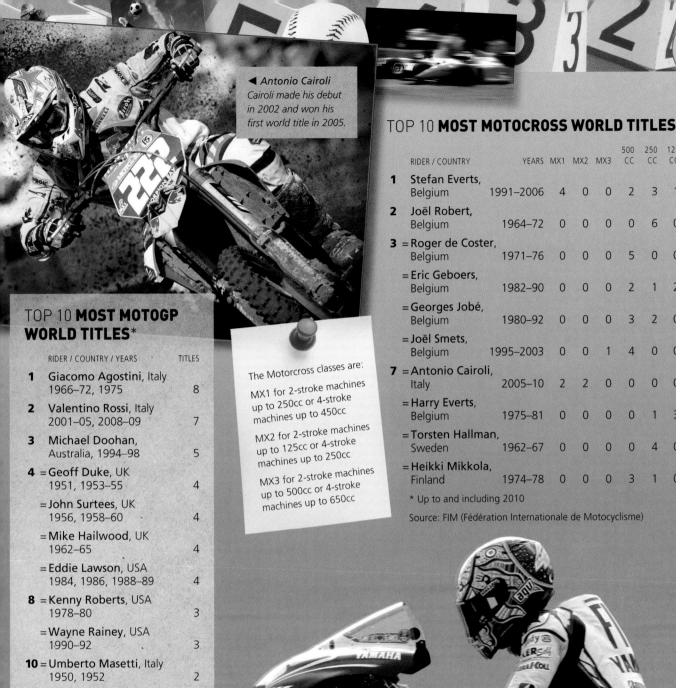

◄ **Antonio Cairoli**
Cairoli made his debut in 2002 and won his first world title in 2005.

TOP 10 **MOST MOTOCROSS WORLD TITLES**

RIDER / COUNTRY	YEARS	MX1	MX2	MX3	500 CC	250 CC	125 CC	TOTAL*
1 Stefan Everts, Belgium	1991–2006	4	0	0	2	3	1	10
2 Joël Robert, Belgium	1964–72	0	0	0	0	6	0	6
3 = Roger de Coster, Belgium	1971–76	0	0	0	5	0	0	5
= Eric Geboers, Belgium	1982–90	0	0	0	2	1	2	5
= Georges Jobé, Belgium	1980–92	0	0	0	3	2	0	5
= Joël Smets, Belgium	1995–2003	0	0	1	4	0	0	5
7 = Antonio Cairoli, Italy	2005–10	2	2	0	0	0	0	4
= Harry Everts, Belgium	1975–81	0	0	0	0	1	3	4
= Torsten Hallman, Sweden	1962–67	0	0	0	0	4	0	4
= Heikki Mikkola, Finland	1974–78	0	0	0	3	1	0	4

* Up to and including 2010

Source: FIM (Fédération Internationale de Motocyclisme)

TOP 10 **MOST MOTOGP WORLD TITLES***

RIDER / COUNTRY / YEARS	TITLES
1 Giacomo Agostini, Italy 1966–72, 1975	8
2 Valentino Rossi, Italy 2001–05, 2008–09	7
3 Michael Doohan, Australia, 1994–98	5
4 = Geoff Duke, UK 1951, 1953–55	4
= John Surtees, UK 1956, 1958–60	4
= Mike Hailwood, UK 1962–65	4
= Eddie Lawson, USA 1984, 1986, 1988–89	4
8 = Kenny Roberts, USA 1978–80	3
= Wayne Rainey, USA 1990–92	3
10 = Umberto Masetti, Italy 1950, 1952	2
= Phil Read, UK 1973–74	2
= Barry Sheene, UK 1976–77	2
= Freddie Spencer, USA 1983, 1985	2

* Moto GP 2002–10, 500cc 1949–2001

The Motorcross classes are:

MX1 for 2-stroke machines up to 250cc or 4-stroke machines up to 450cc

MX2 for 2-stroke machines up to 125cc or 4-stroke machines up to 250cc

MX3 for 2-stroke machines up to 500cc or 4-stroke machines up to 650cc

► **Valentino Rossi**
As of the the end of 2010, Rossi had taken 138 podiums out of 181 MotoGP starts.

HORSE SPORTS

THE 10 LATEST WINNERS OF THE US TRIPLE CROWN*

YEAR	HORSE	JOCKEY
1978	Affirmed	Steve Cauthen
1977	Seattle Slew	Jean Cruguet
1973	Secretariat	Ron Turcotte
1948	Citation	Eddie Arcaro
1946	Assault	Warren Mehrtens
1943	Count Fleet	Johnny Longden
1941	Whirlaway	Eddie Arcaro
1937	War Admiral	Charley Kurtsinger
1935	Omaha	Willie Saunders
1930	Gallant Fox	Earl Sande

* Up to and including 2010

The US Triple Crown consists of the Kentucky Derby, Preakness Stakes, and Belmont Stakes. Gallant Fox is the only Triple Crown winner to have sired another Triple Crown winner—Omaha. The only other horse to win the Triple Crown is Sir Barton in 1919, ridden by jockey Johnny Loftus.

THE 10 FASTEST WINNING TIMES OF THE KENTUCKY DERBY*

	HORSE	YEAR	JOCKEY	TIME (MINS:SECS)
1	Secretariat	1973	Ron Turcotte	1:59.40
2	Monarchos	2001	Jorge F. Chavez	1:59.97
3	Northern Dancer	1964	Bill Hartack	2:00.00
4	Spend A Buck	1985	Angel Cordero, Jr.	2:00.20
5	Decidedly	1962	Bill Hartack	2:00.40
6	Proud Clarion	1967	Bobby Ussery	2:00.60
7	Grindstone	1996	Jerry Bailey	2:01.06
8	Fusaichi Pegasus	2000	Kent Desormeaux	2:01.12
9	War Emblem	2002	Victor Espinoza	2:01.13
10	Funny Cide	2003	Jose Santos	2:01.19

* Up to and including 2010

TOP 10 MONEY-WINNING JOCKEYS IN THE BREEDERS CUP

	JOCKEY*	YEARS	WINS	MONEY WON ($)#
1	Pat Day	1984–2004	12	23,033,360
2	Jerry Bailey	1986–2005	15	22,006,440
3	Frankie Dettori, Italy	1990–2010	10	17,831,172
4	Garrett Gomez	1994–2010	12	17,758,600
5	Chris McCarron	1984–2001	9	17,669,600
6	Mike Smith	1990–2010	13	17,274,760
7	John Velazquez, Puerto Rico	1995–2010	9	14,873,930
8	Gary Stevens	1984–2005	8	13,723,910
9	Corey Nakatani	1990–2006	7	9,965,480
10	Edgar Prado, Peru	1992–2010	4	8,729,180

* All jockeys from the USA unless otherwise stated.
# Up to and including 2010

Source: Breeders' Cup

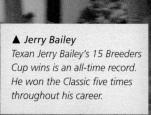

▲ Jerry Bailey
Texan Jerry Bailey's 15 Breeders Cup wins is an all-time record. He won the Classic five times throughout his career.

The Hambletonian and Little Brown Jug are the two most prestigious races in the harness racing calendar. The Hambletonian, for three-year-old trotters, was first staged during the 1926 New York State Fair at Syracuse. The race is named after Hambletonian, the greatest sire in harness racing history. Since 1981 the permanent home of the race has been the Meadowlands Race Track in East Rutherford, New Jersey.

TOP 10 **MOST WINS IN THE HAMBLETONIAN AND LITTLE BROWN JUG** *

	DRIVER	YEARS	H#	LBJ#	TOTAL
1	John Campbell	1977–2006	6	4	10
2	= Billy Haughton	1955–80	4	5	9
	= Mike Lachance	1988–2003	4	5	9
4	Stanley Dancer	1961–83	4	4	8
5	Ron Pierce	1993–2010	3	3	6
6	= John Simpson Sr	1956–64	2	3	5
	= Frank Ervin	1949–66	2	3	5
8	= Ben White	1933–43	4	0	4
	= Joe O'Brien	1955–73	2	2	4
10	= Henry Thomas	1937–44	3	0	3
	= Del Cameron	1954–67	3	0	3
	= Howard Beissinger	1969–78	3	0	3
	= Bill O'Donnell	1985–86	1	2	3
	= Ron Waples	1983–92	1	2	3
	= Jack Moiseyev	1991–96	1	2	3

* Up to and including 2010
\# H = Hambletonian; LBJ = Little Brown Jug

▲ Hambletonian
The Hambletonian is one of three races that make up the Triple Crown for harness racing trotters.

TOP 10 **OLYMPIC EQUESTRIAN NATIONS** *

	COUNTRY	DRESSAGE	EVENTING	JUMPING	TOTAL
1	Germany	11	4	6	21
2	Sweden	7	7	3	17
3	France#	3	3	6	12
4	= USA	0	6	5	11
	= West Germany†	7	1	3	11
6	Netherlands	3	5	2	10
7	Italy#	0	3	4	7
8	= Australia	0	6	0	6
	= Great Britain	0	5	1	6
	= USSR	4	1	1	6

* Based on gold medals won in the three main disciplines: Dressage, Three-Day Eventing, and Show Jumping, up to and including 2008
\# France and Italy totals include one shared gold in the now-discontinued High Jump event held in 1900
† Not including the five gold medals won by the United Germany team, 1956–64

▲ Galloping to gold
The most successful German in Equestrian Events is Dr. Reiner Klimke, who won six Dressage gold medals between 1964 and 1988. He also won two bronze medals.

WATER SPORTS

TOP 10 OLYMPIC AND WORLD CHAMPIONSHIP WATER POLO MEDAL-WINNING COUNTRIES

	COUNTRY	GOLD	SILVER	BRONZE	TOTAL*
1	Hungary	13	10	4	27
2	USA	4	7	7	18
3	Italy	8	4	4	16
4	Yugoslavia	5	5	4	14
5	USSR	4	3	4	11
6	= Russia	0	1	7	8
	= Spain	3	4	1	8
8	Netherlands	2	3	2	7
9	Belgium	0	4	2	6
10	Australia	2	1	2	5

* Up to and including the 2008 Olympic Games and 2009 World Aquatics Championships

TOP 10 MOST WORLD AND OLYMPIC DIVING GOLD MEDALS*

	DIVER / COUNTRY	M/F	YEARS	OLYMPIC GAMES	WORLD CHAMPS	TOTAL
1	Guo Jingjing, China	F	2001–09	4	10	14
2	Greg Louganis, USA	M	1978–88	4	5	9
3	Dmitri Sautin, Russia	M	1994–2003	2	5	7
4	= Fu Mingxia, China	F	1991–2000	4	2	6
	= Wu Minxia, China	F	2001–09	2	4	6
6	= Klaus Dibiasi, Italy	M	1968–76	3	2	5
	= Gao Min, China	F	1986–92	2	3	5
	= Qin Kai, China	M	2007–09	1	4	5
	= Wang Feng, China	M	2001–09	1	4	5
10	= Pat McCormick, USA	F	1952–56	4	0	4
	= Phil Boggs, USA	M	1973–78	1	3	4

* In individual and synchronized events at the Olympic Games 1904–2008 and the World Aquatics Championships 1973–2009

TOP 10 MOST WORLD AQUATIC CHAMPIONSHIP TITLES*

	SWIMMER / COUNTRY	YEARS	IND.	RELAY	TOTAL
1	Michael Phelps, USA	2001–09	13	9	22
2	Ian Thorpe, Australia	1998–2003	6	5	11
3	= Grant Hackett, Australia	1998–2005	7	3	10
	= Aaron Peirsol, USA	2001–09	7	3	10
5	= Kornelia Ender, East Germany	1973–75	4	4	8
	= Libby Lenton, Australia	2005–07	4	4	8
7	= Jim Montgomery, USA	1973–78	2	5	7
	= Kristin Otto, East Germany	1982–86	3	4	7
	= Jenny Thompson, USA	1991–2003	3	4	7
	= Michael Klim, Australia	1998–2007	2	5	7
	= Leisel Jones, Australia	2001–07	4	3	7
	= Ryan Lochte, USA	2005–09	3	4	7

* In individual long course events and relays up to and including 2009

◀ *Guo Jingjing* Chinese diving champion Guo Jingjing was just 18 when she won her first Olympic medal—a silver at Sydney in 2000.

THE 10 **FASTEST WINNING TIMES IN THE SYDNEY TO HOBART RACE***

	YACHT / COUNTRY	YEAR	ELAPSED TIME#
1	Wild Oats XI, Australia	2005	1:18:40:10
2	Nokia, Denmark	1999	1:19:48:02
3	Wild Oats XI, Australia	2008	1:20:34:14
4	Wild Oats XI, Australia	2007	1:21:24:32
5	Alfa Romeo, Australia/New Zealand	2002	2:04:58:52
6	Wild Oats XI, Australia	2010	2:07:37:20
7	Wild Oats XI, Australia	2006	2:08:52:33
8	Alfa Romeo II, Australia/New Zealand	2009	2:09:02:10
9	Nicorette, Sweden	2000	2:14:02:09
10	Morning Glory, Germany	1996	2:14:07:10

* Up to and including 2010
# days:hours:minutes:seconds

TOP 10 **MOST FORMULA ONE POWERBOAT WORLD TITLES**

	DRIVER / COUNTRY	YEARS*	TITLES
1	Guido Cappellini, Italy	1993–2009	10
2	Scott Gillman, USA	1997–2006	4
3	Renato Molinari, Italy	1981–84	3
4	=Jonathan Jones, UK	1991–98	2
	=Sami Seliö, Finland	2007–10	2
6	=Bob Spalding, UK	1985	1
	=Fabrizio Bocca, USA	1992	1
	=Gene Thibodaux, USA	1986	1
	=Jay Price, Qatar	2008	1
	=John Hill, UK	1990	1
	=Roger Jenkins, UK	1982	1

* There was no championship 1987–89

Source: UIM

The first Sydney to Hobart race took place in 1945 and was initially going to be an informal cruise, until British naval officer John Illingworth suggested it should be a race. It starts in Sydney Harbour at 1.00 pm on Boxing Day each year, and takes in 628 nautical miles. One of the toughest yacht races in the world, it is regarded as a sporting icon in Australia, alongside the Melbourne Cup and Ashes Test matches.

▶ *Guido Cappellini*
Between 1993 and 1996 Italian Cappellini won the Formula One Powerboat world title a record four consecutive years. He also won three consecutive titles in 2001–03.

WINTER SPORTS

TOP 10 MOST ALPINE SKIING WORLD CUP RACE WINS (MEN)

SKIER / COUNTRY	FIRST/LAST WIN	WINS*
1 Ingemar Stenmark, Sweden	1974–89	86
2 Hermann Maier, Austria	1997–2008	54
3 Alberto Tomba, Italy	1987–98	50
4 Marc Girardelli, Luxembourg	1983–96	43
5 Pirmin Zurbriggen, Switzerland	1982–90	40
6 Benjamin Raich, Austria	1999–2009	35
7 Bode Miller, USA	2001–10	32
8 Stephan Eberharter, Austria	1998–2004	29
9 Phil Mahre, USA	1976–1983	27
10 Franz Klammer, Austria	1973–1984	26

* Up to and including 2011

Source: FIS

The very first winner of a men's World Cup event was Heinrich Messner of Switzerland, who won the slalom at Berchtesgaden, West Germany, on January 5, 1967.

◀ **Hermann Maier**
Austria's Hermann Maier won four overall World Cup titles, two Olympic gold medals, and three World Championship gold medals.

▼ **Vreni Schneider**
Switzerland's Vreni Schneider was voted her country's "Sportswoman of the 20th Century."

TOP 10 MOST ALPINE SKIING WORLD CUP RACE WINS (WOMEN)

SKIER / COUNTRY	FIRST/LAST WIN	WINS*
1 Annemarie Moser-Pröll, Austria	1970–80	62
2 Vreni Schneider, Switzerland	1984–95	55
3 Renate Götschl, Austria	1993–2007	46
4 Anja Pärson, Sweden	1998–2011	42
5 Lindsey Vonn (née Kildow), USA	2004–11	41
6 Katja Seizinger, Germany	1991–98	36
7 Hanni Wenzel, Liechtenstein	1973–84	33
8 Erika Hess, Switzerland	1981–86	31
9 Janica Kostelic, Croatia	1999–2006	30
10 Marlies Schild, Austria	2004–11	299

* Up to and including 2011

Source: FIS

The first winner of a women's World Cup race was Nancy Greene of Canada, who won the slalom in West Germany, on January 7, 1967.

TOP 10 **MOST INDIVIDUAL SKI-JUMPING MEDALS AT THE NORDIC WORLD SKI CHAMPIONSHIPS**

	JUMPER / COUNTRY	YEARS	G	S	B	TOTAL*
1	**Birger Ruud**, Norway	1931–48	5	2	0	7
2	**Adam Malysz**, Poland	2001–11	4	1	1	6
3	**Jens Weissflog**, Germany	1985–95	2	1	2	5
4	=**Janne Ahonen**, Finland	1997–2005	2	0	2	4
	=**Martin Schmitt**, Germany	1999–2009	2	2	0	4
	=**Sven Eriksson**, Sweden	1931–36	0	1	3	4
	=**Jari Puikkonen**, Finland	1980–89	1	2	1	4
	=**Masahiko Harada**, Japan	1993–99	2	1	1	4
	=**Reidar Andersen**, Norway	1930–37	0	3	1	4
	=**Andreas Goldberger**, Austria	1993–97	0	2	2	4
	=**Helmut Recknagel**, West Germany	1958–62	2	0	2	4
	=**Matti Nykänen**, Finland	1982–89	1	1	2	4
	=**Simon Ammann**, Switzerland	2007–11	1	1	2	44

* Up to and including the 2011 championship

Source: FIS

▼ *Adam Malysz*
Despite his World Championship successes, Poland's Adam Malysk has not yet won an Olympic gold medal. He took a bronze and silver at Salt Lake City in 2002, and two silver medals at Vancouver in 2010.

THE 10 **FASTEST WINNING TIMES IN THE MEN'S 500 METERS SPEED-SKATING OLYMPIC FINAL**

SKATER / COUNTRY / YEAR / VENUE / TIME (SECS)

1 **Casey FitzRandolph**, USA
2002
Salt Lake City, USA — **34.62**

2 **Joey Cheek**, USA
2006
Turin, Italy — **34.88**

3 **Tae-Bum Mo**, South Korea
2010
Vancouver, Canada — **34.91**

4 **Hiroyasu Shimizu**, Japan
1998
Nagano, Japan — **35.68**

5 **Aleksandr Golubev**, Russia
1994
Lillehammer, Norway — **36.33**

6 **Uwe-Jens Mey**, East Germany
1988
Calgary, Canada — **36.45**

7 **Uwe-Jens Mey**, Germany
1992
Albertville, France — **37.14**

8 **Eric Heiden**, USA
1980
Lake Placid, USA — **38.03**

9 **Sergey Fokichev**, USSR
1984
Sarajevo, Yugoslavia — **38.19**

10 **Yevgeniy Kulikov**, USSR
1976
Innsbruck, Austria — **39.17**

EXTREME SPORTS

TOP 10 MOST WINNERS OF THE BODYBUILDING OLYMPIA CHAMPIONSHIPS*

	BODYBUILDER / YEARS	WINS
1	= Lee Haney 1984–91	8
	= Lenda Murray# 1990–2003	8
	= Ronnie Coleman 1998–2005	8
4	Arnold Schwarzenegger Austria 1970–80	7
5	= Cory Everson# 1984–89	6
	= Dorian Yates, UK 1992–97	6
	= Iris Kyle# 2004–10	6
8	= Kim Chizevsky# 1996–99	4
	= Jay Cutler 2006–10	4
10	= Sergio Oliva, Cuba 1967–69	3
	= Frank Zane 1977–79	3

* Men's and women's championships
\# Female champions

Source: IFBB

The Ironman competition consists of a 2.4-mile open water swim, 112-mile cycle race, and a full marathon of 26 miles 385 yards. The fastest time is 8 hours 4 minutes 8 seconds by Luc Van Lierde of Belgium in 1996. The women's record is 8 hours 54 minutes 2 seconds by Britain's Chrissie Wellington in 2009. Paula Newby-Fraser (Zimbabwe) holds the record for the most wins—8. The men's record is 6, held jointly by Dave Scott and Mark Allen (both USA).

▲ **Hawaiian extremes**
The Ironman World Championship has been held in Hawaii every year since 1978.

All winners are from the USA unless otherwise stated. The Olympia championships are international bodybuilding events organized by the International Federation of Body Building and Fitness (IFBB).

THE 10 LATEST WINNERS OF THE IRONMAN WORLD CHAMPIONSHIP

YEAR	MALE / COUNTRY	FEMALE / COUNTRY
2010	Chris McCormack, Australia	Mirinda Carfrae, Australia
2009	Craig Alexander, Australia	Chrissie Wellington, UK
2008	Craig Alexander, Australia	Chrissie Wellington, UK
2007	Chris McCormack, Australia	Chrissie Wellington, UK
2006	Normann Stadler, Germany	Michellie Jones, Australia
2005	Faris Al-Sultan, Germany	Natascha Badmann, Switzerland
2004	Normann Stadler, Germany	Natascha Badmann, Switzerland
2003	Peter Reid, Canada	Lori Bowden, Canada
2002	Tim DeBoom, USA	Natascha Badmann, Switzerland
2001	Tim DeBoom, USA	Natascha Badmann, Switzerland

▼ *Ronnie Coleman
Coleman's eight Mr. Olympia wins were in consecutive years.*

TOP 10 LEADING GOLD MEDALISTS AT THE SUMMER X GAMES*

ATHLETE# / COUNTRY / SPORT / YEARS	GOLDS
1 Dave Mirra, USA BMX 1996–2005	13
2 Travis Pastrana, USA Moto X/rally car racing 1999–2010	10
3 Tony Hawk, USA Skateboarding 1995–2003	9
4 Andy Macdonald, USA Skateboarding 1996–2002	8
5 = Fabiola da Silva, Brazil In-line skating 1996–2007	7
= Pierre-Luc Gagnon, Canada Skateboarding 2002-10	7
7 = Bucky Lasek, USA Skateboarding 1999–2006	6
= Jamie Bestwick, England BMX 2000–10	6
9 = Bob Burnquist, Brazil Skateboarding 2001–08	5
= Biker Sherlock, USA Street luge 1996–98	5

* Up to and including X Games XVI in 2010.
# All male except Fabiola da Silva

► **Travis Pastrana**
Pastrana won the first three Moto X Freestyle titles in 1999, 2000 and 2001.

Andy Macdonald holds the record for winning the most X Games medals—15 in total. The first ESPN Extreme Games (now X Games) for "alternative" sports were held in June/July 1995. The Games are held every year and since 1997 there has also been an annual Winter X Games.

TOP 10 FASTEST WINNING TIMES OF THE IDITAROD TRAIL SLED-DOG RACE*

	MUSHER#	YEAR	TIME
1	John Baker	2011	8d 18h 46m 39s
2	Martin Buser, Switzerland	2002	8d 22h 46m 02s
3	Lance Mackey	2010	8d 23h 59m 09s
4	Doug Swingley	2000	9d 00h 58m 06s
5	Doug Swingley	1995	9d 02h 42m 19s
6	Lance Mackey	2007	9d 05h 08m 41s
7	Jeff King	1996	9d 05h 43m 13s
8	Jeff King	1998	9d 05h 52m 26s
9	Martin Buser, Switzerland	1997	9d 08h 30m 45s
10	Jeff King	2006	9d 11h 11m 36s

* Up to and including 2011
# All mushers from the USA unless otherwise stated

Source: The Iditarod

▼ **Alaskan extremes**
The Iditarod is held annually, beginning on the first Saturday in March, and is a 1,161-mile (1,868-km) race across Alaska from Willow, near Anchorage, to Nome. First held in 1973 as a test of the best sled-dog mushers and teams, it has now evolved into a highly competitive race.

SPORTS MISCELLANY

TOP 10 HIGHEST-EARNING SPORTSWOMEN

SPORTSWOMAN*	SPORT	EARNINGS ($)#
1 Maria Sharapova, Russia	Tennis	24,500,000
2 Serena Williams, USA	Tennis	20,200,000
3 Venus Williams, USA	Tennis	15,400,000
4 Danica Patrick, USA	Auto racing	12,000,000
5 Kim Yu-Na, South Korea	Figure skating	9,700,000
6 Annika Sorenstam, Sweden	Golf	8,000,000
7 Ana Ivanovic, Serbia	Tennis	7,200,000
8 Jelena Jankovic, Serbia	Tennis	5,300,000
9 Paula Creamer, USA	Golf	5,200,000
10 Lorena Ochoa, Mexico	Golf	5,000,000

* All from the USA unless otherwise stated
\# Based on earnings from prize money, endorsements, and appearance fees in the 12 months to August 2010

Source: *Forbes* magazine

◀ *Maria Sharapova*
Sharapova has won three Grand Slam events: Wimbledon, and the US and Australian Opens.

TOP 10 HIGHEST-EARNING SPORTSMEN

SPORTSMAN*	SPORT	EARNINGS ($)#
1 Tiger Woods	Golf	105,000,000
2 Floyd Mayweather	Boxing	65,000,000
3 Kobe Bryant	Basketball	48,000,000
4 Phil Mickelson	Golf	46,000,000
5 David Beckham, UK	Soccer	43,700,000
6 Roger Federer, Switzerland	Tennis	43,000,000
7 LeBron James	Basketball	42,800,000
8 Manny Pacquiao, Philippines	Boxing	42,000,000
9 Eli Manning	Football	39,900,000
10 Terrell Suggs	Football	38,300,000

* All from the USA unless otherwise stated
\# Based on money earned from salaries, bonuses, prize money, endorsements, and licensing income in the 12 months to July 2010
Source: *Forbes* magazine

◀ *Floyd Mayweather*
Mayweather received around $25 million for fighting Oscar de la Hoya in 2007.

THE 10 **LATEST WINNERS OF THE JESSE OWENS AWARD** (MALE)

YEAR / WINNER / DISCIPLINE

2010 David Oliver
Hurdler

2009 Tyson Gay
Sprinter

2008 Bryan Clay
Decathlete/
heptathlete

2007 Tyson Gay
Sprinter

2006 Jeremy Wariner
Sprinter

2005 Justin Gatlin
Sprinter

2004 Justin Gatlin
Sprinter

2003 Tom Pappas
Decathlete/
heptathlete

2002 Tim Montgomery
Sprinter

2001 Tim Montgomery
Shot putter

Source: USATF

Named after the great sprinter and long jumper, the Jesse Owens Award is the highest accolade that can be bestowed upon an American athlete. There are separate awards for men and women, the 2010 winner of the women's award being sprinter Allyson Felix.

TOP 10 **MOST WATCHED SINGLE SPORTS EVENTS ON US TELEVISION**

EVENT	YEAR	% US HOUSEHOLDS
1 Super Bowl XVI , San Francisco 49ers v. Cincinnati Bengals	1982	49.1
2 Super Bowl XVII , Washington Redskins v. Miami Dolphins	1983	48.6
3 Winter Olympics Figure Skating, Nancy Kerrigan and Tonya Harding	1994	48.5
4 Super Bowl XX, Chicago Bears v. New England Patriots	1986	48.3
5 Super Bowl XII, Dallas Cowboys v. Denver Broncos	1978	47.2
6 Super Bowl XIII, Pittsburgh Steelers v. Dallas Cowboys	1979	47.1
7 Super Bowl XLIV, New Orleans Saints v. Indianapolis Colts	2010	46.4
8 Super Bowl XVIII, Los Angeles Raiders v. Washington Redskins	1984	46.4
9 Super Bowl XIX, San Francisco 49ers v. Miami Dolphins	1985	46.4
10 Super Bowl XIV , Pittsburgh Steelers v. Los Angeles Rams	1980	46.3

MOST VALUABLE SPORTING BRANDS

Forbes magazine works out value of sporting-team brands as a percentage of a team's overall value that is derived from its name, to calculate the most valuable sporting brands. In 2010, Manchester United were deposed by the New York Yankees thanks to their 27th World Series title, which pushed up the brand's merchandising revenue to $328 million. Currently ranking third is Spanish soccer team Real Madrid, whose seven-year $1.4 billion television deal is the largest in professional sports. The Dallas Cowboys and European football teams Barcelona, Bayern Munich and Arsenal all hold Top 10 positions.

◀ *New York Yankees*
The Yankees are the most successful team in Major League Baseball.

THE UNIVERSE & THE EARTH

Caves
caverbob.com
Lists of long and deep caves

Disasters
emdat.be
Emergency Events Database covering major disasters since 1900

Encyclopedia Astronautica
astronautix.com
Spaceflight news and reference

Islands
worldislandinfo.com
Information on the world's islands

Mountains
peaklist.org
Lists of the world's tallest mountains

NASA
nasa.gov
The main website for the US space agency

Oceans
oceansatlas.org
The UN's resource on oceanographic issues

Planets
nineplanets.org
A multimedia tour of the Solar System

Rivers
rev.net/~aloe/river
The River Systems of the World website

Space exploration
spacefacts.de
Manned spaceflight data

LIFE ON EARTH

Animals
animaldiversity.ummz.umich.edu
A wealth of animal data

Birds
avibase.bsc-eoc.org
A database on the world's birds

Conservation
iucn.org
The leading nature conservation site

Endangered
cites.org
Lists of endangered species of flora and fauna

Extinct
nhm.ac.uk/nature-online/life/dinosaurs-other-extinct-creatures
Dinosaurs and other extinct animals

Fish
fishbase.org
Global information on fish

Food and Agriculture Organization
fao.org
Statistics from the UN's FAO website

Forests
fao.org/forestry
The FAO's forestry website

Insects
entnemdept.ufl.edu/walker/ufbir
The University of Florida Book of Insect Records

Sharks
flmnh.ufl.edu/fish/sharks
The Florida Museum of Natural History's shark attack files

THE HUMAN WORLD

FBI
fbi.gov
Information and links on crime in the USA

Health
cdc.gov/nchs
Information and links on health for US citizens

Leaders
terra.es/personal2/monolith
Facts about world leaders since 1945

Military
globalfirepower.com
World military statistics and rankings

Names
ssa.gov/OACT/babynames
Most common names since 1879 from the Social Security Administration

Nobel Prizes
nobelprize.org
The official website of the Nobel Foundation

Religion
worldchristiandatabase.org
World religions data (subscription required)

Rulers
rulers.org
A database of the world's rulers and political leaders

Supercentenarians
grg.org/calment.html
A world listing of those who have reached 110 or older

World Health Organization
who.int/en
World health information and advice

TOWN & COUNTRY

Bridges and tunnels
en.structurae.de
Facts and figures on the world's buildings, tunnels, and other structures

Bridges (highest)
highestbridges.com
Detailed facts and stats on the world's highest bridges

Buildings
emporis.com/en
The Emporis database of high-rise and other buildings

Country and city populations
citypopulation.de
A searchable guide to the world's countries and major cities

Country data
cia.gov/library/publications/the-world-factbook
The CIA's acclaimed *World Factbook*

Country populations
un.org/esa/population/unpop
The UN's worldwide data on population issues

Development
worldbank.org
Development and other statistics from around the world

Population
census.gov/ipc
International population statistics

Skyscrapers
skyscraperpage.com
Data and images of the world's skyscrapers

Tunnels
lotsberg.net
A database of the longest rail, road, and canal tunnels

CULTURE & LEARNING

Art
artnet.com
World art info, with price database available to subscribers

The Art Newspaper
theartnewspaper.com
News and views on the art world

Education
nces.ed.gov
The home of federal education data

Languages
ethnologue.com
Online reference work on the world's 6,909 living languages

Libraries
ala.org
US library information and book awards from the American Library Association

The Library of Congress
loc.gov
The gateway to one of the world's greatest collections of words and pictures

Newspapers
wan-press.org
The World Association of Newspapers' website

The New York Public Library
nypl.org
One of the country's foremost libraries, with an online catalog

The Pulitzer Prize
pulitzer.org
A searchable guide to the prestigious US literary prize

UNESCO
unesco.org
Comparative international statistics on education and culture

MUSIC

All Music Guide
allmusic.com
A comprehensive guide to all genres of music

American Society of Composers, Authors, and Publishers
ascap.com
ASCAP songwriter and other awards

Billboard
billboard.com
US music news and charts data

Classical music
classicalusa.com
An online guide to classical music in the USA

Country Music Hall of Fame
countrymusichalloffame.com
The history of and information about country music

Grammy Awards
naras.org
The official site for the famous US music awards

MTV
mtv.com
The online site for the TV music channel

Recording Industry of America
riaa.org
Searchable data on gold and platinum disk award winners

Rock and Roll Hall of Fame
www.rockhall.com
The museum of the history of rock

Rolling Stone
rollingstone.com
Features on popular music since 1967

ENTERTAINMENT

Academy Awards
oscars.org
The official "Oscars" website

E! Online
eonline.com
Celebrity and entertainment news and gossip

Emmy Awards
emmyonline.org
Emmy TV awards from the National Television Academy site

Hollywood
hollywood.com
A US cinema site with details on all the new releases

Internet Broadway Database
ibdb.com
Broadway theater information

Internet Movie Database
The best of the publicly accessible movie websites; IMDbPro is available to subscribers

Internet Theatre Database
theatredb.com
A Broadway-focused searchable stage site

Tony Awards
tonyawards.com
Official website of the American Theatre Wing's Tonys

Variety
variety.com
Extensive entertainment information (extra features available to subscribers)

Yahoo! Movies
movies.yahoo.com
Charts plus features and links to the latest movie releases

THE COMMERCIAL WORLD

The Economist
economist.com
Global economic and political news

Energy
eia.doe.gov
Official US energy statistics

Environment
epi.yale.edu
The latest Environmental Performance Index rankings

Internet
internetworldstats.com
Internet World Stats

Organization for Economic Co-operation and Development
oecd.org
World economic and social statistics

Rich lists
forbes.com
Forbes magazine's celebrated lists of the world's wealthiest people

Telecommunications
itu.int
Worldwide telecommunications statistics

Travel industry
ustravel.org
Information on US travel

The World Bank
worldbank.org
World development, trade and labor statistics, now freely accessible

World Tourism Organization
world-tourism.org
The world's principal travel and tourism organization

ON THE MOVE

Aircraft crashes
baaa-acro.com
The Aircraft Crashes Record Office database

Airlines
airfleets.net
Statistics on the world's airlines and aircraft

Airports
airports.org
Airports Council International statistics on the world's airports

Air safety
aviation-safety.net
Data on air safety and accidents

Air speed records
fai.org/records
The website of the official air speed record governing body

Car manufacture
oica.net
The International Organization of Motor Vehicle Manufacturers' website

Metros
metrobits.org
An exploration of the world's subway systems

Rail
uic.org
World rail statistics

Railways
railwaygazette.com
The world's railway business in depth from *Railway Gazette International*

Shipwrecks
shipwreckregistry.com
A huge database of the world's wrecked and lost ships

SPORT

Baseball
mlb.com
The official website of Major League Baseball

Basketball
nba.com
The official website of the NBA

Football
nfl.com
The official website of the NFL

Golf
pgatour.com
The Professional Golfers' Association Tour

Hockey
nhl.com
The official website of the NHL

Olympics
olympic.org
The official Olympics website

Skiing
fis-ski.com
Fédèration Internationale de Ski, the world governing body of skiing and snowboarding

Sports Illustrated
sportsillustrated.cnn.com
Sports Illustrated's comprehensive coverage of all major sports

Tennis
lta.org.uk
The official site of the British Lawn Tennis Association

Track and field
iaaf.org
The world governing body of athletics

INDEX

PICTURE CREDITS

Activision
65t Activision Blizzard.

American Motorcyclist Association
189b.

AKG
138-139b Paramount Pictures/album/akg-images;144b Warner Bros./album/akg-images; 152t Photo: Pixar Animation Studios/Walt Disney Pictures/Album/akg-images.

The Art Archive
117t The Art Archive / Musée d'Orsay Paris / Alfredo Dagli Orti .

Bridgeman Art Library
118t Private Collection/Bridgeman Art Library.

Corbis
10b © Mike Agliolo; 11 © Mark M. Lawrence; 18l © Maggie Steber/National Geographic Society; 19l © Russ Heinl/All Canada Photos; 20 © Paul Harris/JAI; 22tl © George Steinmetz; 22c © George Hammerstein; 23t © Stringer/Russia/Reuters; 23b © Matthieu Paley; 25l © Ed Darack/Science Faction; 24b © Jim Zuckerman; 26t © Frans Lemmens; 26b © Ocean; 28 © Andrew McConnell/Robert Harding World Imagery; 28b © Cezaro de Luca/epa; 29b © Ziyah Gafic/VII Network; 30b © Adi Weda/epa; 32-33 © Gerd Ludwig; 34l © Louie Psihoyos/Science Faction; 36c © Brian J. Skerry/National Geographic Society; 37c & 37t© DLILLC; 38-39b © Toshiki Sawaguchi/epa; 39br © Jeff Vanuga; 39tr ©Remy Steinegger/Reuters; 41c © Fred Buyle/Realis Agence; 40-41b © Gallo Images; 40tl © Paul A. Souders; 42-43t © Tom Brakefield; 43b © Frans Lanting; 44t © Thomas Marent/Visuals Unlimited; 45t © Tobias Bernhard; 46tl © Denis Scott; 47tr © Joe McDonald; 48b ©LWA-Dann Tardif; 52t © Frans Lanting; 53c © Beawiharta/Reuters; 54-55 © Matthias Kulka; 57r © Bettmann; 58t © Alessandro Della Bella/Keystone; 59br © Robert Gilhooly/epa; 60b © Gideon Mendel/ActionAid; 62b © Jalil Rezayee/epa; 63t © Imaginechina; 64-65 background © Gideon Mendel/In Pictures; 66bl © Yann Arthus-Bertrand; 67tl © Alai Bazil/epa; 67br © Alan Crowhurst/epa; 68tl © Bettmann; 68b © Mark Wilson/Pool; 69b © Luke MacGregor/Reuters; 70cl © Bettmann; 70cr © Hulton-Deutsch Collection; 70b © Bettmann; 71br © Underwood & Underwood; 72t © Reuters; 73tl © HO/Reuters; 73tr © Luis Galdamez/Reuters; 74-75t © Shepard Sherbell/SABA; 76-77 background © Hulton-Deutsch Collection; 77br © Bettmann; 77c © Bettmann; 76t © Hulton-Deutsch Collection; 80t © Paul Bowen/Science Faction; 80b © Korea News Service/X01654/Reuters; 81b © Ed Darack/Science

Faction; 83t © Paolo Whitaker/X00921/Reuters; 82-83 background © John Van Hasselt; 84-85 © Zhang Chao/Xinhua Press; 86b © Jose Fuste Raga; 87t © Danny Lehman; 88b © Philippe Lissac/Godong; 89b © Martin Harvey; 90b © Khaled Al-Hariri/X00374/Reuters; 91b © Christophe Calais; 92t © Jose Fuste Raga; 92-93b © Joson; 93c © Stuart Freedman/In Pictures; 95t; 96t © Michael Fiala/Reuters; 99t © Richard Klune; 98c © Joseph Sohm/Visions of America; 98t © YNA/epa; 100b © Martial Trezzini/epa; 101b © Martin Jones; 104t © Louise Gubb; 105t © Guo Cheng/XinHua/Xinhua Press; 107t © Kimberly White/Reuters; 109b © Blaine Harrington III; 109c © Blue Lantern Studio; 112tr © HO/Reuters; 112b © Hulton-Deutsch Collection; 113b © Marco Secchi; 115t © Katie Orlinsky; 116b © Robert Holmes; 117b; 119t © Michele Asselin; 118br © Luke MacGregor/Reuters; 120-121 © Rick Maiman/Sygma; 122br © Sunset Boulevard; 123bl © Sozufe Adeleri /Retna Ltd ./Retna Ltd.; 123t © G.J. McCarthy /Dallas Morning News; 124t © Alfredo Aldai/epa; 124b © Michael Ochs Archives; 126t © Giulia Muir/epa; 127t, 130tl & 133b © Neal Preston; 129r © Tim Mosenfelder; 130b © Kirsty Umback; 132-133 background © Owen Franken; 134 © Rune Hellestad; 135t © Barry Lewis/In Pictures; 135br & 136t © Reuters; 137tl © Jörg Carstensen/dpa; 142t © Walter McBride ./Retna Ltd.; 143b © Robbie Jack; 162tl © Schenectady Museum; Hall of Electrical History Foundation; 163bl © Tracey Nearmy/epa; 163tr © Robert Wallis; 165b © Britta Pedersen/dpa; 166t © Kim Kyung-Hoon/Reuters; 172b © Karen Kasmauski; 172-173 background © Jeremy Horner; 174t © Kim Komenich/San Francisco Chronicle; 175tr © Micheline Pelletier; 175bl © Underwood & Underwood; 177tr © Emilio Suetone/Hemis; 180t © Akhtar Soomro/epa; 181bt © Jean-Pierre Lescourret; 182b © Omar Sobhani/Reuters; 184-185 © William Manning; 184t © Blaine Harrington III; 188b © Bettmann; 189t © Wu Hong/epa; 190t © Philip Wallick; 191t & 190-191 background © Dean Conger; 194b © Randy Faris; 195t © Deon Reynolds/Monsoon/Photolibrary; 197 © Christophe Boisvieux; 197 inset © Marcus Brandt/epa; 198tr © Lake County Museum; 200c © Bettmann; 200b © Fueger/dpa; 201 © Kapoor Baldev/Sygma; 202-203 © Kay Nietfeld/epa; 204b © Chen Kai/Xinhua Press; 207t © London 2012/Handout/Reuters; 209t © Olivier Maire/epa; 211r © Reuters; 214t © Bettmann; 214b © Jeanine Leech/Icon SMI; 216t © Andrew Gombert/epa; 216b © Icon Sports Media; 217 © Icon SMI; 218b © Marius Becker/epa; 219t © Zou Zheng/Xinhua Press; 220t © Dave Sandford/NHL Images/Reuters; 222b © Paulo Whitaker/Reuters; 222t © Matthew Ashton/AMA; 223t © Christian

Liewig; 225t © M.J. Masotti Jr./Reuters; 227b © Reuters; 228b © Adam Stoltman; 229t © Justin Lane/epa; 230b © Gerry Penny/epa; 231b © The Augusta Chronicle/ZUMA Press; 232t © George Tiedemann/GT Images; 232-233 © Schlegelmilch;234b © Tim de Waele; 235t © Robin Van LonkHuijsen/epa; 235b © Kai Fösterling/ epa; 237t © Tony Kurdzuk/Star Ledger; 239b © Chen Shaojin/Xinhua Press; 240t © Christophe Karaba/epa; 240b © Jean-Yves Ruszniewski/TempSport; 242t © Bruce Omori/epa; 242b © Reuters; 243t © Bo Bridges; 244t © Ben Radford; 245b © Justin Lane/epa.

ESO
10tl; 12-13 background Y. Beletsky; 13r G. Hüdepohl.

Fotolia
9b © Tristan3D; 17l © Martha Andrews; 18-19 © Eric Isselée; 22l © Yong Hian Lim; 24t © Marta; 26t & 49tl © Eric Isselée 26-27 © Mytho; 27t © zwo; 28t © Antony McAulay; 29t © electriceye; 28-29 background © Tomáš Hašlar; 31t © Kirill Zdorov; 33 inset © SkyLine; 33br © raven; 36b © patpitchaya; 37b © hperry; 38t © Taalvi; 41b © Jakub Krechowicz; 42c © lunamarina; 44b © picturetime; 46b © patrimonio designs; 46c © iPics; 48tl © biglama; 49tr © valdis torms; 50cr © Oleksiy Ilyashenko; 50tl © MilkMilk777; 50t © hazel proudlove; 50cl © gtranquillity; 50b © Konstantin Sutyagin; 51cl © TMAX; 51bl © Tomboy2290; 53br © Herbie; 52-53b © Hagit Berkovich; 56 © cameraman; 56r © TheSupe87; 57c © anankkml; 57b © Olaru Radian; 58b © Irochka; 59bl © Maxim_Kazmin; 58-59 background © zphoto; 60t © Ben Chams; 61b © electriceye; 62tl © TheKid; 62c © Sprinter81; 63b © Taffi; 62-63 background © eyewave; 64l © klikk; 64br ©Ruth Black; 65bl ©godfer; 65c © ben; 66t © JAMCO Design; 66-67 background © Konovalov Pavel; 67tr © DoctorJools; 67tr © Andy Lidstone; 68-69 background © KonstantinosKokkinis; 70tl © Carsten Reisinger; 70tr © Lance Bellers; 70-71 background © Tyler Olson; 72 © SpbPhoto; 72b © Herbert Berends; 73r © picsfive; 73br © Domen Colja; 73c © Tommroch; 74t & 74bl © Gina Sanders; 75tl © Sebastian Kaulitzki; 74-75 background © Tracy King; 77l © ann triling; 78-79 background © life_artist; 79t © sabri deniz kizil; 79b © Danicek; 79tl © Dariusz Kopestynski; 80-81 background © zphoto; 82b © Pixlmaker; 82r © Elena Kovaleva; 85 © Maximo Sanz; 86t © RabidBadger; 86-87 background © Daniel Fleck; 87b © Galyna Andrushko; 88t © Marco Birn; 88t © Anchels; 89t © nezezon; 90t © Kristina Afanasyeva; 91t © Manish; 91tr © Alex; 94bc © Sylvie Thenard; 94bc © Ilja Mašík; 95b © Andrea Seemann;

95tr ©H D Connelly; 96l © NesaCera; 97l ©trancedrumer; 98-99 background © Rainer Plendl; 100t © nali; 100-101 background © Olaru Radian; 101t © Adamus ; 104b © pablo_hernan; 104-105 background © mirpic; 105b © EastWest Imaging; 106b © Carlos Restrepo; 106-107 background © picsfive; 107bl © imagebos; 107br © Taiga; 107tl © tanatat; 108t © Yang MingQi; 108b © pressmaster; 108 background © flucas; 110-111b © Acik; 110-111 background © VAPhoto; 112-113 background © oleschwander; 113tl © Andrezej Tokarski; 114c © absolut; 114-115 background © Jim Barber; 116-117 background © HelleM; 118bl © Yuriy Panyukov; 119b © Paolo Frangiolli; 119br © Andrii Pokaz; 121 br © sharpshot; 122 background © Jim Barber; 122bl © Pedro Nogueira ; 123br & 138-139 background © A Dudy ; 123 background, 126-27 background, 128-129 background & 130t © DWP; 124-125b © dim@dim; 127br © Alx; 128br © Veronika Vasilyuk; 131b © Kristian Peetz; 134-135 background © Annette Chalmers; 136c © Carolina K. Smith MD; 136-137 background © sumnersgraphicsinc; 138br © Kirtsy Pargeter; 143r © Steve Mann; 143 background © jeffrey van daele; 144 & 145 © Albachiaraa; 146bl © Arman Zhenikeyev; 146br © TRITOOTH; 146-147 background © Phuong Nguyen; 148-149 © Argus; 150tl © Christos Georghiou; 150r © Allyson Kitts; 150-151 background © jas ; 151b © jwblinn; 151bl © katatonia; 151c © RTimages; 151c © Irochka; 154-155 background © Sebastian Kaulitzki; 156-157 background © Tr3; 158b © James Steidl; 159c © ZecKa; 160t © Elena Baryshkina; 162b © Andrzej Tokarski ; 162tr © Ian O'Hanlon; 162-163 background © kentoh; 163c © Norman Chan; 163br © Alysta ; 164c © microimages; 164b © dinostock; 164-164 background © Matt Baker; 166b © Vjom; 167tl © Arcady; 169br © sumnersgraphicsinc; 170t © Feng Yu; 170-171 background; 171r © Speedfighter; 172t © Beboy; 173r © sabri deniz kizil; 175br © Ilja Mašík; 176r © Lusoimages; 176cl © Lana Langlois; 176b © volff; 176cr © felinda; 176bl © Giuseppe Porzani; 176br © Bernd Jürgens; 177tl © mashe; 177bl © arkpo; 177br © Hugh O'Neill; 178l © Yahia Loukkal; 178bc © Daniel James Armisha; 178br © Witold Krasowski; 179l © Lack-O'Keen; 179b © Torian; 180b © mtkang; 180 background © Sergey Tokarev; 181tl © NJ; 181 background © Luiz; 182t © Christopher Nolan; 182 background © .shock; 183l © thanh lam; 183r © Yuri Arcurs; 185b © miro kovacevic; 185t © Nimbus; 191b © Ericos; 192 background © lunamarina; 193 © Stocksnapper; 195bl © Arkhipov; 196b © laurent davaine; 199t © Michael Rosskothen; 199cr © Secret Side; 200 © icholakov; 203br © Nobilio; 207l © Nikolai Sorokin; 207r © ErickN;

212b © Sean Gladwell ; 212-213 background © Supertrooper ; 215tr © Steve Degenhardt; 216b © Albo; 218t & 228-229 background © Michael Flippo; 19tl © Giordano Aita; 222-223b © Frog 974; 224-225 background © Mark Herreid; 226-227 background & 227t © lilufoto; 230-231 background © Alexei Novikov; 230b © Sven Hoppe; 231t © zimmytws; 236-237 background © TMAX; 240-241 background © R Roulet; 244 background © Alx; 245t © Lazypit; 245t © Petr Nad.

Getty Images
14t,17b; 31b; 59t; 102-103; 113c; 128r; 161b; 170b; 194t; 196c; 199tr; 204t; 206c, 206b; 210b; 213r; 215b,224t; 225b; 226t; 226b; 230t; 233tr; 237br; 238 & 244b Getty Images;16l Gamma-Keystone; 25r Sylvain Grandadam; 27l Stephen Alvarez; 34b De Agostini; 35b; 61t; 75tr; 82t; 132t; 193t; 205b, 208tl; 212t; 212-213b; 228t; 236b & 242-243 AFP; 40c Yva Momatiuk & John Eastcott; 43r Minden Pictures; 45b Frank Lukasseck; 56t Image by Brittany DeWester; 65t SSPL; 71t Barcroft Media; 78t& 206tr Popperfoto; 93t Gavin Hellier; 110-111tl FilmMagic; 125, 127b, 128l & 137tr; 215t & 219b WireImage; 131t Bob Thomas; 133t & 167t Redferns; 171b Tim Graham; 209b & 241b Bongarts; 220b NHLI; 221 Sports Illustrated.

iStockphoto.com
19r © Bartosz Hadyniak; 30t © Niko Guido; 36b © David Thyberg; 69t © art12321; 48tr © catman73; 107c © Alex Kalmbach; 114t © SAMIphoto; 114t © milosluz; 114-115b © MBCheatham; 142 background © Yarek Gnatowski; 166-167 background © Henrik Jonsson; 178tr © Roydee; 195tl © Hogne Botnen Totland; 198b © 4x6; 205t © Matt Jeacock; 206tl © Darja Tokranova; 206-207 © Hanquan Chen; 208 background © arne thaysen; 214-215 © Joseph Gareri; 224b © Danny Hooks.

The Kobal Collection
49b Walt Disney Pictures; 113tr Nordisk Film; 138t Universal/Playtone; 139t Warner Bros/Regency/Canal +; 140 Danjaq/EON/UA; 141 Columbia/Danjaq/EON/UA; 144t MGM ; 145t 20th Century Fox; 145b Twentieth Century-Fox Film Corporation; 146t Silver Pictures; 147t 20th Century Fox; 147b Warner Bros/Legendary Pictures; 148b MGM ; 149t Danjaq/EON/UA; 150t Forward Pass; 150b Warner Bros/DC Comics; 151t Imagine Ent/Gordon, Melinda Sue; 153t Studio Ghibli; 153c Castle Rock/Shangri-La Entertainment; 153b Dreamworks/Aardman Animations; 154t Universal/Boland, Jasin; 154b Walt Disney; 155b 20th Century Fox; 155t Warner Bros; 156t Columbia Pictures; 156b Warner Bros/James, David;

157t Columbia/Michaels, Darren; 157b Focus Features/Bailey, Alex; 158t First Light Productions/ Kingsgate Films; 159t Marvel/Sony Pictures; 159b 20th Century Fox/Vaughan, Stephen; 160b Warner Bros/Wallace, Merie W ; 161t See-Saw Films; 164t Dreamworks Animation; 167b Marv Films; 174t Columbia Pictures; 199bl 20th Century Fox/Paramount/Wallace, Merie W ; 199br 20th Century Fox.

Mary Evans Picture Library
21c; 203br IBL Collections.

NASA
10-11, 14c, 14b, 15t, 15cl & 15cr; 11r, 12t & 15b JPL-Caltech.

Photolibrary
17r Index Stock Imagery; 20-21 imagebroker.net; 21r OSF; 21b Superstock; 26c Dominic Sansoni; 27r F1 Online; 34 background DEA Picture Library; 35t Highlights for Children; 47b Dinodia; 51t Visions LLC; 78-79b David Hughes; 94bl Walter Allgoewer; 94r Axel Schmies; 95r Karl Johaentges; 96b Robert Harding Travel; 97r Japan Travel Bureau; 99b Phototake Science; 106t Robin Laurance; 168-169 Peter Arnold Images.

Random House
110c from Bog Child by Siobhan Dowd, published by David Fickling Books. Used by permission of The Random House Group Ltd.

Rex Features
121 Skyline Features.

Science Photo Library
8-9 Victor de Schwanberg; 19c Gregory Ochocki; 55 inset A. Barrington Brown; 179r Philippe Psaila.

Siemens
186-187 Curventa/Siemens

Additional photographs were kindly supplied by:
Fotolia.com: © arto; © jut; © travis manley; © picsfive; ©clearviewstock; © Gagarin; ©Rina Okukawa; © Luminis; ©alexkar08; ©Eky Chan; ©Dmitriy Kosterev; ©Antonio Nunes; ©Ben Stoate; ©Giordano Aita; © Ilia Shcherbakov; © Tombaky; iStockphoto.com: © Kirsty Pargeter; © Goldmund Lukic; © Hogne Botnen Totland.

Packager's Acknowledgements
Palazzo Editions would like to thank Richard Constable and Terry Jeavons for their design contributions

ACKNOWLEDGMENTS

Special research
Ian Morrison (sport); Dafydd Rees (music)

Academy of Motion Picture Arts and Sciences
 – Oscar statuette is the registered trademark
 and copyrighted property of the Academy of
 Motion Picture Arts and Sciences
Air Crashes Record Office
Airports Council International
Alexa
Apple
Applied Animal Behaviour Science
Artnet
Art Newspaper
Association of Leading Visitor Attractions
Association of Tennis Professionals
Audit Bureau of Circulations Ltd
BARB
Barclaycard Mercury Prize
BBC
Roland Bert
Billboard
Boeing
Peter Bond
Box Office Mojo
BP Statistical Review of World Energy
Richard Braddish
Breeders' Cup
Thomas Brinkhoff
BRIT Awards
British Academy of Songwriters, Composers
 and Authors (Ivor Novello Awards)
British Association of Aesthetic Plastic Surgeons
British Film Institute
British Library
British Phonographic Industry
Cameron Mackintosh Ltd
Carbon Dioxide Information Analysis Center
Charities Direct
Checkout
Christie's
Duggan Collingwood
Computer Industry Almanac
ComScore.com
Stanley Coren
Crime in England and Wales (Home Office)
Department for Culture, Media and Sport
Department for Environment, Food and
 Rural Affairs
Department for Transport
Department of Trade and Industry
The Economist
Philip Eden
Emporis
Environmental Performance Index
Ethnologue
Euromonitor International
FA Premier League
Federal Bureau of Investigation
Fédération Internationale de Football
 Association
Fédération Internationale de Motorcyclisme
Fédération Internationale de Ski
FIFA
Film Database
Financial Times
Food and Agriculture Organization of the
 United Nations

Christopher Forbes
Forbes magazine
Forbes Traveler
Forestry Commission
Fortune
FourFourTwo
General Register Office for Scotland
Global Education Digest (UNESCO)
Global Forest Resources Assessment (FAO)
Gold Survey (Gold Fields Mineral Services Ltd)
Russell E. Gough
Governing Council of the Cat Fancy
Robert Grant
Bob Gulden
Highestbridges.com
Home Office
Barney Hooper
The Iditarod
Imperial War Museum
Indianapolis Motor Speedway
Interbrand
International Air Transport Association
International Association of Athletics
 Federations
International Association of Volcanology and
 Chemistry of the Earth's Interior
International Centre for Prison Studies
International Energy Association
International Federation of Audit Bureaux of
 Circulations
International Game Fish Association
International Labor Organization
International Obesity Task Force
International Olympic Committee
International Organization of Motor Vehicle
 Manufacturers
International Paralympic Committee
International Rugby Board
International Shark Attack File, Florida Museum
 of Natural History
International Telecommunication Union
International Union for Conservation of Nature
 and Natural Resources
Internet Movie Database
Internet World Stats
Inter-Parliamentary Union
Claire Judd
Kennel Club
Ladies Professional Golf Association
Major League Baseball
Man Booker Prize
Chris Mead
The Military Balance (International Institute for
 Strategic Studies)
MTV
Music Information Database
National Academy of Recording Arts and
 Sciences (Grammy Awards)
National Aeronautics and Space Administration
National Basketball Association
National Football League
National Gallery, London
National Hockey League
National Statistics
Natural History Museum, London
AC Nielsen
Nielsen Media Research
Nobel Foundation

Northern Ireland Statistics Research Agency
NSS GEO2 Committee on Long and Deep Caves
Office for National Statistics
Organisation for Economic Co-operation and
 Development
Organisation Internationale des Constructeurs
 d'Automobiles
Roberto Ortiz de Zarate
Oxford English Corpus
Julian Page
Power & Motoryacht
Professional Bowlers Association
Professional Golfers' Association
Population Reference Bureau
PRS for Music
Railway Gazette International
River Systems of the World
Royal Aeronautical Society
Royal Astronomical Society
Royal Opera House, Covent Garden
Royal Society for the Protection of Birds
Peter Sabol
Eric Sakowski
Screen Digest
Screen International
Robert Senior
Sotheby's
State of the World's Forests (FAO)
Stockholm International Peace Research
 Institute
Stores
Sustainable Cities Index (Forum for the Future)
Tate Modern, London
Trades Union Congress
The Tree Register of the British Isles
twitterholic.com
United Nations
United Nations Educational, Scientific and
 Cultural Organization
United Nations Environment Programme
United Nations Population Division
United Nations Statistics Division
Universal Postal Union
US Census Bureau
US Census Bureau International Data Base
US Geological Survey
Lucy T. Verma
Ward's Motor Vehicle Facts & Figures
World Association of Girl Guides and Girl
 Scouts
World Association of Newspapers
World Bank
World Broadband Statistics (Point Topic)
World Christian Database
World Development Indicators (World Bank)
World Factbook (Central Intelligence Agency)
World Health Organization
World Metro Database
World Organization of the Scout Movement
World Population Data Sheet (Population
 Reference Bureau)
World Silver Survey (The Silver Institute/Gold
 Fields Mineral Services Ltd)
World Resources Institute
World Sailing Speed Record Council
World Tennis Association
World Tourism Organization
World Trade Organization